"Veola Vazquez, Joshua Knabb, Charles L(a very helpful and biblically based book that describes their HEAL model for having healing conversations on race focusing on humility, empathy, acceptance, and love. The authors humbly and transparently share their own stories and struggles and provide practical skills and steps for engaging in the process of building racial understanding and unity and overcoming racism. Highly recommended!"

Siang-Yang Tan, senior professor of clinical psychology at Fuller Theological Seminary and senior pastor emeritus of First Evangelical Church Glendale, California

"The history of the church when it comes to race is a mixed bag. Some Christians have done great work to build bridges and work toward racial healing and justice. Others have used their interpretations of the Bible to make things worse. This book is a welcome step in the right direction. The authors bring together their personal and professional experience to provide a practical road map to help Christians who want to become more like Christ and bring about healing in their communities. If that describes you, this book will help light the path."

Joshua N. Hook, professor of psychology at the University of North Texas

"The next generation of scholarship in the world of integration (of Christianity and psychology) needs to speak more directly to the problems of everyday life experienced by both Christians as well as non-Christians. And as I reflect on the many social ills of our day, I cannot think of an issue that is more pressing than the topic of race, and I cannot think of a work more compelling than the cultivation of Christ-inspired healing and shalom. I am so pleased to offer my endorsement of *Healing Conversations on Race*—it is an honest, personal, and practical resource informed by recent scholarship."

David Wang, Cliff and Joyce Penner Chair for the Formation of Emotionally Healthy Leaders at Fuller Theological Seminary

VEOLA VAZQUEZ, JOSHUA KNABB,
CHARLES LEE-JOHNSON,
AND KRYSTAL HAYS

HEALING
CONVERSATIONS
ON RACE

FOUR KEY PRACTICES
FROM SCRIPTURE
AND PSYCHOLOGY

ivp
Academic
An imprint of InterVarsity Press
Downers Grove, Illinois

InterVarsity Press
P.O. Box 1400 | Downers Grove, IL 60515-1426
ivpress.com | email@ivpress.com

InterVarsity Press® is the publishing division of InterVarsity Christian Fellowship/USA®. For more information, visit intervarsity.org.

All Scripture quotations, unless otherwise indicated, are taken from The Holy Bible, New International Version®, NIV®. Copyright © 1973, 1978, 1984, 2011 by Biblica, Inc.™ Used by permission of Zondervan. All rights reserved worldwide. www.zondervan.com. The "NIV" and "New International Version" are trademarks registered in the United States Patent and Trademark Office by Biblica, Inc.™

While any stories in this book are true, some names and identifying information may have been changed to protect the privacy of individuals.

The publisher cannot verify the accuracy or functionality of website URLs used in this book beyond the date of publication.

Cover design and image composite: David Fassett
Interior design: Daniel van Loon

ISBN 978-1-5140-0392-3 (print) | ISBN 978-1-5140-0393-0 (digital)

Printed in the United States of America ∞

Library of Congress Cataloging-in-Publication Data
A catalog record for this book is available from the Library of Congress.

| 29 | 28 | 27 | 26 | 25 | 24 | 23 | | 13 | 12 | 11 | 10 | 9 | 8 | 7 | 6 | 5 | 4 | 3 | 2 | 1 |

Veola Vazquez

This book is dedicated to my husband, my sons, and my many ethnically and culturally diverse family members. You each challenge me in your own ways and spur me on to love and good works.

Joshua Knabb

This book is dedicated to my wife, Adrienne, and children, Emory and Rowan, who motivate me on a moment-by-moment basis to love like Jesus loves.

Charles Lee-Johnson

This book is dedicated to my amazing daughter, Chacity, whose fight for life in her battle against lupus, kidney failure, and chronic illness inspires and encourages me to express the fullness of the gifts, vision, and love that God has deposited within my spirit. Your fight for life, passion for our people and justice, and commitment to the Lord motivate me to go harder in everything I do.

Krystal Hays

This book is dedicated to my husband, children, and extended family, who have guided and inspired me to live out my God-given calling and purpose, even when it's hard.

CONTENTS

ACKNOWLEDGMENTS

VEOLA VAZQUEZ

I would like to thank my husband, Carlos, for his ongoing support and love and for the way he challenges me to think deeply and seek Christ daily. I would also like to thank my sons, Luke and Mark, for the joy and laughter they bring into my life and for regularly reminding me to slow down and connect. Thank you also to my coauthors, Joshua Knabb, Charles Lee-Johnson, and Krystal Hays, for your boldness and encouragement throughout this journey of developing the HEAL model. Thank you also to our editor, Jon Boyd, for his support and championing of this project. I also want to acknowledge my students who regularly kindle reminders to remain humble, listen deeply, and grow. Above all, I thank my Lord and Savior, Jesus Christ, for his faithfulness to patiently teach me and shine light into new areas of my life. He is faithful to stimulate new life in areas that appear barren.

JOSHUA KNABB

First, I would like to thank my wise, talented coauthors, Drs. Veola Vazquez, Charles Lee-Johnson, and Krystal Hays, who have served as reliable traveling companions over the last few years as we humbly attempt to have Christlike conversations on race. Second, I would like to offer appreciation to Jon Boyd at InterVarsity Press, who believed in and enthusiastically supported this project from the moment he first heard about it. Third, I would like to acknowledge the anonymous reviewers, who offered thoughtful comments in order to strengthen earlier drafts of the manuscript. Fourth, I would like to thank the many students in the Doctor of Psychology (PsyD) and Doctor of Social Work (DSW) programs at California Baptist University who participated in HEAL events over the last few years and offered helpful feedback as they interacted with and experienced firsthand the HEAL model. Fifth, I would like to acknowledge the dean for the College of Behavioral and Social Science at CBU, Dr. Jacqueline Gustafson, who generously provided her leadership and support as we planned and implemented HEAL trainings and steadily wrote the book. Finally, I would like to thank the "head of the body," Jesus Christ, who perfectly modeled humility, empathy, acceptance, and love as he fulfilled his earthly mission of reconciliation.

CHARLES LEE-JOHNSON

All praises and glory to God, whose mercy, love, and favor continuously humble and challenge me to be better. To my amazing wife, Monalisa, who is my best friend, my rock, my love, and the consistent voice of God in my ear pushing me to be the best version of myself every day; I am so thankful that I get to do life with you. I am blessed to father the most amazing children: Chacity, Jazmine, Destiny, Ajamn, and Kokayi—you guys are the wind beneath my wings, always pushing me higher than I can imagine; I love you with a love that words could never describe. To my grandchildren: Darrel Jones (Dj), Zuri Miles, and Zion Wheeler—your zeal for life and love for your Papa keep me moving forward on the most difficult days and intensify the call within me to make this world a better place. To my mother, Joyce Kitchen, I could never thank you enough for the sacrifices you made for me as a single mother in Los Angeles to ensure that I could obtain the best of what God intended for my life; you're the greatest, and I am so thankful that I am your son. To my father, Ron Johnson (rest in heaven), who came into my life when I was eight years old, taught me how to be a man, and placed the crown of excellence upon my head; your legacy and memory will forever live through me. To my California Baptist University (CBU) family, I am so thankful for all of you and grateful to be a part of such an amazing family.

And last but not least, to The Life Church (TLC) family that allows me to pastor and lead in Riverside, California, I am so thankful to serve the Lord and our community with you.

KRYSTAL HAYS

I first want to give thanks and praise to God for choosing me to do his work. I need to acknowledge the generations of Black people who came before me and paved the way for my accomplishments. I am grateful to my forebears, many of whom were enslaved and denied the right to their full humanity and dignity. They suffered and sacrificed that I might have the privilege to pursue my dreams. I would also like to thank my husband, Maurice, and children Natalie, Nathaniel, and William, for their love and support. Additionally, I appreciate the inspiration I receive from my social worker community, which seeks justice and equity for the marginalized. I'm grateful to my professional family at California Baptist University and my spiritual church family for allowing me to do life among like-minded believers. I would also like to thank my coauthors for bringing me along on this journey of discovery and healing.

INTRODUCTION

WHEN THE TOPIC OF RACE RELATIONS arises in conversation, the resulting emotions are often fear, uncertainty, and anger. For many people, confusion seems to permeate these conversations, with no shortage of solutions being circulated for addressing the present-day suffering, turmoil, and injustices surrounding race. Like many people, and maybe just like you, the authors of this book have struggled to understand how to respond to the pain associated with race and racism and within cross-racial relationships. Prior to writing this book, we sought to understand what, exactly, healing and racial unity in the twenty-first century might look like and how we were going to get there. As Christians with advanced degrees in the helping professions, we knew we had an important role to play in bringing together our Christian brothers and sisters of different racial and ethnic backgrounds. We each saw the growing anger, disconnection, and disunity in our own communities and recognized that, with our commitment to Christlikeness and biblical unity, as well as our combined years of study, we could potentially make a difference. As we held informal conversations about race-related events, we found that hearing each other's stories and experiences built a growing empathy and understanding for differing views. We also found that we continually returned to the importance of a biblical view of significant race-related events and the importance of demonstrating Christlikeness to build racial unity. As we engaged in these powerful conversations, which included laughing together, lamenting together, and, ultimately, understanding and responding to each other's pain, we gradually developed a model for how to have healing conversations on race. This book is the culmination of these deep conversations. Throughout the book, we will guide you through our model by first providing explanations of the components of the model and then walking with you through the various activities. However, before you enter into this journey with us, we invite you to get to know each of us by hearing our personal stories.

ABOUT THE AUTHORS

Veola Vazquez, PhD. If asked to describe myself, the first thing I will mention is that I am a child of God and that I cannot think of myself outside of my relationship with Christ. Since the age of fifteen when I first gave my life to Christ, I have committed my life to his service. Yet, you would not fully know me unless you understood more about my racial history and background. My parents, a White woman and a Black man, married in 1966, a year before the Supreme Court of the United States ruled that laws against interracial marriage were unconstitutional. This means that my parents' marriage was illegal in many states at the time they married. Due to this, they experienced significant discrimination as a young married couple. My parents later divorced, for reasons unrelated to their races, after having three children. As a biracial female, I have also experienced discrimination, and I have often felt that others do not understand my experience of being a part of both racial worlds. These experiences have strongly influenced who I am today and, if asked to describe myself, I will also include the racial part of my identity. However, beyond being a Christian, and a biracial female, I am also interculturally married, and I am a licensed psychologist and a professor at a Christian university in a diverse area of Southern California. I teach courses on cultural diversity and serve as the diversity coordinator within a doctor of psychology program. These multiple identities, and their related experiences, combine to motivate me to help Christians of different racial/ethnic backgrounds to break down the walls of disunity by living out the fruit of the Spirit (Galatians 5:22-23) in cross-racial relationships.

Despite my deep motivation for this work, writing this book and developing the HEAL model has not been easy. As we wrote each chapter, I wrestled with how to honor Christ while also accurately and truthfully portraying the deep need for racial healing within our world, representing as much as possible the different voices and experiences of those who continue to experience the pain of racial injustice, racial injury, and/or disunity in their cross-racial relationships. I have sought to vulnerably approach these issues with "fear and trembling," recognizing that, despite spending much time in prayer, reading, conversation, and digging through the Word of God, the final HEAL model is not the ultimate method for healing racial disunity. I recognize that any human-derived model will always have faults, despite our desire to center our approach in Christlikeness and a biblical worldview. I humbly recall that while I wait for heaven, I can only "know in part" what Christlikeness looks like. Someday, however, we will be with him face-to-face and will "know fully" (1 Corinthians 13:12). Until then, we prayerfully present to you this unique approach to healing racial disunity.

Joshua Knabb, PsyD, ABPP. Although almost four long decades have passed, I can still vividly remember the interaction. My kindergarten teacher eagerly approached me one seemingly uneventful school day as I was lost in classroom play. As she slowly leaned down to my level, I noticed she had a new student with her, an unfamiliar face. "Will you be Dae-Ho's first friend in America?" she asked, anticipating my enthusiastic, "Yes!" Although Dae-Ho had just moved from South Korea and did not speak much English, I spent the rest of the school year learning how to communicate with him, sharing my world with him (and vice versa), and, ultimately, building unity with my new friend from another part of the world.

Throughout my childhood, in fact, I was blessed to be surrounded by people from a wide variety of racial backgrounds, given I lived in lower-middle-class, multiracial neighborhoods in several different cities. As a

White child in Southern California, on any given day I might be riding bikes with a Black friend, then playing football with a Latino friend, only to scurry off to spend the night at an Asian American friend's house to round out the day. Early on in life, therefore, I felt a tremendous amount of confidence in my ability to create and maintain lasting, meaningful connections with people from a plethora of different backgrounds.

Yet, several salient changes occurred in my adolescent years that deeply impacted my experience of, and confidence in, unity. In middle school, my father moved in and out of the home several times in one year, ultimately choosing to divorce my mother and start another family about an hour away. During this same time, I observed that my multiracial group of friends appeared to be reorganizing into separate, more homogeneous racial groups, which meant I had less and less contact with racially different others. Then, about halfway through my time in middle school, I was frequently bullied by a classmate—and his friends—who were from a different racial background than my own. As I struggled to understand the disunity of my adolescence, I carried with me the hurt of feeling rejected by my father, compounded by a painful yearning to simply be accepted by racially different others. "Why, God, is it so hard for people to love one another, as you've taught us to do?" I frequently cried out in these tumultuous years of separation and isolation.

Fast-forward to the twenty-first century, and I continue to ruminate on this pressing question, both personally as a Christ-follower and professionally as a board-certified clinical psychologist. With all the struggles our society experienced in 2020—whether toiling to truly heal race relations in the United States or struggling to understand and respond to a pandemic that has humbled even the brightest of scientists and politicians—I've been more determined than ever to do my part to promote Christlike, loving unity. Given I believe the Bible offers the requisite blueprint for healing conversations on race, with certain insights from the contemporary psychology literature providing many of the needed building blocks, I am excited about the potential for the current project to contribute to lasting unity, one relationship at a time. Reminiscent of my childhood years, I still believe that, as brothers and sisters in Christ, we can create and maintain lasting connections in our local faith communities in order to be a shining example of unity for the world.

Charles Lee-Johnson, MSW, DMin. As a Black man who loves Jesus Christ, preaches the Word of God as a pastor of a predominately Black church, and serves as the associate dean of the Division of Social Work at a Christian university, in my engagements with some of my White Christian brothers and sisters, I've often asked myself the question, *Do we know the same Jesus?* This question frequently arises in my mind, and others like me, as we interact with our White brothers and sisters in Christ. We know these brothers and sisters are Bible-loving, church-attending, and gospel-spreading believers, but they seem to lack understanding, compassion, and empathy around numerous social issues, especially race. The Jesus I met when I was five years old cared for the poor, cared for the oppressed, stood up for the marginalized, challenged injustice, welcomed the rejected of society with open arms, and engaged in healing conversations with everyone he encountered. I was introduced to the Jesus of Luke 4, who said, "The Spirit of the Lord is on me, because he has anointed me to proclaim good news to the poor. He has sent me to proclaim freedom for the prisoners and recovery of sight for the blind, to set the oppressed free, to proclaim the year of the Lord's favor" (Luke 4:18-19).

I often battle to understand which Jesus my Christian siblings are following when they don't empathize when unarmed young Black men are murdered by police officers; when they argue support for the confederate flag and confederate leaders; when they support political officials that parade in blatantly racist ideology; when they participate in and perpetuate birtherism and similar conspiracy theories; when they lack compassion around protecting and humanely caring for immigrants; when they deny structural racism; when they invalidate the experiences and realities of people of color; when they are nonsupportive of reparations or major social change movements; when they are unwilling to recognize the connection between slavery, Jim Crowism, and the current conditions of people of color; and, most recently, when they attack any theories or trainings that appear to cast a negative light on sins of racism. This is not a new phenomenon. Dr. Martin Luther King Jr. also struggled to understand how his White brothers and sisters believed in the same Christ he did and yet failed to see the inhumanity and ungodliness in the racism of American law and practice.

For years, I and many people of color have lived with severely entrenched skepticism of White Christians and White theology. Beyond what I mentioned earlier, there is also a long history of White Christians using the Bible and the Christian faith to justify slavery, segregation, suppression, and subjugation of people of color. The devil would love to use this history and our ongoing struggles to keep us divided, bitter, and angry at one another. I am excited about this book because it pushes us toward one another, instead of away from one another. The tension and trauma of racism encourage us, like Adam and Eve when they sinned, to hide from God. This book, on the other hand, invites us to acknowledge our sin, come out of hiding, and discover the mercy and grace of our heavenly Father, and to extend that same mercy and grace to one another. In the HEAL model, I have found a new way to engage my White brothers and sisters in Christ, and using these precepts has allowed us to have authentic, heartfelt, and transformational conversations with one another that have healed our souls. Working with my colleagues on this model and book has changed my life, given me new tools to engage others, and enhanced my ability to live in harmony with those who have different experiences and outlooks than mine. I have become a better Christian and discovered peace like never before.

Krystal Hays, PhD, LCSW. I watched a television program that featured various Black Americans responding to the question, "When is the first time you realized you were Black?" As I pondered this question myself, I discovered that I cannot recall ever living without the knowledge of my Blackness. I always knew I was Black and had parents and a community that made being Black a wonderful thing. I think the more salient question for me is, "When is the first time you realized being

Black was a problem?" The realization that others would perceive me as inferior because of my racial identity began as a young child. For me, racism feels like death by a thousand cuts. Being followed around the store by the store clerk for fear that I might steal something. Riding in the car with my father as he is followed home by the police for no apparent reason. Receiving comments like, "Wow, you're so articulate," as if they expected me not to be. Watching my husband be heckled and called a "nigger"[1] by a neighbor driving by. These are just a few examples of my experiences of racism over the years. There is not one single incident that leaves an indelible mark and solidifies my experience with racism; there are thousands.

My identity as a Black woman was inherited at birth; however, my identity as a Christian has grown and evolved throughout my life. Over the years, my love for Christ has deepened and my understanding of God's purpose and plan for humanity has become clearer. The problem is that the more I know God as a God of love and justice, the more conflicted I become about my dual identity as a follower of Christ and a Black woman. I am continually challenged by individual and collective responses from those that profess a belief in Christ, and love me as a Christian, yet have no problem perpetuating violence against me (and other Black Americans) because of my racial identity. I cannot quite understand how some of my White brothers and sisters can claim to love the same God I do, and read the same Bible, yet hold such drastically different interpretations and responses to the issue of racism. This passion for justice is further driven by my identity as a licensed clinical social worker committed to justice and equity. The social work profession

---

[1]Throughout the book, we have included our personal stories, as well as other true stories that have been altered to protect the identity of the people involved. However, when recounting stories or personal experiences, we will use the language of the original speaker. We recognize the extreme pain and historical injury connected with words such as these. However, we have purposefully chosen to leave these words within the given accounts to accurately portray, and not water down, the true and painful experiences of racism and race-related injury that many people experience. We encourage you, as you read the stories within this book, to intentionally return to your commitment toward Christlikeness, healing, and learning to use the HEAL model as the method to respond to these true accounts.

is deeply committed to the pursuit of social justice, and as the director of a doctor of social work (DSW) program at a Christian institution I am leading others to actively pursue justice as well. My identity as a follower of Christ, a Black woman, and a social worker are all integral parts of my human experience.

My growing inner conflict with racism, particularly among Christians, along with the recent racial uprisings that occurred in 2020, have motivated me to join my colleagues in identifying a solution to ongoing racial injury and disunity. The process of developing this model and writing this book has been healing for me in many ways. I will admit that I continue to struggle with feelings of anger and sadness as I see God's vision for a diverse community of believers from every tribe, tongue, and nation (Revelation 7:9) contrast against our current reality of race-based hierarchy and division. Yet, this book provides me with hope that it is possible to pursue God's vision of heaven and manifest it here on earth. I pray that as you embark on this journey you will become our partner in the pursuit of racial healing and unity and that we may become more like the vision of diverse love and unity God presents to us.

ABOUT OUR READERS

In reading our stories, you have likely seen our passion and commitment to helping Christians grow in racial unity. We want to invite you to add our model for healing cross-racial relationships to your own story. Before you begin this journey, it will be important for you to understand our assumptions about you, the reader, and how you might use this book. This book can be used individually or with a partner or group. For example, you might choose to read it at home alone, in a weekly group Bible study, with a counselor or therapist when seeking out professional mental health services, in a training within a church or parachurch organization, or in a classroom environment to facilitate experiential learning related to diversity. You can read the book along with a racially different or similar partner, as a part of a book club, or for your own personal study and growth. No matter the context in which you use the book, it is important that you know that this book is founded on a Christian worldview and biblical principles; therefore, as coauthors, we make the following assumptions about you and your interactions with the activities within the book:

1. You are a Christian and desire to demonstrate Christlikeness during conversations on race, race-related events, and racism.

2. You believe that racism exists, it is sinful, and it displeases God.

3. You are motivated to increase unity and grow deeper in your relationships with others, especially others who come from racially different backgrounds. (We do not have any one specific combination of racially different Christians in mind when applying our model for healing conversations. Rather, the focus is on cultivating Christlike unity among any two individuals who come from different racial backgrounds.)

4. You want to enter into conversations on race with intentionality and humility.

While some readers may use this book for personal growth, this is not a substitute for professional mental health services. Although we draw on psychological principles in this book, some readers may need a professional level of care because of more enduring, ongoing psychological and personal struggles or impaired daily functioning. If you believe you need pastoral counseling, professional counseling, or psychotherapy, please schedule an appointment with a mental health professional.

Finally, before continuing to the next chapter, prayerfully consider whether you are ready to begin this journey. If you are ready to begin, let's get started!

1

RACE RELATIONS

THE PROBLEM AND THE SOLUTION

A new command I give you: Love one another. As I have loved
you, so you must love one another. By this everyone will know
that you are my disciples, if you love one another.

JOHN 13:34-35

JODY, A WHITE 23-YEAR-OLD *pastor's daughter, fidgets*
with a lock of her auburn hair as she waits on the steps leading
to the front door of her parents' Detroit home. Her stomach roils
as she practices the speech prepared for her 6'3", barrel-chested
father. Jody can guess what he is going to say but prays she is
wrong. Before she builds up the nerve to enter the home, her
mother flings open the front door. Mother's green eyes are wide
with worry. "What are you doing out here by yourself? Is
something wrong?" she questions.

Jody is not ready to face her family, but there would never be a
right time for this conversation. She stands, gives her mother a
wry smile, and slides past her into the house. "Dad!" she calls,
finding him sitting in his easy chair reading the Bible, his regular

Saturday afternoon routine. The house smells of chocolate, and Jody breathes in the sweet aroma as her pulse quickens when her eyes meet her father's.

Dad offers a smile and seems about to speak, but Jody launches into her speech, fumbling over the words, "I love William, and we're getting married. And I want you to love him too."

A soft gasp comes from behind Jody. She turns and finds her mother with one hand pressed against her heart and the other grasping the edge of the sofa. "But he's Black,"[1] Mother whispers.

Jody turns back to her father. He slowly closes his Bible and sets it on the coffee table. He stands and looks down at Jody. "I love William," he says. Jody feels a slight release of the tightness growing in her chest. "But you are not marrying a Black man."

In her father's gaze, Jody sees his love for her, while also clearly recognizing the steadfastness of his statement. A tear wells in her eye. She doesn't know what to do.

THE PROBLEM AND SOLUTION: A BIBLICAL PERSPECTIVE

Imagine yourself sitting with Jody over a cup of coffee as she recounts the story of her father's reaction to her wedding plans. If she ended the story as we ended it here, you might wonder, Did she argue with her father? Did she storm out? Did she give in to her parents' wishes? When we hear stories like this, we often want to fill in the details and follow the story to completion. Who doesn't like a good story?

Narratives, or stories of connected events, draw us in, stirring a need for a deeper understanding of the world, ourselves, and others. We use the stories of our own and others' past experiences to make sense of the world and our place in it, knitting together seemingly isolated occurrences to find meaning in our lives. For example, reading Jody's story may have

---

[1] Although various terms may be used to describe racial and ethnic groups, throughout the book, we will use terms consistent with the recommendations of the American Psychological Association (2019, 2021).

reminded you of your own prior experiences or circumstances of your friends or family members. We store narratives like these in our memories and often refer back to them. In fact, you may find that you have a number of race-related stories that come to mind when thinking about Jody's experience and may have even thought, *That reminds me of the time when . . .*

We regularly think about and draw from our past narratives (and those that others have shared with us) because they help us to describe and consolidate our thoughts, feelings, and behaviors. You may have your own race-related stories to tell (no matter your racial/ethnic background), and, when pieced together with the other stories of your life, these provide a greater narrative of who you are, what you think about race-related issues and racism, and how your experiences have affected your relationships with others. Over time, we incorporate these into our view of the world. We then use these integrated stories to help us better understand each new circumstance and make predictions about our own and others' behaviors. At times, these predictions serve us well, helping us to effectively navigate an uncertain world and ambiguous relationships. At other times, when responding to racially driven events and/or having discussions about race and racism, these predictions hinder us and cause disunity in relationships, as we may weave together these stories of our prior experiences with misinformation, emotional pain, and previous relational conflict. For example, you may find that you have heard a story like Sam's:

> *Sam, a White male, was excited about his new job. The only uncertainty he felt surrounded his relationship with his new coworkers. One of his coworkers, Taj, was a dark-skinned man from Iran. Each time he interacted with Taj, Sam couldn't help but think about his sister-in-law's stories from New York after the terrorist attacks of September 11, 2001. Taj's nationality had Sam worried that Taj might have terrorist thoughts. Sam realized that some people might think he was overreacting or even xenophobic, but he couldn't help but remember his own*

fear after 9/11. He didn't know how to interact with Taj when he
thought about the past.

Sam's story is one example of the ways we use our own and others' stories (narratives) to make sense of the world around us and to make predictions about others' behaviors and choices about our own behaviors. Unfortunately, these integrated stories may leave us with inaccurate and even hurtful predictions and subsequent behaviors.

Since humans invariably think in stories, as we thread these together, we begin to develop a cohesive account of ourselves and our histories. As we do so, we create a grand narrative, or big-picture depiction, of our lives and relationships. For centuries, humans have attempted to create cohesive narratives to make sense of crosscultural and interethnic relationships. Today, for example, many societal and cultural narratives try to help us make sense of, and respond to, race relations and the suffering brought on by racism. You may have read some of these "narratives" within the most popular contemporary books on the topic of race relations. Many of these works use different stories to explain current race-related disunity. Although some of these may certainly be helpful, they often draw from the author's own worldview (greater meta-narrative), which may be quietly residing in the background, unacknowledged and unidentified.

In many ways, both individuals and cultural groups have attempted to make sense of the world and endure hardship and relational suffering by regularly returning to the salient narratives of their culture or belief system. Like hundreds of jigsaw puzzle pieces scattered on a large dining room table with no puzzle box top picture to reveal how to place them carefully together,[2] contemporary Christians can get easily overwhelmed by this plethora of competing, fragmented ideas on the problem of, and the solution to, disunity in race relations. However, within our model, we define the problem as a lack of a coherent and integrated biblical view of racial disunity. Succinctly put, we are using the wrong meta-stories to make sense of race relations and racism.

---

[2]Thanks to the Christian theologian M. Todd Bates for a version of this metaphor.

For Christians, the Bible reveals a well-defined meta-narrative for understanding the problem of racial disunity. This meta-narrative, or the *grand narrative of Scripture*,[3] tells us of God's relationship with humankind, assisting us in answering the important questions about who we are, what is wrong in our world and relationships, and what the solution is.[4] Although contemporary advancements in the social sciences have filled in some gaps to help us grasp the current problems in our society, we believe the Bible's far-reaching, timeless plan better helps us make sense of our divided, unstable, and unpredictable world. In other words, God's "resilient relationship story"[5] helps Christians to understand the problem and solution to suffering, especially the suffering we endure in relationships. To be clear, the Bible offers us a grand story of relationships that we can apply to race relations.

The grand narrative of Scripture. Beginning in Genesis, the first two humans were "dependent on God," recognizing that their Creator was at the center of existence; yet, they infamously wanted to be "like God." No longer content to draw their understanding of the world from him, they quickly placed themselves at the center, futilely attempting to acquire human knowledge of good and evil. By prioritizing themselves above God, they lost the unity that defined their existence, relied on their own inaccurate story to make sense of the world, and began to judge their experience outside of God's perfect love and wisdom.

However, despite their notorious attempt to turn from him, God continued to pursue humankind. We see his loving pursuit in story after story recounted in the Old Testament. Then, in the New Testament, we read that God entered history in human form to reconcile humans to himself (John 3:16). Because of this crucial act of love, we have the opportunity for the following:[6]

---

[3]Anderson et al. (2017); Bonhoeffer (1955); Wolters (2005).
[4]Anderson et al. (2017).
[5]Johnson (2008).
[6]Grudem (1994).

- Restoration of relationship with God as a friend, rather than an enemy (justification).

- Indwelling of the Holy Spirit to empower us to become more like Jesus Christ (sanctification).

- Walking with God moment to moment, day to day, and year to year, until we are one day together with God, face-to-face, forever in perfect unity with him and fellow believers (glorification).

After Jesus' ascension to heaven, the first-century church was tasked with bringing together and unifying Christ-followers from all different walks of life and cultural backgrounds, solidifying their identity, first and foremost, in Jesus Christ (John 17:20-21; Galatians 3:26-29; Ephesians 4:1-6). In this story of all stories, we can see the movement from creation to fall to redemption to restoration, with love and reconciliation as the central themes. These themes are seen in Paul's letter to the Colossians:

> The Son is the image of the invisible God, the firstborn over all creation. For in him all things were created: things in heaven and on earth, visible and invisible, whether thrones or powers or rulers or author- ities; all things have been created through him and for him. He is before all things, and in him all things hold together. And he is the head of the body, the church; he is the beginning and the firstborn from among the dead, so that in everything he might have the su- premacy. For God was pleased to have all his fullness dwell in him, and through him to reconcile to himself all things, whether things on earth or things in heaven, by making peace through his blood, shed on the cross. (Colossians 1:15-20)

Ultimately, the biblical story is one of rebuilding unity and community as Christians move from justification to sanctification to glorification on this side of heaven, placing God at the center of the human experience. Although humans were created in God's image to be in relationship with him and others, the fall and humanity's sinfulness led to disunity and brokenness, including racial disunity, racial injustice, racism, and strain in cross-racial relationships. However, by taking on human form roughly two thousand years ago, God demonstrated his love for humankind, personally revealing his desire for restored communion and unity, with love as the antidote to division, disunity, hate, and injustice. In other words, racial disunity and racism are a result of humanity's sinfulness, and it is God's desire to restore our broken cross-racial relationships.

The grand narrative of Scripture and race relations. To summarize our view of the way a biblical meta-narrative helps to make sense of the problem of, and solution to, disunity in race relations, next we offer a succinct statement that captures our guiding principles. First, it is important to understand that we believe race relations exist along a continuum. You may have noticed that, thus far in the book, we have referred to "racial disunity," "racial injustice," "strain in cross-racial relationships," and "racism." We believe these terms/descriptors provide a snapshot of the negative end of the continuum and describe unhealthy and painful ways race relations may be experienced in our fallen world. On the positive end of the continuum, we may experience productive and healthy cross-racial relationships, with the extreme positive end of the continuum exemplified by intentional racial unity and Christlike love in cross-racial relationships. By contrast, on the extreme negative end, you might find intentional racism and purposeful disunity, founded in ungodliness. Presumably, apathy toward race relations may fall somewhere in the middle of the continuum. However, along this continuum, we believe that cross-racial relationships and race relations can be experienced in innumerable ways. (See figure 1.1 for a depiction of how this continuum might look.)

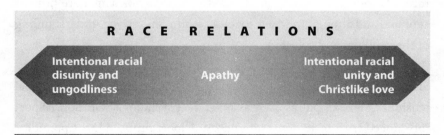

Figure 1.1. Continuum of race relations

Therefore, the biblical meta-narrative helps us to understand the following as the problem of, and solution to, ongoing difficulties in race relations (we will unpack these ideas as we move into the upcoming chapters):

Problem: Sin is the root of all of humanity's problems in race relations, including racism and racial disunity. Racism itself is a sin and the result of sin.

Solution: Christlikeness is the solution to all of humanity's problems in race relations, including racism and racial disunity. The qualities of Christlikeness, such as love, servanthood, and self-denial, are incompatible with racism and compel us toward racial unity.

THE PROBLEM AND SOLUTION: A SOCIAL, PSYCHOLOGICAL, AND HISTORICAL PERSPECTIVE

Although a biblical meta-narrative provides a response to the problem of, and solution to, racial disunity, in our present time, it can be challenging to find an agreed-upon root cause of racial injustice, racism, and cross-racial strain in the secular literature and within the church. This is especially true because there is no shortage of narratives for making sense of the racially fragmented world around us. In fact, there are some individuals within society who believe that racism no longer exists. For those who recognize the ongoing truth of racism's existence, these cultural narratives include both systemic (macro-level) and individual (micro-level) explanations for the problem of, and solution to, racial tension, injustice, and racism. To be sure, in the context of contemporary race relations, there are a variety of stories, many of which are human-centered and attempt to weave together a human-derived understanding of the problem and solution.

Within the field of diversity studies, for years psychologists and sociologists have researched and attempted to provide answers to resolve racial tensions. For example, as early as 1954, the psychologist Gordon Allport introduced Intergroup Contact Theory. Allport proposed that prejudice, for instance, could be reduced by contact between groups when optimal conditions were met.[7] These conditions included equal status, cooperation, common goals, and support of authorities. Research has repeatedly supported the effectiveness of these conditions in improving cross-racial relationships and decreasing prejudice.[8] Others have found that other factors beyond those described by Allport can also be helpful remedies for improving cross-racial relationships, such as knowledge about the other person, emotional responsiveness, and empathy/perspective-taking.[9]

The current psychological literature also supports the idea that people who want to engage in helpful and healing conversations with racially different others must do so with a degree of foundational knowledge about the other person's experience, self-awareness, other-awareness, specific communication skills, and cultural humility.[10] Cultural humility has come to be seen as one of the key healing factors in cross-racial relationships.[11] A culturally humble person recognizes their limitations in understanding culturally different others, seeks opportunities to learn, and accepts that learning will be a lifelong process.

Although social scientists have historically sought remedies for racial tensions, as these tensions have grown in recent years efforts have increased to help both professional and lay audiences respond proactively to these issues. As such, the general public has increased race-related awareness and actions. In 2020, the American Psychological Association's *Stress in America* survey[12] found that 59% of Americans had recently taken action against racial injustice. One-third of these people reported that this action included having meaningful conversations about race. What is more, 24% of Americans reported purposefully and actively learning more about the topic. With 70% of the American population identifying as Christian,[13] these conversations have likely included individuals of the Christian faith.

---

[7]Allport (1979).
[8]Pettigrew and Tropp (2006).
[9]Pettigrew and Tropp (2008); Rodenborg and Boisen (2013).
[10]Hays (2016); Hook et al. (2017).
[11]Hook et al. (2017).
[12]American Psychological Association (2020).
[13]Pew Research Center (2015).

As an example of Christ to the world, Christians and the Christian church, the bride of Christ, play a pivotal role in responding to, and answering the question about, the problem and solution to racial disunity. However, historically the church's response to race relations has often been problematic. As such, we turn briefly to a review of race relations in the church.

A brief history of race relations in the United States and Christian church. Christianity in the United States developed and continues to dwell within the country's historical context as a nation. Historical factors that have influenced and been influenced by American Christianity include actions/events such as the enslavement of Black Americans, the encroachment on Native American land, the internment of Japanese Americans, post-9/11 xenophobia toward Middle Easterners, and constantly changing immigration laws, to name a few. Unfortunately, American Christianity cannot disentangle itself from these past or current circumstances, nor their ongoing effects on relationships within the church and the church's relationship with the community. However, awareness of historical and current events, especially when placed against the backdrop of a biblical meta-narrative, can help drive us toward personal and relational change. Although a thorough review of the history of the Christian church and race relations is beyond the scope of this book,[14] we provide a brief overview to set the context of our current purposes.

Even though the focus of Christianity within the United States has historically been one of evangelism, this has not always included the idea of equality or freedom of oppressed peoples.[15] In fact, in the 1800s and early 1900s, Scripture was often used as confirmation of God's desire that enslaved people conform to the oppressive and violent actions of advocates for slavery and that indigenous peoples be civilized through oppression.[16] This approach to Scripture has been denounced as a

---

[14]See Priest and Nieves (2006), for example, for additional information on this topic.
[15]Priest and Nieves (2006).
[16]McSloy (1996).

failure to recognize the important role of ethnic culture and experience in shaping biblical interpretation [which] can produce damaging results because it can lead a culturally dominant community to insist that its own interpretations of the Bible are "objective" and "official" to the exclusion of all others.[17]

Although these views and practices gradually changed with Christian leaders' growing acknowledgment of the unbiblical nature of them, this did not outright change race relations within the church. For example, early American church congregations were split along racial lines, with racial/ethnic congregations serving as places of worship for congregants of non-White groups who were not allowed to worship alongside White parishioners. Racism also continued to plague early Christianity in more subtle ways. Many commentators refer to Martin Luther King Jr.'s "Letter from Birmingham Jail" to point out the insidious nature of racism within Christianity. Dr. King described individuals he referred to as the "White moderate." He wrote of the Christian and Jewish White moderate who

is more devoted to "order" than to justice; who prefers a negative peace which is the absence of tension to a positive peace which is the presence of justice; who constantly says, "I agree with you in the goal you seek, but I cannot agree with your methods of direct action." . . . Shallow understanding from people of good will is more frustrating than absolute misunderstanding from people of ill will.[18]

Dr. King's writings to his "Christian and Jewish brothers" highlighted a more indirect, yet no less harmful, form of racial injustice, the lack of action that led to the further perpetuation of these injustices. More recently, biblical scholar and author Esau McCaulley echoed this idea, stating, "Moderation or the middle ground is not always the loci of righteousness."[19] Subtle racialized behaviors and ideas such as those described by Dr. King and more overtly negative race-related actions and

---

[17]Romero (2020, pp. 181-182).
[18]King (1963).
[19]McCaulley (2020, pp. 68-69).

racism have historically caused significant racial division within the church.

Current race relations within the church: The need for healing. More recently, some positive changes have occurred within the church. During the fourteen-year period between 1998 and 2012, the number of multiracial churches in America (churches with less than 80% of members of the same race/ethnicity) grew by 6%, comprising a total of 12% of US congregations.[20] Although this is still only a small proportion of US churches, this growth has developed alongside changes in attitudes within the church. In 2015, approximately 40% of White churchgoers said their churches needed to become more ethnically diverse.[21] This finding mirrors the more recent 2021 findings that the majority of Black Americans who attend traditional Black churches believe that their churches should also become more racially and ethnically diverse.[22]

However, despite this change in the church's racial/ethnic composition and the apparent desire of many church members to have a less segregated church experience, Christians continue to see difficulties with race relations within the church. Many congregants (of all racial/ethnic backgrounds) continue to affirm that they "strongly disagree" with the idea of their churches becoming more ethnically diverse.[23] The continued evidence of this is seen on Sunday mornings, in that most churches continue to be segregated by race.

In addition to these disparities in church composition and ideas about church integration, predominantly White and predominantly ethnic churches differ in their approaches to race-related issues. For example, many historically Black churches see one of their primary roles as helping congregants respond to racism and discrimination in society.[24] In contrast, within many primarily White congregations, it is not uncommon to see attempts at smoothing the color line by focusing on

---

[20]Dougherty and Emerson (2018).
[21]Smietana (2015).
[22]Mohamed (2021).
[23]Smietana (2015).
[24]Ellison et al. (2017).

similarities among races rather than differences, taking the spotlight off race and racism.[25] Often, ethnic churches also maintain cultural traditions, including holding services in their native language and celebrating traditional holidays and festivals. These churches seek ways to highlight and preserve the culture of their ethnic group, rather than assimilating to the mainstream culture. At times, primarily White churches will host an ethnic congregation within their building. Still, it is not uncommon for members to avoid crossing cultural lines (sometimes never even seeing each other on the same campus).

Although church members have differing views about the necessity of increasing ethnic integration within their congregations, we have seen the potential harm that different approaches to racial/ethnic issues can cause as we have listened in on conversations within congregations. They may go something like this:

> *Bryan, a Black pastor, says to Frank, a White pastor, "I'm upset about ongoing racism, even among Christians. As pastors, we need to do something." Frank says to Bryan, "The members of my congregation think that Black people are making a big deal out of this. Talking about it seems to be causing more problems than it's fixing." Bryan does not know how to respond. He is hurt and feels unheard. He nods his head and says nothing more. Yet, he leaves the conversation with Frank vowing never to talk to him about race-related issues again.*

> *After a church service, Susan, a Chinese American woman, tells Sandra, a Mexican American woman, "I wish everyone would stop blaming the Chinese for the coronavirus. People are acting like it's my fault that they have to wear masks." Sandra responds with, "Well, it did come from China. It's just a fact." Susan feels stung by Sandra's response and quips, "You're a great example of Christian love!" and leaves the sanctuary with a stomp of her foot, thinking that all people of Mexican descent must think the*

---

[25]Emerson and Smith (2000).

same way. She vows to avoid people with that background for fear that they will act in racist ways toward her in the future.

The two examples above are aggregates of the types of race-related conversations that may take place among Christians; yet, these approaches tend to divide church members and Christians further. There are some Christians, however, who are seeking ways to have more productive and loving conversations, especially in light of the events during the last several years that have brought race relations in the United States back into focus. You may have picked up this book for just this reason.

THE PROBLEM AND SOLUTION: AN INTEGRATIVE BIBLICAL AND PSYCHOLOGICAL MODEL FOR HEALING CONVERSATIONS

Our healing conversations on race approach and methodologies are founded, foremost, on the goal of helping Christians to grow in Christlikeness and apply Christlikeness to cross-racial conversations and relationships. Our goal is not to merely translate the most popular secular ideas of the day.[26] Instead, we start with the Bible as a firm foundation and build our approach on sound biblical doctrine and theology. In other words, although each of us may have slightly different theological beliefs within Protestant Christianity, our collaborative approach is to promote biblical unity and a shared narrative for healing cross-racial relationships and facing racism together, regardless of our theological backgrounds or denominational affiliations. Like a Venn diagram that displays each of our theological and denominational backgrounds in four separate circles, we have attempted to focus on our similarities, not differences, by presenting the overlapping content.

---

[26]We recognize that there are a variety of helpful contemporary approaches to responding to racial disunity within both secular *and* Christian communities. In fact, from a Protestant perspective, we believe God offers his grace to even secular communities, meaning that certain psychological and social insights and advancements, when it comes to race relations, can occur outside of the body of Christ (for a more in-depth, contemporary discussion, see Mouw, 2002). Thus, as Christian authors trained in the behavioral sciences, we in no way seek to dismiss other helpful approaches. Instead, here we simply wish to differentiate our approach by firmly anchoring our understanding of the problem of, and solution to, racism to the biblical meta-narrative in order to aid Christian communities.

With this strategy in mind, we believe, with boldness and confidence, that the Bible is authoritative as God's Word and a personal relationship with Jesus Christ is needed to be reconciled to God.[27] Indeed, as Christ-followers, we believe that Jesus is the head of the church and holds everything together (Colossians 1:15-20). As Christians, our main purpose while on this planet is to worship and enjoy God.[28] This means he is at the center of healing conversations on race, offering us the empathy, mercy, and grace we need in these pivotal encounters with racially different others (Colossians 1:15-20; Hebrews 4:14-16). What is more, we believe that racism exists, it is sinful, and it displeases God.

In our model, we combine God's "special grace" that he offers to Christians with God's "common grace,"[29] which includes psychological advancements in our contemporary understanding of race relations and positive relational change. Therefore, moving beyond our biblically grounded model, we also draw on several bodies of literature within contemporary psychology, including attachment theory, emotionally focused therapy (EFT), and the psychology diversity literature.[30] Within each of these areas, practicing mental health professionals have found success in healing hurting relationships through scientifically proven theories and techniques. Keep in mind, in drawing on these theories, we aim to honor God in our effort to present a Christian-distinctive model, attempting to benefit from the best of psychological science in the process. As you read through this book and engage in the provided activities, we will regularly return to Scripture as the foundation, while also guiding you through principles and steps toward having healing conversations on race.

Some Christian authors may describe our approach as either *integration* or *Christian psychology*.[31] In either case, our goal is to start with a clear and specific scriptural view of God, reality, people and sin, values,

---

[27]Larsen (2007).
[28]See Protestant Christianity's famous Westminster Shorter Catechism.
[29]Kuyper (2015).
[30]Hays (2016); Hook et al. (2017); Johnson (2019a, 2019b); Mikulincer and Shaver (2017).
[31]Johnson (2010).

and redemption.[32] Building on this foundation, we utilize research-supported methods from within the psychology literature. Within our model, the psychology literature can be helpful because it describes and explains, in fairly significant detail, key relational processes and patterns that have been reliably observed over time. Psychology can also help us delve deeper by giving language to our experiences and practical solutions to common struggles.

See figure 1.2 for a visual depiction of how we prioritize the various writings we have drawn from, placed within the process of Christian spiritual and psychological growth. Notice that we start with Christlikeness and sanctification as a central aim. Sanctification is sandwiched between the steps of justification and glorification, given that Christians are called to emulate Jesus Christ as we move from being reconciled to God in Christ to being face-to-face with God in heaven.

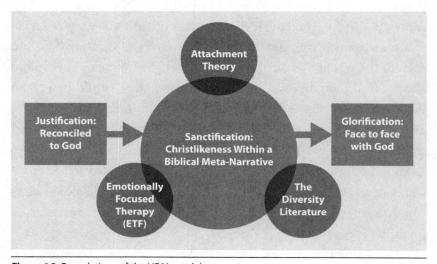

Figure 1.2. Foundations of the HEAL model

The model is founded on a biblical meta-narrative that places God at the center. As we actively love God and others, we can anticipate being face-to-face with him in heaven one day. This is the proverbial

---

[32]Knabb et al. (2019).

"already but not yet" of the sanctification process. As Christians, we are justified through Christ's work on the cross, and our position before God is firm because we are sealed with the Holy Spirit at our conversion (Ephesians 1:13). However, we are called to "continue to work out [our] salvation with fear and trembling" (Philippians 2:12), putting off our old ways and putting on new ways. Therefore, we seek to "put on" the fruit of the Spirit that Paul speaks of in his letter to the Galatians: "love, joy, peace, forbearance, kindness, goodness, faithfulness, gentleness and self-control" (Galatians 5:22-23). Historically, Christlikeness has been the foundation and goal of the spiritual disciplines. Thus, we will draw from the spiritual formation literature as a guide for activities (lectio divina) and our understanding of Christlikeness.[33]

We believe our approach to healing conversations on race is rather unique, grounded in a biblical view of reality, human nature, values, and redemption. Rather than finding ways to fight against racism by being *less* racist, our model advocates for being *more* Christlike. If Christlikeness—and the corresponding fruit of the Spirit—is a central aim in this life, the process of sanctification should be at the core of Christian conversations on race (Galatians 5:22-23).[34]

Our approach emphasizes one-on-one and small group conversations to elicit change on a *micro* (individual, personal) level, cultivating safety, trust, and unity in one relationship at a time. Modeled after God entering into human history to *personally* respond to our estrangement and suffering and Jesus entering into specific relationships to *personally* effect change, we prioritize the healing power of individualized attempts to create loving, unifying, and, ultimately, enduring Christlike exchanges with others. We believe that micro-level (individual) changes such as these have the power to influence and lead to macro-level (systemic) changes, thereby dually creating changes within individual relationships and within communities and churches.

---

[33]Boa (2009); Calhoun (2005); Chandler (2014); Foster (2018); Graybeal and Roller (2007); Howard (2018); Mulholland (2016); Willard (2002).
[34]Wright (2017).

We believe that healing conversations on race start and end with four pivots. Helping you learn to pivot in these ways during healing conversations on race is our goal for you as you journey through this book. We invite you to set these pivots as ongoing goals:

1. Pivot from a human-centered understanding of race relations and racism to a God-centered understanding.

2. Pivot from a focus on self to a focus on Other (God) and others.

3. Pivot from disunity to unity.

4. Pivot from judgment of others ("like God") to Christlike love ("dependent on God").

We pray that you will learn to effectively use our model for healing conversations on race. We use the acronym HEAL to provide you with an easy-to-remember device to use when having these conversations, which we will unpack more as we move through this book. Therefore, another ongoing goal for you is that you will learn to use the following practices during these conversations:

- *H*umility—Prayerfully Reflect
- *E*mpathy—Identify Emotion and Need
- *A*cceptance—Consent to God's Loving Presence
- *L*ove—Respond with Christlikeness

The pivots and practices of the HEAL model are meant to be ongoing and work hand in hand, with no expiration date, dividing lines, or clearcut boundaries. Instead, they are enduring and permeable, in the sense that they are pursued on a daily basis, there is overlap between them, and they are all needed as you slowly move toward Christlike unity with racially different others.

Although in subsequent chapters we will encourage you to focus on an individual pivot that corresponds with a particular practice of the model (for example, the first pivot, from a human- to God-centered understanding, is discussed in the chapter on the first practice, humility), the pivots are meant to be cultivated collectively and on an ongoing basis, in no particular order. Similarly, the practices of the HEAL model overlap and work in unison, in that you can regularly return to the different practices during any given conversation on race as needed. However, we have developed the model using an easy-to-remember acronym so that you can call to mind each of the practices (and pivots) as you seek to engage in healing conversations on race. Therefore, as you dive deeper into this book and the activities within, we invite you to work toward flexibly and holistically engaging in the four practices (and pivots).

We recognize that movement toward these practice- and pivot-related goals will be an ongoing process, as is our growth in Christlikeness. This is just as true for the Christian reading this book who is new to these ideas as it is for the reader who has been devouring every book on race relations that they can find. Also, depending on your personal background, race/ethnicity, and experiences, the way you proceed through the book may look different when compared to how a friend or neighbor might do so. Remember, a culturally humble person recognizes that they are still growing and in the process of sanctification, and each person is on a different journey, given God created every human being as distinct, with particular talents and skills and unique, original, non-replicable relationships with God and others.

> As a biracial psychologist, I (Veola) figured that I was relatively well-versed in cultural issues. I had spoken at events about race relations, completed a dissertation focused on spirituality, acculturation, and interracial marriage, and taught college courses on cultural diversity. However, I was not prepared for the confusion that hit when the racial uprising of 2020 began. I suddenly felt forced to choose a side, White or Black. I felt disconnected from my Black family members, while also fearing that I might be attacked by a group of White youth while jogging in my neighborhood. Although constantly aware of my race and the possible meaning of it within certain environments, it had

never been such a raw emotional experience. As I attempted to speak with friends, family, and colleagues about racial issues, I found myself wondering how to do so in a way that honored both parts of my biracial identity, while also honoring God as my first priority. I realized I had much to learn and much more self-awareness to gain. For me, the HEAL model was an outgrowth of this growing awareness. I admit, though, that I will continue to learn more about myself and others. I accept this as a part of living with Christlike humility and a part of my sanctification process. (If you would like to know more of my story or that of my coauthors, refer back to the introduction and keep reading as we will share our stories throughout the book.)

Shortly after the murder of George Floyd in 2020, I (Josh, a White male) attended a faculty meeting with several university colleagues, one of whom (Charles, a Black male) is a coauthor of this very book. During the opening moments, Charles authentically expressed the deep, ongoing pain of watching the viral video footage, which vividly captured yet another unarmed Black man being killed. As he passionately shared his heartfelt emotions and powerfully declared the many reasons for the injustice of the event, I remember experiencing a tremendous amount of confusion, not knowing what to say or do and remaining silent for the duration of our time together. Although I am a board-certified clinical psychologist by trade and have helped countless clients over the years to more confidently identify, verbalize, and accept their inner pain, in this 60-minute time span, I was utterly speechless and unable to fully process what I was going through. I was, simply put, lost in my own inner experience. Despite being in this clouded state for most of the meeting, at the very end, I recall thinking, "I have to say something, anything." Therefore, with a shaky, uncertain voice, I conjured up just enough energy to say, to paraphrase, "I've been silent today because I don't know what to say. But I want to listen and learn, and my silence doesn't mean I don't care." Immediately after the meeting, I started a much longer journey of processing why, when my colleague and friend needed my support, I remained quiet and unresponsive. In prayerful reflection, I gradually gained insight into what had occurred—I was experiencing a unique combination of fear, powerlessness, and shame. First, I felt scared that, as a White male who could not fully understand my colleague's experience as a Black man in America, I would somehow say the wrong thing, offend him, or embarrass myself. Second, I felt powerless because, as a White male, I was convinced I had nothing to offer and could not contribute or help in any meaningful or effective way. Third, I felt good old-fashioned shame, since I struggled (and still struggle) with feeling naive and ignorant and, as a White male, like I have no real cultural heritage of my own to embrace. Yet, in that very moment, I needed to display Christlike humility, empathy, acceptance, and love, pivoting from a self-derived understanding and self-focused preoccupation to God's understanding and a more unifying, outward-facing, action-oriented love. Although I did not know it at the time, Charles's pain, coupled with my own, would serve as a much-needed launching pad, propelling me toward more ongoing, authentic conversations on race, race relations, the need for greater unity among racially different Christians, and ultimately, the HEAL model.

WHAT TO EXPECT

Whether you read this book alone or with a partner or group, the content and activities within each chapter are designed to be engaged slowly, approximately one chapter per week. Our prayer is that your engagement with these activities will culminate in a conversation with a racially different partner and a commitment to apply this biblically tethered model to Christ-likeness within the church, one relationship at a time.

Follow each chapter, completing the exercises and discussing your thoughts and progress with others. If you find that you struggle with the content of a specific chapter, feel free to slow down to rest, pray through the material, and engage with the journaling activities until you feel you are ready to proceed. After all, because God is at the center, not on the periphery, he will ultimately be your guide as your heavenly Father who understands your vulnerabilities and invites you to receive his grace, which is readily available in the present moment (Colossians 1:15-20; Hebrews 4:14-16).

In the following chapter (chapter two), we will focus on *humility* (H), and you will gain foundational biblical knowledge about race relations and the psychological concept of cultural humility to help you pivot from a human-centered understanding to a God-centered under-standing of race relations. The activities provided in this chapter are designed to help you solidify this key material as a starting point. In chapter three, we will focus on *empathy* (E), and you will learn about the importance of listening to others' stories and lamenting the pain of racial tension and racism. You will engage in activities focused on reflecting on your own cultural and spiritual journey, learning others' stories, and lamenting race-related injuries. The goal is to help you pivot from self to God and others. In chapter four, we will focus on *acceptance* (A). You will learn key Christian mental skills to use during difficult conversa-tions on race to trust in, and consent/yield to, God's active, loving presence. We include activities that will help you practice these skills and pivot from disunity to unity, with God serving as the proverbial glue. Chapter five will focus on *Christlike love* (L), and you will learn to apply key psychological skills for use during conversations on race. The pro-vided activities will help you practice these psychological skills and pivot from human judgment to Christlike love. Chapter six will provide you with a step-by-step guide for having a healing conversation on race, and we will guide you through this conversation with a racially different partner. Chapter seven will provide encouragement for holding on to the lessons learned within the book and guide you in responding to challenges along the way.

To help you easily move through the ideas within this book, we have organized each chapter in the same way. We will begin with a brief story, then provide a biblical view of the chapter's focus. In turn, we will discuss a psychological perspective on the same topic. From there, we will integrate the biblical and psychological views, prioritizing Scripture. Within each chapter, we will also include breaks with instructions for journaling. After the initial biblical view of the topic is presented, we will ask you to engage in an exercise called lectio divina as a strategy for developing connectedness, Christlikeness, and the fruit of the Spirit.

Lectio divina. Lectio divina is an approach to reading Scripture that has been referred to as an act of "divine reading."[35] As a spiritual discipline, lectio divina is a means of pursuing spiritual formation, transforming into the image of Christ in our relationships with God and others. We believe that reading Scripture this way can deepen your understanding of biblical principles, help you to internalize and apply Scripture to race relations, and help you to cultivate connectedness with racially different others. In our view, lectio divina is a vehicle through which we can pursue "an ever-transforming intimacy with God,"[36] which we can take into our relationships with racially different others as we have healing conversations on race. The process of lectio divina[37] involves the following steps:

- *Read*—Read a chosen passage in Scripture and slowly allow yourself to take in its content. To use the famous metaphor of eating food to describe lectio divina, this first step is like taking an initial bite of food.

- *Reflect/meditate*—Take one key verse from the chosen passage and ponder and meditate on it. Slowly and gently recite the selected

---

[35]Wilhoit and Howard (2012).
[36]Wilhoit and Howard (2012, pp. 224-225).
[37]Benner (2010); Guigo II (2012); Wilhoit and Howard (2012).

verse, thinking deeply about what it means. To return to the food metaphor, this second step is like chewing a bite of food.

- *Respond/pray*—Spend time in prayer with God, asking him to help you apply what you have learned from the chosen verse in meaningful ways. Cry out to God, asking him to fill your heart so that God's perfect love consumes you at the center of your being. To again revisit the food metaphor, this third step is like tasting a bite of food.

- *Rest/contemplate*—Slowly and gently repeat a word from the chosen verse, focusing on this word and allowing God to fill your heart with his love and a deeper meaning of his Word. Sit silently with God in contemplation, allowing him to penetrate your heart and change you from the inside out. To draw on the food metaphor one final time, this fourth and final step is like savoring a bite of food.

Journaling breaks. In each chapter, we will also provide journaling exercises. We will ask you to think deeply about your race-related experiences, emotions, and relationships. We encourage you to spend adequate time completing the journaling exercises both within each chapter and at the end of each chapter. You will use the material you produce from these activities during an intentional healing conversation on race. We will guide you through this conversation in chapter six, and you will need access to your responses to the journaling activities from the conclusion of each of the previous chapters.

TIPS FOR A SUCCESSFUL EXPERIENCE

Be intentional. The information and activities in this book are essential components to prepare you for healing conversations on race. Block out some uninterrupted time whenever you read to focus on the information and activities. Throughout the book, we offer some background on each topic, which will take time to absorb, given the importance. We believe that a deeper knowledge of this material is necessary to prepare you for the activities, which will help you shift how you engage racially different others in a healing manner. Ultimately, you are encouraged to slowly complete the tasks within each chapter with intentionality and deep focus.

Be open. Your commitment to self-reflection, deeper thought, and emotional awareness and vulnerability will prepare you to engage in healing conversations. This process may be challenging at times. You may find yourself thinking about events and experiences you have not thought about in a while. Be open to new information and experiences as you embark on this process of development and growth. Paradoxically, the more vulnerable you can be with both God and your fellow brothers and sisters in Christ, the more you will be able to promote Christlike unity, with God at the center as *the* source of love (1 John 4:7-21). Although the journey may be difficult, we want to encourage you that it is well worth it.

Be prayerful. Be mindful that God is at the center of this entire experience. Fully enter into each activity of this journey, asking God to open your heart and mind to receive what he has for you.

To begin your preparation for this journey, before moving on to the next chapter, grab a journal or paper and pencil and spend some time responding to the following questions, then close the chapter by following along with the prayer:

1. On a scale of 1 to 10, how ready are you to begin this journey (with 10 indicating that you are very ready)? Why did you choose this number? What current or past factors are motivating you to begin learning how to have healing conversations on race?

2. What fears, worries, or concerns do you have about beginning this journey? What support do you need to help respond to these concerns? Who can help, and what can they do? What will you do to access this support?

3. How would you describe your current relationship with God? What conversation with him do you need to begin so that he can serve as your trustworthy traveling companion on this trek toward deeper unity and connection within his church?

To end this chapter and begin our journey together, we offer the following prayer, famously written by the late Trappist monk Thomas Merton. As you read through the prayer, try to make a commitment to fully yield to God as your trustworthy guide. He is with you right now, leading you toward racial unity within his body of believers:

> My Lord God, I have no idea where I am going. I do not see the road ahead of me. I cannot know for certain where it will end. Nor do I really know myself, and the fact that I think that I am following your will does not mean that I am actually doing so. But I believe that the desire to please you does in fact please you. And I hope I have that desire in all that I am doing. I hope that I will never do anything apart from that desire. And I know that if I do this you will lead me by the right road, though I may know nothing about it. Therefore I will trust you always, though I may seem to be lost and in the shadow of death. I will not fear, for you are ever with me, and you will never leave me to face my perils alone.[38]

---

[38]Merton (1958, p. 79).

2

HUMILITY

PURSUING CHRISTLIKENESS

But the fruit of the Spirit is love, joy, peace, forbearance, kindness,
goodness, faithfulness, gentleness and self-control.

GALATIANS 5:22-23

IMANI (WHO IS BLACK) IS ANGRY. *She sets down her*
phone after scrolling through Instagram for the last 30 minutes.
Her best friend, Ava (who is White), had filled her story with
selfies at the beach, but Ava had posted nothing about the recent
race-related unjust murder of an unarmed Black teenager by a
White neighborhood patrol member. Imani internally stews as
she considers how to respond to her best friend's silence. She
cannot help but think, "Silence is Violence," as she has seen
several friends post, and thinks that Ava should know this by
now. Imani begins to wonder if Ava is secretly withholding racist
ideas and considers whether she should stop following Ava on
Instagram or stop being friends altogether.

Alone in her bedroom, Ava sits scrolling through her Instagram
feed, reading the many different responses others have had to the

recent murder. She wants to post something, but does not know what to say or how to say it. Partly, she feels like she has no right to respond or post, especially as a White teen. She wonders aloud, "Maybe saying nothing is better than saying the wrong thing." She closes the Instagram app, sets down her phone, and stares at the ceiling as she tries to fall asleep, still uncertain if she made the right choice.

Statements by Dr. Martin Luther King Jr. in response to the silence of his White pastoral friends during the civil rights movement have been paraphrased in the following way: "Our lives begin to end the day we become silent about things that matter. . . . In the end we will remember not the words of our enemies, but the silence of our friends. . . . A time comes when silence is betrayal."[1] Imani's pain over her best friend Ava's silence exemplifies the betrayal often felt by people of color, and the often non-intentional harm of their White friends, as both parties try to make sense of race-related experiences. On the other hand, Ava's uncertainty about how to show her concern exemplifies the confusion often felt by White individuals as they seek to find ways to respond to these painful situations. This struggle is not just a Black and White experience. People from all races and ethnicities often go through similar relational struggles as they try to make sense of their race-related experiences.

As we discussed in the last chapter, we tend to view each new racialized event, like Imani's and Ava's experience, from within the context of our many other race-related experiences. As we build and integrate our repertoire of these stories, we gradually create a more and more consistent response to each new circumstance. As Christians, unless our understanding of these experiences is grounded in the grand narrative of Scripture—which includes recognizing that we were created in God's image to be in relationship, struggle to do so because of the deep impact of sin, and need God as our redeemer to restore our broken unity—we miss opportunities for demonstrating Christlikeness and developing healing relationships.

---

[1] Paraphrase from King as cited by Mayer (2014).

Returning to the story of Imani and Ava, while there is nothing wrong with Ava posting pictures of herself at the beach, if they seek to respond in a manner consistent with Christlikeness and the grand narrative of Scripture, both Ava and Imani might humbly consider the importance of restoring broken unity. For Ava, this might include seeking to be responsive to the pain that Imani and possibly other people of color may feel in hearing that someone from their racial group has been killed due to race. Although there are a variety of responses Ava and Imani might choose, we believe that healing in racial encounters begins first with humility.

Therefore, as a first step in helping you learn how to respond in situations like Imani's, in this chapter we focus on the practice of humility (H of the HEAL model). We provide a biblical view of people, relationships, and race relations, and explore what humility looks like in cross-racial relationships. We anchor our discussion mostly to the spiritual formation literature because of its emphasis on the importance of being formed into the image of Christ. In becoming more like Jesus Christ, we are called to display humility through the fruit of the Spirit (love, joy, peace, patience, kindness, goodness, faithfulness, gentleness, and self-control)[2] as we work to develop true biblical community with our brothers and sisters in Christ. Ultimately, we were created in God's image to be in relationship, with Jesus Christ humbly modeling for us the love we are to have for each other (John 13:34-35). Therefore, we believe that healing conversations on race begin and end with cultivating humble Christlikeness in our relationships with diverse others.

As you read this chapter and seek to grow in your own understanding of humility, biblical community, and Christlikeness, we invite you to move beyond your "head" (a mere cognitive understanding) to your "heart" (a more holistic understanding) by humbly and prayerfully reflecting on your personal response to the information we present. As

---

[2]In Galatians 5:22-23, the New American Standard Bible (2020) uses "patience," whereas the New International Version Bible (2011) uses "forbearance." We will use both terms throughout the book, but often defer to "patience."

you do this, you may find that you are beginning to rewrite your story and your responses to race relations, with God serving as your trustworthy guide. Ultimately, we seek to help you start your story with a biblical, Christ-centered perspective as your foundation as you humbly pivot from a human-centered understanding of race relations to a God-centered understanding.

HUMILITY AND RACE/ETHNICITY: A BIBLICAL PERSPECTIVE

The concept of race is not discussed in the Bible. Instead, biblical distinctions among people groups are based on clan (family group), nationality (nation of origin), religion (followers of the one true God or idolaters), and ethnicity (common religious beliefs or traditions that bond a group together).[3] The distinction by nationality is seen frequently in the Old Testament when the writers refer to people groups like the Egyptians, Moabites, or Canaanites.[4] Also, New Testament texts commonly distinguish between Jew and Gentile. The Samaritans serve as an example of a group that was distinguished by both religion and ethnicity.

In fact, the Samaritans were a unique group in the New Testament era. They stood out as being both religiously and ethnically distinct.[5] Jews did not associate with Samaritans (John 4:9) due to specific religious beliefs that separated this group from Israel as a nation. These distinct beliefs ("but you Jews claim that the place where we must worship is in Jerusalem," John 4:20) were part of the ongoing conflict between the Jews and Samarians. This key disagreement about how to faithfully worship God is an example of how the two groups were distinguished ethnically and religiously. The story of the "good" Samaritan (which we will return to for the lectio divina exercise at the end of this section) exemplifies the conflict between these groups, while also demonstrating a Christlike response to alleviate the conflict and increase unity. Race, or distinctions based on skin color, were not relevant to the separation between these

---

[3]Priest and Nieves (2006); Erickson (1998).
[4]See Exodus and Numbers.
[5]Priest and Nieves (2006).

two groups, nor is race used as a differentiator among people groups throughout Scripture or when talking about the kingdom of God. Discussing the story of the good Samaritan, pastor and author Timothy Keller stated,

> By depicting a Samaritan helping a Jew, Jesus could not have found a more forceful way to say that anyone at all in need . . . is your neighbor. Not everyone is your brother or sister in faith, but everyone is your neighbor, and you must love your neighbor.[6]

Therefore, how do we humbly respond to issues of race when viewing them through a biblical lens? We believe that Scripture's depiction of the kingdom of God provides a foundation for understanding how to actively live humbly with others, including as racially diverse brothers and sisters in Christ.

The kingdom of God and race/ethnicity. According to Scripture, the kingdom of God includes peoples from "every nation, tribe, people and language" (Revelation 7:9). God's love for all people is highlighted in examples throughout the grand narrative of Scripture.[7] In the Old Testament, these examples include Ruth (see the book of Ruth), a Moabite woman, and Rahab (see Joshua 2, 6), a prostitute, both of whom were ancestors of Jesus. Within the New Testament, the examples of the Samaritan woman (John 4), which we will explore in depth later in this chapter, the Syrophoenician woman (Mark 7:24-30), and the Roman centurion (Matthew 8:5-13)[8] all provide further evidence of God's love for all people and that God does not want "anyone to perish, but everyone to come to repentance" (2 Peter 3:9). This is clearly seen in the Old Testament when, despite Jonah's attempt to avoid God's will, God calls Jonah to preach repentance to the Ninevites (Jonah 1–4).

The common thread that weaves together the stories of these historical individuals is their choice to humble themselves before God and serve

---

[6]Keller (2010a, pp. 67-68).
[7]Erickson (2013).
[8]See Erickson (2013) for a discussion of race (nationality) and God's love for all people.

and worship him (or the consequences of not doing so, as is the case with Jonah). Despite different national and ethnic backgrounds, these individuals were called to be a part of the kingdom of God. This new heavenly community of peace that emanates from God's plan of redemption and restoration will be one without sin, injustice, oppression, or conflict.[9] This new community, with Christ at the center, brings together individuals from every racial and ethnic background.

> God's vision for his people is not for the elimination of ethnicity to form a colorblind uniformity of sanctified blandness. Instead, God sees the creation of a community of different cultures united by faith in his Son as a manifestation of the expansive nature of his grace. This expansiveness is unfulfilled unless the differences are seen and celebrated, not as ends unto themselves, but as particular manifestations of the power of the Spirit to bring forth the same holiness among different peoples and cultures for the glory of God.[10]

On this side of heaven, with Christ at the center, we can begin to live out God's will for true biblical community with all people. We see humility, at its root, as the active demonstration of Christlikeness in community through the fruit of the Spirit.

Christlikeness, the fruit of the Spirit, and race/ethnicity.

Do nothing out of selfish ambition or vain conceit. Rather, *in humility value others above yourselves*, not looking to your own interests but each of you to the interests of the others.

In your relationships with one another, have the same mindset as Christ Jesus:

Who, being in very nature God,

did not consider equality with God something to be used to his own advantage;

rather, *he made himself nothing*

by taking the very nature of a servant,

being made in human likeness.

---

[9]Boa (2009).
[10]McCaulley (2020, pp. 106-107).

And being found in appearance as a man,
    he humbled himself
    by becoming obedient to death—even death on a cross!
Therefore God exalted him to the highest place
    and gave him the name that is above every name,
that at the name of Jesus every knee should bow,
    in heaven and on earth and under the earth,
and every tongue acknowledge that Jesus Christ is Lord,
    to the glory of God the Father. (Philippians 2:3-11, italics added)

Paul's encouragement to the early believers in Philippi provides us with a framework for biblical humility: "to value others above ourselves." This value of others is a call to see beyond our own social location, with an openness to the hearts, hurts, understandings, experiences, perspectives, and even values of other people. This is not easy work. Paul explains that we have a Savior who considered relationship with us so important that Christ physically, psychologically, socially, and spiritually lowered himself for us, lived among us, modeled humility for us, died for us, and, ultimately, was resurrected for us, in demonstration of the depth of sacrifice that is required to create peace, harmony, and unity. As children of God in the process of sanctification, we are likewise called to lower ourselves, live among one another, model holiness, and die to self in the struggle for one another, knowing we will be resurrected one day and brought to our Savior, prayerfully having what was required of us to create peace, harmony, and unity within our world, to the best of our ability. This is the call of every Christian, in response to every person, of every race, tribe, nation, and tongue.

Therefore, in this process of sanctification, we can grow in our ability to love God, live humble lives, and prioritize God's will, learning to love diverse others in our communities the way that God desires. Again, in the text cited above, Paul stated that Jesus "made himself nothing" (Philippians 2:7). Here the Greek word *kenōsis* is used, which describes "self-emptying of one's will in support of God's divine will."[11] We are exhorted by Paul to this same mindset (Philippians 2:5). *Kenotic* self-emptying is meant to be an ongoing, purposeful act in our lives.[12] Building on this understanding, as Christ-followers, we are to pivot from our own self-serving, fallen will to the will of God, allowing God's fruit to be on display in our lives. More specifically, author C. J. H. Wright suggests that Paul's command to the Galatians to cultivate the fruit of the Spirit is the foundation for emulating Christ.[13] Therefore, we are most able to demonstrate humility and Christlikeness through the Holy Spirit's "love, joy, peace, forbearance, kindness, goodness, faithfulness, gentleness and self-control" (Galatians 5:22-23) displayed in and through us each second of our day, including in our interactions and conversations with ethnically/racially diverse people and responses to racism. Stated differently, Christ is living in us, and we must intentionally choose to die to self, demonstrating humility in each passing instance so that Christlikeness, exemplified in the love of God and others, can manifest in all our relational encounters, including our cross-racial encounters.

With humility as our goal, and sanctification as our focus, each fruit of the Spirit and their combined results form the foundation for healing conversations on race as we seek to build unity in cross-racial relationships within the body of Christ. C. J. H. Wright describes the fruit of the Spirit in the following ways (adapted to include race relations):[14]

- *Love*—As we demonstrate Christlike love toward others, we seek deeper connection with both God and others, despite racial differences. This includes loving racially different others in action and with compassion, even when we do not feel loving and when self-sacrifice is involved.
- *Joy*—Joy is not just a feeling of happiness, but a faithful response of hope to the promise of eternity from God. Joy is demonstrated in

[11]Chandler (2014, p. 47).
[12]Beasley-Topliffe (2003).
[13]Wright (2017).
[14]Wright (2017).

rejoicing and thanksgiving for God's eternal and daily blessings. Yet, Christians also rejoice and find joy amid suffering, racial disagreements, and conflict because of their faith in God, knowing God is at the center to see them through.

- *Peace*—Peace is intimately connected with joy. Just as with joy, peace is not simply a feeling. It is, instead, a gracious gift of God. As we trust God's provision and sovereignty, we experience peace, rather than anxiety or fear. Not only is peace God-given, but Christians are commanded to grow in peace and to cultivate peace in our daily lives and relationships, including our interactions with racially different others.

- *Patience/Forbearance*—Christians are commanded to demonstrate patience through bearing with and enduring the faults of others, the sin of the world, suffering, and our own frailties. Patience involves forgiveness and relinquishing anger, even when we come from different racial backgrounds, do not completely agree on race-related matters, and do not fully see the problem of, and solution to, racism in the exact same way.

- *Kindness*—Kindness, like the other fruit of the Spirit, involves self-sacrifice and the act of placing others' needs before one's own. This kindness is demonstrated in Christ's character through his love and mercy. We demonstrate kindness by compassionately meeting the needs of others, even when they contradict our own needs or come from a different racial background and have vastly different experiences than our own.

- *Goodness*—Goodness is a characteristic of righteousness and demonstrated through morally good behaviors and actions and a trustworthy character. When we demonstrate goodness, we have no falsehood in ourselves and can be said to have integrity. The "good" person will make the right choice or choose the right behavior, even when it may cause themselves pain. Justice is a form of goodness, which includes racial justice and pursuing morally good behaviors and integrity in race relations.

- *Faithfulness*—We can be both faithful to God and demonstrate faithfulness in our relationships with others by persevering in the fruit of the Spirit. Faithfulness involves commitment to our beliefs and relationships over the long term. A faithful Christian is consistent and persistent in trustworthiness and will do what they say, even amid pain and struggle in race relations.

- *Gentleness*—Those with gentleness patiently endure suffering and the faults of others. Yet, they do so without retaliation, with a soft response, and with a controlled temper, which is especially relevant for healing conversations on race. Gentleness does not imply doing nothing when hurt by others, but, instead, responding with humility and a recognition of our own limitations and sinfulness in our pursuit of racial unity. A gentle Christian is firm in biblical convictions, but approaches others with self-control, modeling God's gentleness to others even when others are not acting as they should be.

- *Self-control*—With the strength provided by the Holy Spirit, we can gain control over sinful desires/behaviors. This includes cultivating control over the temper, the tongue, and attitudes. We can exercise self-control by avoiding conflict and seeking peace, especially in the context of difficult conversations on race. In this way, self-discipline benefits others and ourselves in our pursuit of racial unity.

You may notice that a commonality among the fruit of the Spirit is self-denial (humility), modeling our lives and behaviors after the humble character of Christ. This may feel like a challenge in terms of race relations, as it can be difficult to humbly endure and forgive racial injustice and injury. In fact, to the person of color, this talk of "self-emptying" and humility may seem like a call to forget the past, detach from historical oppression, or minimize the racial injustices we see in the world today. However, ignoring or denying injustice is not part of our call to "walk humbly" (Micah 6:8). Often in interactions with dominant groups, persons from marginalized groups feel challenged to bottle their feelings and to view each act of injustice as a separate incident and disconnected from historical violence and oppression. Christlikeness is not demonstrated in denying feelings, experiences, or realities, but rather in allowing the Holy Spirit to work so powerfully through us that we can express ourselves cross-racially in a way that honors the kingdom of God. Peter Scazerro, in his book *Emotionally Healthy Spirituality*, states,

> To feel is to be human. To minimize or deny what we feel is a distortion of what it means to be image bearers of God. To the degree that we are unable to express our emotions, we remain impaired in our ability to love God, others, and ourselves as well. Why? Because our feelings are a component of what it means to be made in the image of God. To cut them out of our spirituality is to cut off an essential part of our humanity.[15]

Let's look at an example:

> *Jamal is a Black student in a predominately White Christian college. During a discussion in a history class, one of his White classmates, Blake, states, "I don't see why Black people are so angry about slavery. They've gotten so many benefits since then, like affirmative action, welfare, scholarships, and government programs to give them a lift. If I had all that help, I'd be fine." Jamal is furious, but is worried that responding will further ostracize him in a school where he's already struggling to fit in.*

In a situation like that of Blake and Jamal, how does each person demonstrate humility and Christlikeness and also accept the validity of the emotional response elicited by the experience? For Blake, the answer is clear. To demonstrate self-denial and humility, he would need to reflect on the pain his statements caused and seek to repair the relationship with Jamal. Relying on the fruit of the Spirit, Blake might demonstrate peace,

---

[15]Scazerro (2014, p. 24). We will return to a deeper discussion of emotions in chapter 4.

kindness, goodness, and gentleness by seeking forgiveness and also demonstrate love by learning more about Jamal's experience.

For Jamal, there is no easy answer to the question of how he might respond. As a Christian who seeks to walk humbly (self-emptying), Jamal might feel like he should just let it go and bear the weight of the racist[16] and hurtful expressions of his classmates. He may think, *After all, enduring this type of persecution is exactly what Jesus did, right?*

We are not suggesting that Christlike humility is God's requirement that the hurt or harmed person be thoughtless, voiceless, or actionless. In fact,

> Jesus shows us that healthy Christians do not avoid conflict. His life was filled with it! He was in regular conflict with the religious leaders, the crowds, the disciples, and even his own family. Out of a desire to bring true peace, Jesus disrupted the false peace all around him. He refused to spiritualize conflict avoidance.[17]

Our challenge to the Jamals of the world is to encourage a humble response by turning to the Holy Spirit as a guide for living out the fruit of the Spirit, always remembering that God can be glorified through pain. In returning to their story, we provide an example of what humility might look like in this situation for both Blake and Jamal.

> *Seeing the expression on Jamal's face after his comments, Blake felt ashamed of what he'd said, which too quickly dismissed Jamal's experience as a Black man living in a country with an enduring legacy of slavery and systemic racism. Blake took a moment to recognize and accept his own emotions, including shame, then turned his attention to what Jamal might be experiencing. He recognized the pain he caused, and as class ended, he asked Jamal if they could talk. Blake apologized to Jamal and asked for forgiveness for his comments. He then*

---

[16]You can return to chapter 1 to review our view of the continuum of racism. Also see the remainder of this chapter for our discussion on the manifestations of racism.

[17]Scazerro (2014, p. 32).

> *promised Jamal that he would spend some time learning more*
> *about the experiences of people of color.*
>
> *Immediately after hearing Blake's initial comments during class,*
> *Jamal was sad and angry. Although his emotions were strong,*
> *Jamal took a moment to reflect on his feelings and his desire to*
> *voice his concerns. Instead of reacting in anger, he took a*
> *moment to accept and identify his deeper, more vulnerable*
> *emotions, inviting God to provide him with peace and Christlike*
> *love in the present moment. Certainly, he felt righteous anger*
> *because of the far-reaching injustices of slavery and systemic*
> *racism. Yet he also felt a deeper sadness and loneliness, given he*
> *truly wanted his classmates to understand and accept, often to*
> *no avail, his unique experiences as a Black student in a*
> *predominantly White college. As class ended, Jamal was*
> *surprised when Blake asked to talk and was hesitant to hear*
> *what Blake had to say. However, Blake's honest apology and*
> *willingness to learn helped Jamal to feel more understood and*
> *less isolated, which is what he really wanted from the beginning.*

Responding to microaggressions, like what Jamal experienced (discussed in the next section), and other injustices with humility and Christlikeness (demonstrated through the fruit of the Spirit—love, joy, peace, patience, kindness, goodness, faithfulness, gentleness, and self-control), as Blake and Jamal attempted to do, glorifies God. This leading of the Holy Spirit was at the center of the largest movement toward racial healing in the United States, the civil rights movement, in which Dr. Martin Luther King Jr. and countless others fought hate with love and brought radical legal and heart changes to America. Reflect on this quote from Dr. King: "Returning violence for violence multiplies violence, adding deeper darkness to a night already devoid of stars. Darkness cannot drive out darkness: only light can do that. Hate cannot drive out hate, only love can do that."[18] Remember, Jesus, as our model, famously

---

[18]King (1963, p. 37).

declared on the cross of all places, "Father, forgive them, for they do not know what they are doing" (Luke 23:34).

JOURNALING BREAK: LECTIO DIVINA

Before moving on to the next section, take a moment to reflect on the biblical perspective of humility presented in the chapter thus far. Lectio divina will help you move from your head to your heart as you reflect on race/ethnicity and Christlikeness and learn to humbly display the fruit of the Spirit in each and every interaction with others.

READ: Read the story of the Samaritan in Luke 10:25-37. Read slowly and allow yourself to take in the content of the passage.

REFLECT: Take one key verse from this story to ponder and meditate on, such as, "But a Samaritan who was on a journey came upon him; and when he saw him, he felt compassion" (Luke 10:33 NASB). As you slowly and gently recite this verse, think deeply about what it means to have humble compassion for someone who you believe is vastly different from you, especially as you see them suffering.

RESPOND: Spend a few minutes praying to God, asking him to fill your inner world with humble compassion as you consider the ways in which you can have more compassion for racially different others by demonstrating the fruit of the Spirit. In other words, cry out to God, asking for Christlike humility and compassion to fill your heart so that you are consumed by God's perfect love at the center of your being.

REST: Slowly and gently repeat the word *compassion*, reminiscent of the Samaritan mentioned in Luke's Gospel, "But a Samaritan who was on a journey came upon him; and when he saw him, he felt compassion." Sit in silence with God, resting in his presence as you are filled with God's compassion from the inside out.

Before you move on to the next section of this chapter, which focuses on a contemporary psychological view of humility and the problem of, and solution to, racism, pick up your journal and reflect on the following questions:

1. Who do you currently know who may be hurting or feel disconnected from others due to their race/ethnicity? Or who do you know who may feel like they are different from, or unaccepted by, those around them?

2. What feelings are you aware of as you think about this person and their experience? Have you ever felt disconnected from others or that you are different from, or unaccepted by, those around you? What emotions does this evoke?

3. What might it look like to display humility, the fruit of the Spirit, and Christlike compassion toward this person? How might you go about doing so in behavioral terms, reminiscent of the Samaritan, who took clear, concrete steps to lovingly care for someone who was vastly different from him?

HUMILITY AND RACE/ETHNICITY: A PSYCHOLOGICAL PERSPECTIVE

Within the psychology diversity literature, humility (*cultural humility*) has been found to play a key role in helping individuals respond to diverse others in productive and healthy ways. As a beginning point, the cultural humility literature calls for an understanding of others' experiences,[19] which includes an understanding of race and racism. Overall, the diversity literature within psychology and sociology views race as an idea developed and determined by society.[20] Generally, *race* has been used to describe the differing phenotypic characteristics (outward appearance and skin color) of groups, whereas *ethnicity* typically describes groups based on shared culture, language, and traditions. Specifically, the use of skin color as a differentiator among people is a more recent historical occurrence. Rather than color of skin, in earlier centuries, people were differentiated by clan, kinship, or national origin.[21] Today, within the psychology literature, we use terms like "people of color" or "person of color" (POC)[22] or Black, Indigenous, and People of Color (BIPOC)[23] when referring to non-White racial and ethnic groups.

With a focus on skin color to define people groups and characteristics, humans will often use stereotypes to predict behavior. These stereotypes,

---

[19]Hook et al. (2017).
[20]Priest and Nieves (2006).
[21]Priest and Nieves (2006).
[22]American Psychological Association (2019).
[23]American Psychological Association (2021).

or the beliefs or expectations we have about groups of people,[24] often stretch beyond basic expectations to assumptions that impact relationships and can even result in negative treatment toward others and prejudice, discrimination, and racism. According to the diversity literature, cultural humility and healthy connectedness may be helpful ways of alleviating these difficulties in cross-racial relationships.[25] Yet without an understanding of racism, the ways in which it manifests, and its impact on BIPOC, our ability to demonstrate cultural humility is limited.

Manifestations of racism. Racism has been defined in several ways. Different ways to conceptualize it include a belief in the "inferiority of a person caused by prejudice against their ethnic group, phenotypic characteristics or purported biological nature"[26] and "a system of advantage based on race that is created and maintained by an interplay between psychological factors (such as biased thoughts, feelings, and actions) and sociopolitical factors (such as biased laws, policies, and institutions)."[27] Therefore, racism can manifest in both individual and societal forms. Although the ways it can manifest are numerous, some examples follow of the way BIPOC may experience racism in their daily lives.

The assumption of sameness. Each person develops a sense of their cultural and racial identity at a different pace, including BIPOC and others.[28] However, at times we can assume that all members of a certain racial group are similar and experience their race and ethnicity similarly.[29] For example, being Black means different things to different Black people.

> I (Veola) have brown skin. My father is Black and mother is White. Although society may look at me and consider me to be Black, I see myself as a biracial female. I connect with both the

---

[24]Hays (2016).
[25]Hook et al. (2017); Pettigrew and Tropp (2006); Rodenborg and Boisen (2013).
[26]Bryant-Davis and Ocampo (2005).
[27]Roberts and Rizzo (2021).
[28]Tatum (1992).
[29]Trimble and Bhadra (2013).

> White side of my identity and the Black side of my identity, not
> one or the other.

Colorblindness. You may have heard others say, "I don't see color." In the psychology literature, this is referred to as colorblindness.[30] Although colorblindness is often seen as altruistic, with the goal of creating unity,[31] some BIPOC may see it as a form of invalidation of their experiences.[32] Racial colorblindness may also have negative effects on BIPOC and increase negative attributions toward them from White people.[33]

> I (Krystal) am a Black woman and have been told by a very
> close White friend, "I don't see you as Black." This was very
> insulting and deeply painful. I assume that her intention was to
> communicate that she didn't judge me negatively because of my
> race. However, I think my blackness is beautiful. I love my Black
> culture and the history of my people. To not see me as Black is
> both dishonest and invalidating. It's like saying "I don't see you
> as a woman" or "I don't see you as a scholar." Instead, I wish that
> she had been able to articulate that she loves who I am,
> including the fact that I am Black, instead of pretending to
> ignore this important part of who I am.

Microaggressions. Racial microaggressions are the seemingly minor and subtle ways in which BIPOC may be invalidated or insulted. For example, they may be served last in a restaurant, be watched more closely by a clerk in a store, or be seen as the same as all other BIPOC. Behaviors such as these are often experienced in brief interactions with others and may be verbal or nonverbal. These interactions often appear to be inconsequential. However, microaggressions can have an additive characteristic and affect BIPOC negatively.[34]

---

[30]Emerson and Smith (2000).
[31]Emerson and Smith (2000).
[32]Zou and Dickter (2013).
[33]Zou and Dickter (2013).
[34]Sue et al. (2007).

Isabel is a 28-year-old Black female. She is single and lives near her parents in a quiet suburb outside a major metropolitan area. She is a full-time student currently completing a PhD in neurobiology at a public university. She has attended a historically Black church most of her life and relied on her faith in God to persevere toward her academic and professional goals. Isabel recently dropped off a package at the UPS store. While standing in line, a White man behind her struck up a conversation. "So, what do you do?" he asked. Isabel sometimes felt uncomfortable telling others what she was studying. People often did not know what to say or how to respond. Typically, this was because they did not understand what someone with a PhD in neurobiology does. This meant she was in for a long explanation of her studies. Despite the temptation to tell the man that she was a waitress, she admitted, "I'm in school studying for a PhD in neurobiology." She smiled at the man and waited for his response, expecting him to ask her, like most people did, "What's that?" Instead, his eyes grew wide, and he stared at Isabel and said, "Really?" Isabel nodded and the man sputtered, "Wow, I didn't expect you to say that. That's awesome . . . you're a powerful Black woman." This was not the response Isabel expected and she didn't know how to react. Why did he have to mention her race?

Implicit bias. Although many of our beliefs, attitudes, and values are clearly expressed and recognized (explicit), we all also harbor unintentional and deep-seated feelings, attitudes, stereotypes, and beliefs, buried in our consciousness (implicit biases) that guide our actions, assumptions, and treatment of others.[35] Some of these implicit biases and attitudes toward others are positive, but often they are negative. Therefore, we must constantly pause, reflect, pray, and be open to correction to insure we are not harming others.

---

[35]Hook et al. (2017).

> *I (Charles) was warned by friends and family, and battled*
> *internally, before taking a job as a faculty member at a*
> *conservative Christian evangelical university. As a Black man,*
> *raised in and pastoring a predominately Black congregation, I,*
> *and those who loved me, assumed my perspectives, theology, and*
> *person would be under constant attack, forcing me to "be White"*
> *in my thinking, pedagogy, and scholarship. Both I and those who*
> *love me were wrong. My perspectives are valued, supported, and*
> *encouraged, and, in more places than I could have imagined,*
> *they are in complete alignment with many of my White*
> *colleagues who equally stand against the evils of racism and*
> *oppression. What if I refused to take the job based on my*
> *assumptions and the assumptions of those who love me?*

Systemic or institutional racism. Structures within society can perpetuate unequal and inequitable treatment and outcomes for BIPOC. We may not readily notice these forms of racism because they tend to be insidious, but their impact is no less powerful. Examples include disproportionate underrepresentation of BIPOC in high-status positions in the United States, misrepresentation and underrepresentation of BIPOC in the media, disproportionately lower median income rates for BIPOC, and a disproportionate lack of access to medical and mental health treatment for BIPOC.[36]

> *Despite living in a highly populated area of a major city, when*
> *Miguel contracted Covid-19, he was not able to immediately find*
> *health care. Miguel, a Latino man who lived in a majority*
> *Latino neighborhood, did not have a car, and the closest clinic*
> *was 15 miles away. His neighbor, Bruno, had the same problem*
> *when he became sick a few months earlier and never received*
> *treatment because he couldn't get to the clinic. Although Bruno*
> *eventually recovered, Miguel watched Bruno struggle to breathe*
> *for days. Miguel wasn't going to let that happen to him. Too*

---

[36]Hays (2016); Roberts and Rizzo (2021).

> *many people were dying from Covid-19. Even if he had to ask for*
> *change from everyone in his building to get to the clinic, he*
> *would do it. He just didn't understand why no one thought to*
> *put a clinic in his neighborhood.*

As we noted earlier, these examples provide a limited perspective of what racism may look in the daily lives of BIPOC. However, the preponderance of the evidence in the psychology literature demonstrates that racism is linked to negative psychological, emotional, physical, and relational outcomes.[37] A culturally humble response to these manifestations of racism provides a foundation for healing conversations on race and other cross-racial interactions.

Cultural humility: Psychology's response to racism. Although multiple solutions have been provided within the psychology literature to respond to racism and build cross-racial connections, scholars have found that one of the most impactful ways to respond to race-related issues and racism is through cultural humility.[38] Understanding racism and the experiences of BIPOC is one way to begin to develop cultural humility. However, a culturally humble person cultivates a number of important characteristics. A person who desires to show cultural humility accepts that they are a lifelong learner, with a continual awareness of the diversity of others, and seeks opportunities to understand others' cultural experiences. Culturally humble people are open to developing greater comfort in thinking and talking about cultural issues and seek ways to respond to and eliminate racism.[39]

Responding with cultural humility to race-related issues involves seeking to understand others' perceptions of racism and race-related experiences. Cultural humility can be cultivated through individual growth experiences, such as attending cultural events or reading about other cultural/ethnic groups, but is best developed within relationships. As you have seen, our model focuses on the relational aspects of humility,

---

[37]Carter et al. (2017); Vazquez et al. (2019); Vazquez et al. (2021).
[38]Hook et al. (2017).
[39]Hook et al. (2017).

and the psychology literature has much to say about the cultivation of positive social relationships and deep emotional connections with others. In the next section we will describe attachment theory to provide a psychological perspective on how cultural humility can be cultivated through relationships.

   Attachment theory: A psychological understanding of connectedness and race relations. Attachment theory is one of the most studied approaches to helping us make sense of the psychology of human relational functioning. We believe that attachment theory can also help us to understand our cross-racial relationships. According to this theory, throughout the lifespan, humans are wired to be in relationship with others.[40] At birth, the *attachment behavioral system* is active, causing infants to seek connection and relatedness with caregivers and caregivers to seek connectedness with their infants. As the relationship develops, if a caregiver has been consistently nurturing and loving, the child develops a secure connection (attachment) with the caregiver. This secure attachment is characterized by a sense of worth and lovableness on the part of the child and the child's expectation that the caregiver will be loving and available. The child then internalizes these experiences, and these beliefs/expectations are applied to future relationships. If caregivers are not consistently nurturing and, instead, the child/caregiver relationship is characterized by inconsistency, emotional disconnection, or a lack of emotional safety, the child may develop an insecure attachment style. In this case, the child creates an internalized view of self and others (an *internal working model* of relationships), which is often carried into future relationships with avoidance (a positive view of one's own worth but a negative view of others' lovingness and/or availability) or anxiety (a negative view of one's own worth, but a positive view of others' lovingness and/or availability).[41] With the former, we may end up avoiding close relationships altogether, given we expect them to inevitably fail, whereas the latter might involve being preoccupied with, and

---

[40]Bowlby (1982).
[41]Bartholomew and Horowitz (1991); Mikulincer and Shaver (2017).

in anxious pursuit of, close relationships, since we believe that the only way people will stick around is if we do all of the work.

On the other hand, secure attachment styles in childhood are linked to attachment security in later adult relationships.[42] In fact, secure adult attachment styles appear to have a number of psychological benefits. Securely attached people appear to be more compassionate and altruistic[43] and may demonstrate greater forgiveness, gratitude, and humility than individuals with anxious or avoidant attachment styles.[44] Generally, people with secure attachments demonstrate greater emotional and psychological well-being.[45] These individuals often experience relationships with others in a balanced way. They may trust others to be available and caring and believe that they are also worthy of love from others. In turn, their relationships are more likely to be characterized by mutual caring, trust, and security. Therefore, we believe that enhancing secure connections with racially different others is an important step in healing cross-racial relationships and can result from practicing humility in these relational encounters. In fact, negative/insecure attachment styles (anxious or avoidant) can be changed to positive/secure attachment styles as we experience new patterns of interaction with others.[46] (We will return to the discussion of attachment in upcoming chapters, filling in additional details about the importance of secure attachments and deep emotional connections with racially different others as a means of building unity within the body of Christ.)

JOURNALING BREAK: PERSONAL REFLECTION

Before moving on to the next section, take a few moments to reflect on the topics of racism, cultural humility, and connection/connectedness in your journal.

1. In what specific racial groups, if any, do you most feel a sense of connection? What emotions arise when you consider this connection?

---

[42]Hazan and Shaver (1987); Hazan and Zeifman (1999).
[43]Mikulincer and Shaver (2005).
[44]Dwiwardani et al. (2014).
[45]Marrero-Quevedo et al. (2019); Mikulincer and Shaver (2017).
[46]Crowell et al. (2002).

2. With which racial groups, if any, do you least feel a sense of connection? What emotions arise when you consider this lack of connection?

3. With which racial groups do you feel you can demonstrate the greatest cultural humility? With which groups do you feel you may demonstrate the least cultural humility? What emotions arise when you consider each of these groups and your ability to demonstrate humility?

4. How would you describe your connection to God? What emotions arise when you consider this connection (or lack of connection)?

RACE RELATIONS AND THE NEED FOR HUMBLE CONNECTEDNESS: AN INTEGRATED BIBLICAL AND PSYCHOLOGICAL PERSPECTIVE

As we seek to integrate a biblical meta-narrative and psychological principles for understanding how to demonstrate humility in race relations, we prioritize Scripture first and foremost as the foundation for building racial unity within the body of Christ. Remember, our goal is to help you humbly pivot from a human-centered understanding to a God-centered understanding of race relations. However, we believe that both biblical and psychological perspectives on connectedness, racism, and humility can help make sense of contemporary race relations.

Connectedness and Christlikeness. First, we believe that cross-racial relationships are best understood in the context of connectedness. From a biblical perspective, grounded in the grand narrative of Scripture, we learn that God created us as relational beings—in his image.

> Then God said, "Let us make mankind in our image, in our likeness, so that they may rule over the fish in the sea and the birds in the sky, over the livestock and all the wild animals, and over all the creatures that move along the ground." (Genesis 1:26)

Within the spiritual disciplines literature, the image of God or *imago Dei* is considered the foundational characteristic of humanity that allows us to be in relationship with God and grow in Christlikeness.[47] Being

---

[47]Chandler (2014).

created in God's image has been interpreted to have various meanings. The most common interpretations describe the *imago Dei* as God's image in humanity that allows for thinking and reasoning, emotions and relationality, and dominion over the earth; moreover, the ultimate goal of humanity is to be formed into God's image.[48] A holistic perspective of the *imago Dei* takes all of these interpretations into account. For our current discussion, we will focus on the importance of our creation as emotional and relational beings.

Throughout Scripture, we see that God created humanity to be in deep relational connection with both himself and others.[49] Being "children of God," "adopt[ed] to sonship," and "co-heirs with Christ" (Romans 8:14-17), we are provided a connection with God and other believers in a new heavenly family. Furthermore, the importance of our emotionality and relationality is seen in Jesus' command to love God and others, which are considered the two greatest commandments (Matthew 22:37-40). Ultimately, God created humans as finite and dependent beings in need of relationship with himself as the source of life and ultimate source of relational connection.[50] The aim, therefore, of all human relationships is to emulate Christ through our connectedness with each other. As pastor and author Eric Mason states, "The gospel is supposed to bring people together who wouldn't naturally be together."[51]

Connectedness, as we mentioned, is a primary driving psychological motivation for humans, and we can only demonstrate true humility in connected relationships. Returning to the attachment literature, psychologists have also studied the ways in which people demonstrate this motivation in relationship with God. Scholars have found that humans' attachments to God often correspond to the attachment styles we experience in early relationships and adult relationships. Generally, secure attachments to others often predict secure

---

[48]Chandler (2014).
[49]Chandler (2014).
[50]Knabb et al. (2019).
[51]Mason (2018, p. 57).

attachment (connection) to God, while insecure attachments to others often predict insecure attachment to God. However, for some people, insecurity in their early relationships drives them toward God as an attachment figure and they find a sense of safety and security in relationship with him.[52] In either case, the research on attachment to others and attachment to God highlights the importance of safety and security in human relationships, as well as in relationship with God himself. As these relationships appear to reciprocally influence each other, growth in one area of relationship may influence growth in the other. Put another way, as we grow in secure relationships with others, we may also grow in security with God, and as we grow in security with God, we may grow in security with others. In cross-racial relationships, our healing conversations model attempts to provide opportunities for such growth, beginning with the practice of humility during conversations on race.

Jesus provides an important example of humble relational connection in his interaction with the Samaritan woman. In this historical account, Jesus begins by first breaking the social rules against interactions between Jews and Samaritans, his initial step of humility (John 4:1-42).[53] Despite her cultural and ethnic/religious background, Jesus approaches the woman as she draws water from a well and asks that she also draw water for him. Cultural and ethnic differences are not barriers in Christ's interaction with her. Instead, Jesus' humility is on display as he models the fruit of the Spirit (love, patience, gentleness).[54] He offers the woman "living water," Christ himself, so that she "will never thirst" again (John 4:10-13). As the woman questions Jesus to better understand his purposes and the meaning behind his statements, Jesus humbly demonstrates patience, kindness, and goodness. Jesus' approach to this woman draws her into relationship with him, and she leaves her interaction with

---

[52]For further discussion of the compensation and correspondence views of God attachment, see Davis et al. (2013), Granqvist (1998), and Granqvist et al. (2010).
[53]Chandler (2014).
[54]Chandler (2014); Erickson (1998).

Jesus declaring his deity: "Many of the Samaritans from that town believed in him because of the woman's testimony" (John 4:39).

The account of the Samaritan woman presents us with a model for
how to overcome barriers by demonstrating humility toward those who
are different from us. The fruit of the Spirit draws others into connectedness with us, while also empowering us to positively and humbly
connect in spite of differences. This deep human emotional connection
is a God-given need and characteristic of the image of God. Unfortunately, our connections with others can be impacted by pain and suffering experienced in prior relationships. Growth and healing in cross-
racial relationships, therefore, must begin with a humble and positive
connectedness, while also being founded on a biblical understanding of
race and racism.

A biblical approach to racism. From a biblical perspective, racism,
and its many manifestations as described in the diversity literature, is a
byproduct of the fall of humankind, which left us severed from each
other and God. It is a means of devaluing others, whether it is experienced individually or systemically. When we engage in or support
racism or when we fail to repair racial disunity, we fail to consider the
meta-narrative of Scripture and the *imago Dei*. In other words, the meta-
narrative of Scripture reminds us that God created humankind in his
image, which means everyone is worthy of dignity and respect. Clearly,
disregarding another person's worth and dignity by devaluing them
based on their race, or avoiding opportunities for the healing of cross-
racial relationships, can be considered sin, especially since God created
diversity and calls us to unity and to love one another.

In general, sin is both a state (sinfulness) and behavior (specific sins),
emanating from the fall of humankind.[55] More specifically, the Christian
notion of sin can be succinctly defined as idolatry and turning away from
God (Exodus 20:3).[56] From a Christian perspective, sinfulness (as a state)
and sin (as a behavior) are collectively:

---

[55]McMinn (2008).
[56]Keller (2010b).

- an inherent, original condition; something we are born with because we live in a fallen, broken world;

- aberrant, immoral behaviors *we* freely choose, based on our own life decisions, which offend God, violate his prescribed law for humankind (loving God and others), and undermine healthy human relatedness;

- and aberrant, immoral behaviors *others* freely choose, based on their own life decisions, which offend God, violate his prescribed law for humankind (loving God and others), and undermine healthy human relatedness.[57]

Because sin is an unfortunate, yet ubiquitous, part of the fall of humankind, we continue to spurn humility and hurt ourselves and others to this very day by chronically turning away from God, violating his law for human relations in the process (Matthew 22:37-40). In the more specific context of race relations, devaluing others, disunity in cross-racial relationships, or even apathy toward the struggles of BIPOC is the result of sin. We deduce that racism fits within God's command to "hate what is evil; cling to what is good" (Romans 12:9). Using a simple syllogism—which employs deductive reasoning by moving from a general point to a specific conclusion—can help us to make sense of the sin of racism for Christ-followers:

God hates sin.

Racism is a sin.

God hates racism.

At times, this simple syllogism can be seen by some BIPOC as invalidating, as it can be experienced to mean that racism should not receive more attention or importance than any other sin. However, from a Christian viewpoint, the sin of racism has deep and regular effects in many areas of life, is passed down from one generation to the next, and permeates individual, group, and systemic functioning. Therefore, as we consider biblical humility, the sin of racism may be considered an

---

[57]McMinn (2008).

opposing behavior. It is opposed to Christ's humble "self-emptying," powerfully described by the apostle Paul (Philippians 2:6-8). Yet, the sin of racism is often unacknowledged, given that Christians struggle to recognize sinfulness in daily living, and needs to be acknowledged and changed as Christians authentically attempt to cultivate Christlikeness and unity within the body of Christ. Thus, as we grow in biblical humility we are better able to acknowledge these potentially unrecognized weaknesses. On the effects of sin, the famous Christian philosopher Alvin Plantinga fittingly offered the following:

> There is a deep and obvious *social* side of sin. We human beings are deeply communal; we learn from parents, teachers, peers, and others, both by imitation and by precept. We acquire beliefs in this way, but just as important (and perhaps less self-consciously), we acquire attitudes and affections, loves and hates. Because of our social nature, sin and its effects can be like a contagion that spreads from one to another, eventually corrupting an entire society or segment of it.[58]

Ultimately, human sinfulness commonly involves a lack of personal awareness, an ignorance of the devastation of turning away from God and violating his law. Because we are blind to sinfulness, attempting to prioritize our own imperfect will above God's perfect will in the process, we may end up hurting the very people that God has called us to love. Still, as Christians, we are called to humility and to love, not hate, one another, which involves a healing reunification process that the late Trappist monk Thomas Merton called "the resetting of a Body of broken bones."[59] Certainly, we are called like King David to humbly seek God's guidance in prayer as we work to understand ourselves and others in the context of race relations: "Search me, God, and know my heart" (Psalm 139:23). We are also called to recognize the sentiment of Jeremiah: "The heart is deceitful above all things, and desperately wicked" (Jeremiah 17:9 KJV21).

---

[58]Plantinga (2000, p. 49); see also McMinn (2008).
[59]Merton (1961).

With this line of thinking in mind, some Christian theologians have even gone as far as to say that we are completely and totally depraved[60] and thus our thoughts are often untrustworthy and vain because of our fallen nature.[61] Therefore, as Christians, we need to dually seek God's wisdom in prayer and anchor ourselves to Scripture when responding to racism. In doing so, a deeper awareness of and conviction for the reality of sin may organically emerge, which, paradoxically, can actually make room for God's loving, merciful presence in this fallen, broken world. Indeed, on the path of sanctification, this form of humility helps us to recognize the impact of sin and surrender our imperfect will to God, exchanging our will for God's will over and over again.

Racism has such a deep and painful impact that the Christian idea of weeping with tears captures the need to humbly and authentically grieve and repent over this sin, seek God's forgiveness, and surrender our human will to God, all in an effort to empty ourselves and cultivate an inner transformation.[62] In fact, when we authentically shed tears because of a deeper sadness for sin, we may, in turn, experience true joy, peace, and acceptance in knowing we are forgiven and redeemed by a perfect God.[63] Applied to the sin of racism, as Christians, we need to humbly connect to a deeper sadness on a regular basis, weeping for both the lost opportunity to cultivate and maintain Christlike unity and our own brokenness in contributing to the rampant disunity among humankind. Put another way, because of our fallen nature, we, too, contribute to division in a whole host of devastating ways, many of which we are unaware of from day to day. Yet, in grieving by connecting to and more fully experiencing a core sadness that resides beneath pride and anger, then actually shedding tears for the sin of racism, we are able to both diagnose and accept the reality of our brokenness and make room for God to heal us and prepare our hearts for the change process to occur.

---

[60]Erickson (1998).
[61]Goodwin (2015).
[62]Scorgie (2011).
[63]Scorgie (2011).

By authentically experiencing sadness and sorrow for the sin of racism, can we begin to let go, relinquishing our own will in favor of the will of God, which is to put others first with Christlike humility. (In the next chapter, we will discuss joint lamentation as a means of crying out to God with others over the pain of racism.)

> *As a White male, I (Josh) have a hard time fully understanding the painful experiences that persons of color endure on a moment-by-moment basis in a predominantly and historically White America. In fact, on any given day of the week, I may quickly move from goal to goal, without ever slowing down to consider the devastating impact that the sins of slavery and systemic racism have had on Christians of color, who are, just like me, created in God's image and my brothers and sisters in Christ. To be honest, as I scurry about on "automatic pilot," lost in my own self-focused thinking and moving from task to task in relatively safe, comfortable environments, probably the last experience I want to connect to is one of sadness, grief, and the historic Christian practice of shedding tears. This is especially true if I erroneously convince myself that I'm not contributing to the problem because "I don't support racism," "I have friends who are Christians of color," and "I didn't personally play a role in creating or maintaining the institution of slavery or racist systems of the past." Yet, in remaining prideful and numb to the enduring impact of racism, I am essentially turning away from the reality of both individual and corporate sin and pain that my racially different brothers and sisters in Christ still experience on a daily basis. Thus, in personally slowing down to allow God to work in and through this deeper sadness and the humble experience of shedding tears, I believe I am dying to self, setting aside my own busy, anesthetized life so as to recognize the devastating impact that human sin—whether larger or small,*

> *corporate or individual—has had on Christians from different*
> *racial/ethnic backgrounds.*

Biblical humility and cultural humility. Christlike humility, when considering the fruit of the Spirit, involves the overarching element of self-denial. This self-emptying described in Philippians 2:6-8 is without pride or arrogance; instead, it is demonstrated with the heart of a servant. As we respond to racially different others, then, we are commanded to humbly respond, seeking to place others' needs above our own. This is a responsibility of all Christians, no matter their racial or ethnic background. We are to demonstrate goodness, self-control, and kindness in race relations. The psychological principle of cultural humility can be integrated with this idea. As Christians, when we recognize our own limitations and seek to be lifelong learners, we open ourselves to the opportunity to grow in unity with other believers. We can demonstrate both biblical and cultural humility as we desire to understand others' perspectives and accept others' differences, while actively working to build deep relational connections. However, as Christians, it is God who is at work within us to help us cultivate the fruit of the Spirit and this attitude of humility. Therefore, as you begin the process of integrating a biblical perspective with the psychological principles we have described, seeking God's help in cultivating humility will be at the heart of the process. Self-emptying, prayerfully reflecting with humility (H), is the first practice in our model for having healing conversations on race. In chapter six, we will walk with you through the specific steps of a conversation using the HEAL model. At that point, we will provide practical examples of how to demonstrate humility in your conversations on race by taking time to prayerfully reflect on your own emotions, connections with God and others, and readiness to demonstrate the fruit of the Spirit.

CONCLUSION

Practicing humility begins with a biblical view of race, race relations, and racism. We believe a biblical view of these issues includes both sorrow for the sin of racism and a Christlike and humble response to those who are racially different from us. This includes a recognition that God's love extends to people "from every nation, tribe, people and language" (Revelation 7:9), as well as the reality that we are imperfect and broken in a fallen world and need to let go of our own will to make room for God's will from moment to moment. Once we do so, we allow the fruit of the Spirit to be on display in our daily life. As we practice Christlike humility, we seek to love others and grow in a desire for deep emotional connectedness when having conversations on race. Weeping with joy fittingly captures a Christian response to racism—we are able to dually (a) express true sadness and repentance for our unique role in contributing to the problem, given we all contribute to the brokenness of this fallen world on at least some level, and (b) experience the forgiveness, love, mercy, healing, and restored unity that only God can provide. Humbly building on this Christian paradox of weeping with joy, we are slowly learning to stand together in racial unity knowing that we have a true redeemer who is leading the way. Step by step, we are being sanctified by Christ to be more like him as he heals us from the inside out and displays his fruit through us.

As you conclude this chapter, we again encourage you in the process you have begun. We know this process can be challenging, but we invite you to humbly and prayerfully reflect (H of the HEAL model) on the biblical view of race and race relations that we have presented. Review your responses to the "Lectio Divina" and "Personal Reflection" prompts and then complete the following activities.

PRAYER AND JOURNALING EXERCISES

In the concluding exercises that follow, we invite you to go deeper by reflecting on the content of the chapter. Grab your journal and reflect on the following:

1. As you think about upcoming conversations on race, attempt to humbly reflect on the idea of racism (and its various manifestations) as sin. How can a deeper sorrow for the sin of racism help you to display humility, compassion, and

forgiveness in the midst of healing conversations on race? How can the joy of redemptive hope, found in Christ, be a response to the sin of racism?

2. Reflect on the ways humility and the fruit of the Spirit can help to heal the sin of racism, and journal about any thoughts, feelings, or questions that arise.

3. As you think about upcoming conversations on race, how ready are you to display the fruit of the Spirit and biblical/cultural humility? What personal sins may be keeping you from demonstrating Christlikeness as you consider having healing, Christ-centered conversations about racial experiences with others? How can sorrow for these sins help you to let go of your own will and make room for Jesus' perfect love?

Below, we have provided an example of a journal entry for Isabel as she reflects on humility and the sin of racism based on her experience of microaggressions, described earlier in this chapter.

EXCERPT FROM THE JOURNAL OF ISABEL: A 28-YEAR-OLD BLACK FEMALE

I'm not sure where to start this "humble reflection" on racism as sin. Of course it's a sin. That's a no-brainer. But I guess I'm supposed to think a little deeper about it. "Microaggressions" is the term I'm thinking about. And I guess I'm supposed to write about my thoughts, feelings, or questions. Well, I don't think I have questions. But I do have thoughts and feelings.

Microaggressions are awful! The incident at the UPS store really set me off. Just thinking about it gets my blood boiling! It hurts that people can be so unaware of how they treat others.

If I think about it more deeply and reflect on ways humility and the fruit of the Spirit can help heal the sin of racism, I can feel the pain of it even more. And I know I'm not the only one that this has happened to. There's so much pain attached to racism, and the brokenness of this world can be so, so heavy. Somehow, I need to find a way to allow the Holy Spirit to enter my experience and help me to see it humbly through Christ's eyes. I need to learn to feel compassion for the people who act like this. It's hard to do that though. The only way I can feel compassion is to think about Jesus and his compassion for others. Like it says in Romans, "While we were still sinners, Christ died for us." If Jesus could say, on the cross of all places, "Father, forgive them, for they do not know what they are doing," maybe I can grow in humility and find a different way to think about others' fallenness, especially when they say racially ignorant things. I guess this can be a step in healing the sin of racism. Thinking about Jesus' example helps. I also know that someday there will be no more racism. Praise God for that!

God, thank you for being with me during that situation. Help me to learn how to handle these things with your kind of humility. Work within me to display your fruit so I can reflect your love in all that I do.

FINAL STEPS

End this chapter's activities with a time of prayer. Briefly thank God for his presence and ask for his continued guidance and grace as you continue to reflect on what you have learned throughout the coming days.

3

EMPATHY

SHARING STORIES AND LAMENTING TOGETHER

Whoever has ears, let them hear.

MATTHEW 11:15

OSCAR IS A 52-YEAR-OLD MEXICAN MAN. *He is married with three elementary-aged children and lives in a rural community in Central California. He grew up in a happy home with his parents and four brothers in a rural farming community. He has a master's degree in business from a diverse public university. He and his wife lead small discipleship groups at their local Spanish-speaking church. Imagine sitting in Oscar's living room, listening intently as he tells a story from his youth.*

"I remember riding in the back of Mama's station wagon every Friday and Saturday at midnight. She'd wake up me and my four brothers and carry each of us, one at a time, and place us in the back portion of the car, where there were no seats. Despite the slight smell of oil that always lingered in the back of the wagon, we'd fall asleep again, covered in blankets, knowing the routine. Mama drove 45 minutes each way to pick up Papa from his *dishwashing job. We were too young to be left alone at night, so we had become accustomed to the midnight awakening. There is one chilly, October night that I will never forget. Papa slammed the car door when he entered and startled me out of sleep. At first, I tried to fall asleep again, but Papa's clothes smelled like fried foods, and he was talking so loudly. He told Mama that he'd been fired. 'Despedido!' he said in a harsh whisper, smacking a hand against the dash. At eight years old, I didn't know exactly what it meant, but I could hear the fear and anger in Papa's voice. I peered over the back seat to watch my parents. No light entered the car, and I couldn't see Mama's face, but I knew she was crying as muffled sobs filtered to the back seat. 'He called me a dirty Mexican,' Papa said. I hurt so much hearing those words, but it was worse to hear the pain in my Papi's voice and the sobs Mama tried to hide. I'll never forget that night. I've held anger toward that White man since that time. And I'm still not sure if I can trust White people."*

As you listen in on Oscar's story, it's likely that you have many thoughts and feelings. Stories affect us in this way by drawing us into the images, feelings, and experiences of the storyteller. Throughout the book so far, we have used the metaphor of narratives and stories, specifically describing the importance of situating an understanding of race relations within the grand narrative of Scripture. Beyond this starting point, next, we want to guide you through understanding the role of individual stories, like Oscar's, in helping to build empathy and emotional connection in cross-racial relationships. Sharing stories about our racial histories or race-related experiences can be a powerful way to heal relational wounds and build Christlike racial unity, especially as they help us develop greater self-awareness and an awareness of others' emotions, needs, and perspectives with the core skill of empathy. Certainly, connecting on a deeper level with others' stories helps us to pivot from self to other, while doing so with Christlikeness also shifts our perspective from self to God (Other). As we specifically listen to others' stories of their race-related experiences, racial injury, and/or racism, we have the opportunity to connect with their emotional experience, grow in empathy, and grieve and lament together over the pain of our broken world. In general, stories teach us, guide us, and help us to develop a greater understanding of individual experiences, but also of the larger social world around us. The best example of a master storyteller is God himself, who has revealed his love for humankind through his use of story within the Bible.

In the pages that follow, we will walk you through a biblical perspective on the core practice of empathy (E of the HEAL model) and the importance of storytelling/narrative and joint grief/lamentation as a means to growing in this key emotional and behavioral response. We will then offer a psychological perspective on these topics and conclude with an integrated view of how to apply the concepts surrounding empathy, listening to narratives, and lamentation to your cross-racial relationships and conversations. As you read this chapter, we pray that you will grow in empathy as you learn to take steps to responsively enter into the experiences and emotions of others, patiently seeing others and their experiences through the lens of Christlike love.

EMPATHY, NARRATIVE, AND LAMENTATION: A BIBLICAL PERSPECTIVE

In our view, empathy is a core component of having healing conversations on race. Yet to develop empathy, an emotional and behavioral responsiveness to others, we must engage with others and lean into understanding their experiences. We believe that immersing ourselves in the stories of others is integral to this task. Before we set the stage for the importance of listening to individual stories, we first begin with a biblical perspective on why this is important. The first key factor to consider is God's model for us in his use of story as a means to draw us into relationship and emotional and behavioral connection with him. As discussed in chapter one, the grand narrative of Scripture is the story that is our starting point for understanding our relationship with God and our relationships with others. This great story of all stories includes re-lational themes focused on creation, fall, redemption, and restored unity, culminating with the goal of perfect community with God and others in heaven. Moreover, with this greater perspective of unity and resto-ration of humanity to God and to each other found within the meta-narrative of Scripture, we can deduce the importance of God's use of story to help humans understand the world around them and grow in their relationships.

Delving deeper into God's grand story, a review of Scripture reveals story after story within the Old and New Testaments that illustrate the core relational themes described above.[1] As we explore the various genres of Scripture, we see evidence of God's providential use of narrative in expressing these themes and in teaching us how to live Christlike lives in our world and relationships.[2] For example, across different biblical authors, we see historical examples depicting God's character, how to know him, the nature of people and sin, the person and work of Christ and the Holy Spirit, salvation, the church, and the last days.[3] In the cre-ation story depicted in Genesis 1–2, we first learn of God's creation of humanity in his image (the *imago Dei*) and his desire to be in continual communion with his people. Here, we also see the depiction of the fall, as the Old Testament writer told the story of Adam and Eve's separation from God due to their sin. Moving throughout the Old Testament, God depicts the stories of both faithful and unfaithful followers and the methods he used to draw his people back to him. For example, in the books of the major and minor prophets, we see God's use of prophets to preach messages of repentance and restoration. In the Psalms, we see examples of God's love and goodness in relation to his people, despite times of trouble and uncertainty (see the lament psalms described below). The New Testament furthers God's story in relation to his people. From the birth of Christ to the book of Revelation, God continues to provide

---

[1]Knabb and Emerson (2013).
[2]Knabb and Emerson (2013)
[3]Erickson (1998).

a picture of his pursuit of humankind and his desire for relationship with *all* people.[4] Jesus entered into human history and died on the cross as the ultimate act of God's love. This act of sacrificial love demonstrated God's caring responsiveness to our need for a Savior and our inability to reach out to him on our own.

Ultimately, the grand narrative of Scripture depicts Christ entering human history and understanding our weaknesses and identifying with our sufferings (Hebrews 2:18; 4:15). Empathy involves demonstrating Christlikeness through identification with the needs, emotions, and experiences of others as we seek to grow in our cross-racial relationships. The various stories of the Bible have a relational theme as their foundation and God's responsiveness to our needs is actively shown from creation, through the fall to redemption and restoration. As Paul stated in 2 Timothy, all Scripture is "God-breathed and is useful for teaching, rebuking, correcting and training in righteousness" (2 Timothy 3:16-17). Therefore, we can return to the stories and greater narrative of the Bible for examples of how to live Christlike lives in our relationships with others and how to demonstrate empathy and emotional responsiveness in our cross-racial relationships. As we emulate Christ, we can learn to respond to the emotions and needs of others, with a loving and compassionate understanding of others' experiences (empathy). Jesus provided additional examples of the use of story (parables) as illustrations of God's loving pursuit of humanity and caring, empathic responsiveness.

Jesus' example, empathy, and Christlikeness. The New Testament provides multiple examples of Jesus' use of story (parables) to teach his followers. Within the spiritual formation literature, the writers often refer to the parables of Jesus as a guide to follow as we seek to be formed into his image day by day.[5] The parables of Jesus provide accessible examples of God's character, heart, and desires, and serve to guide us in our transformation into his image.[6] Jesus understood the deepest

---

[4]Graybeal and Roller (2007).
[5]Graybeal and Roller (2007); Chandler (2014).
[6]Chandler (2014).

spiritual and emotional needs of humanity and met his listeners exactly at the point of their needs. In fact, before recounting one of his parables, Jesus stated, "Whoever has ears, let them hear" (Matthew 11:15). Jesus wanted his parables to affect the hearers, while also recognizing that there were some individuals present who would not receive his message. However, as the hearers of the message were drawn into the stories of Jesus, they were provided with the opportunity for self-reflection and to pivot from a focus on the self to a focus on God and, in turn, to repent (turn from their sinful ways) and be saved. As listeners began the life of following Christ, they learned to be more like him, reflecting the fruit of the Spirit (Galatians 5:22-23) in their relationships. Jesus' parables provide a guide for this, often centering on the overarching scriptural themes of redemption and restoration, reminding us of God's pursuit of all humanity and his desire for each of us to live Christlike lives and pursue Christlike relationships (as examples, see the parable of the lost son in Luke 15:11-32 and the parable of the lost sheep in Luke 15:1-7).

Whether through the overarching narrative and themes of Scripture (creation, fall, redemption, restoration) or through specific stories and parables, God uses story to teach, discipline, guide, and convict. With relationship, restoration, spiritual formation, sanctification, and Christlikeness as additional undergirding themes, we believe that the restoration of our relationships should also be a theme in our life stories, and this is facilitated by empathy. Emotional and behavioral responsiveness to the needs of others is demonstrated throughout the themes of Scripture and in individual stories. Furthermore, these stories are a powerful spiritual teacher and can convict to the response of repentance and evoke interpersonal and spiritual healing. Many biblical stories are, in essence, used to convey God's loving, patient pursuit of humankind; thus, they can help us to make better sense of the need, as followers of Christ, to patiently and lovingly pursue restored unity with others, displaying empathy and the fruit of the Spirit along the way. In the context of healing conversations on race, as we are formed into the image of Christ, stories about racism, race relations, and so forth can be used to help us make sense of our relationships and grow in empathy as we move toward unity, reminiscent of God's use of story in the Bible. Again, Jesus himself provides the ultimate example of one who did not just use stories to teach and guide but also heard the stories of others and responded with empathy, compassion, and love.

We call your attention once again to Jesus' interaction with the Samaritan woman in John 4, during which his self-emptying love is on full display. Although earlier we used this story to depict Jesus' humility, here we want to focus on Jesus' empathy. During this interaction, Jesus was responsive to the woman's deepest concerns and needs, although unspoken:

> Jesus answered, "Everyone who drinks this water will be thirsty again, but whoever drinks the water I give them will never thirst. Indeed, the water I give them will become in them a spring of water welling up to eternal life."
>
> The woman said to him, "Sir, give me this water so that I won't get thirsty and have to keep coming here to draw water." (John 4:13-15)

In his responsiveness to her concerns, and in his empathy for her deepest need, Jesus offered the woman the solution to her ongoing disunity with God and others. We see Jesus' empathy in both his emotional and his behavioral response to the woman. This one example, among many, demonstrates the manner in which we are to interact with others as we join with them in seeking unity. By empathically engaging and seeking to respond to deeper needs and emotions, we pivot in our relationships from ourselves to others with Christlike love. During conversations on race, this may not be an easy task, but we believe it is foundational to healing.

Again, in looking to God's story of love and restoration, we see that he lovingly pursues us in our fallen, wayward state, then patiently waits for us to turn to him. As a parallel process, we, too, should be patient and emotionally understanding and responsive (empathic) as we pursue unity and restoration in our cross-racial relationships, despite the possible challenges involved. This is especially true when relating to people who may not be so quick to see the world the way we do or may be struggling in some way, shape, or form. In fact, the New Testament fittingly describes a sort of "long-temperedness," encompassing the qualities of patience, forbearance, and slowness in expressing anger in relationships.[7] As one of the fruit of the Spirit that Paul mentioned in Galatians, "long-temperedness" most accurately captures God's relationship with us, but it can easily be extended to our relationships with others. Because God is patient and responsive to us in our struggle to live a life that is fully reconciled and honoring to him, we should, in turn, display long-temperedness and responsiveness in our relationships with others, even during conversations on race. We should move toward reconciliation in relationships because "God has given to us the ministry of reconciliation. He doesn't give us the luxury of refusing to be reconciled."[8] We believe that part of this challenging, but rewarding, process will include a natural inclination to grieve and lament together over the pain and brokenness in our world and in our cross-racial relationships. In addition, although this may naturally occur during conversations on race, we believe that purposeful joint lamentation is important as another means of growing together in unity and in developing even greater empathy and relational connections.

Joint lamentation and Christlikeness. Throughout the grand narrative of Scripture, the writers provide multiple depictions of the people of God lamenting and grieving as they cry out to God over their suffering, sin, and/or pain. This kind of lamentation may be a natural occurrence during conversations on race, with the people involved being explicit about their grief and pain surrounding racism and injustice. However, we believe that purposeful lament, which includes inviting others into the process with us, can be a means to deeper emotional connection and empathy. Empathy, as one of the driving core practices within our model for healing cross-racial relationships, can

---

[7]Witherington (2012).
[8]Mason (2018, p. 41).

be fueled and supported by joint lamentation that is founded in Christ-likeness. Within a biblical perspective, lamentation is a form of prayer and worship in which the individual and/or community commune with God while expressing deep emotional pain, petition God for help, and rest in God's providential care and love.[9] Most of the laments in Scripture are found in the Psalms, with the first half of the book of Psalms being primarily dedicated to the psalms of lament. These psalms can provide a model for lamentation over the pain of racism and racial injustice.

In his discussion of the Psalms, Walter Brueggemann[10] described them as depicting "seasons" in the life of the followers of God. The inevitable ups and downs of life are seen in the songs of the Psalms, which focus on every season of life, including *orientation* (times of well-being and thankfulness), *disorientation* (times of pain, suffering, or difficulty), and *new orientation* (times of refreshment that arise after difficult seasons). The lament psalms (psalms of disorientation[11]) commonly follow a clear pattern. The psalmist enters a time of suffering or difficulty, crying out to God by expressing the primary emotions of sadness, fear, and anger, then gives thanks to God for hearing the heartfelt cry. In other words, there was a complaint/lament, followed by praise, a both/and experience of suffering within the human condition.[12] If we model our own process of lamentation after this biblical approach of healthy emotional expression, we can learn to cry out to God in pain, while at the same time thanking God for being with us as we grieve. We can present our emotions to God, as well as our relational needs behind the lament, followed by a trusting acknowledgment that God is still present, even though he may seem distant for the time being. Lamenting is, foundationally, a relational act, given we are crying out to God in the midst of pain.[13] When we lament, we are lamenting

---

[9]Graybeal and Roller (2007).
[10]Brueggemann (1984)
[11]Brueggemann (1984).
[12]Brueggemann (1984).
[13]Calhoun (2005); Graybeal and Roller (2007).

to God, not just lamenting. What is more, in the Old Testament, the Israelites' laments were often community activities, with the psalms of lament being read during times of corporate worship.[14] Therefore, although we can certainly lament the pain of race-related injuries, difficulties in cross-racial relationships, and racism alone, healing can begin as we lament communally, with racially different Christian brothers and sisters. As we engage with each other through hearing each other's stories and sharing primary emotions and needs connected to the stories, we can enter into times of lament together, crying out to God for healing, while also placing our trust in him to respond with his providential care.

Put succinctly, by listening to the stories/narratives of others and jointly lamenting the pain of racial division, we can both experience and express God's love in cross-racial relationships and build cross-racial unity through the development of empathy. In fact, we share the stories found throughout this book in their original raw form to provide opportunities for you, the reader, to begin the process of listening and joint lamentation. It was the sharing of stories like these that provided the initial impetus for the writing of this book. Together this sharing facilitated deeper emotional connections and empathy for each other and provided the opportunity to lament the pain of racial division and injustice. This process not only caused our friendships to grow, but it also broke down walls and increased our sense of working together to build the kingdom of God.

> *I (Veola) remember when I initiated conversations with my coauthors about the growing racial unrest in the United States. We couldn't meet in person due to the Covid-19 pandemic; therefore, our first conversations were held via Zoom. As I sat in my makeshift office in my home, I felt my heart begin to beat a little faster as we started our discussion. At first, I wasn't sure I wanted to enter into these conversations because I knew they*

---

[14]Graybeal and Roller (2007).

would be hard. I was tempted to just listen as others shared their experiences. I was concerned about the emotional drain of having conversations about race and the potential strain these conversations might put on my relationships with my colleagues. I thought, "Who wants conflict at work?" Despite my rapid heartbeat and my mind telling me to keep my thoughts to myself, I chose to openly share my feelings about my own experiences and how I was being impacted by world events. Instead of experiencing conflict, I found that my colleagues joined me in my sadness, uncertainty, and fears. Even through the limitations of Zoom, it was their empathy that showed me we were in this together and gave me the courage to continue these conversations.

Throughout my life, as a Black woman, I (Krystal) have experienced that it is generally not safe to lament the pains of racism with White people. Lamenting racism comes easily with Black people and other people of color. However, when sharing about hurt, pain, or fears because of my race with my White brothers and sisters, the response has often been, "Why do you think like that?" "Well, I don't see color," or some other form of dismissing or deflecting. However, as I collaborated with my colleagues on the development of this model, we have had opportunities to share deeply about our race-related experiences. In a moment of vulnerability, I shared with my White brother (Josh) about feeling overwhelmed with sadness and fear for my children after another mass shooting of Black people by a self-proclaimed White supremacist. My pain and frustration radiated through my body as I looked Josh in the eye and told him how I felt. His response was simply, "I can't begin to understand how that feels. As a parent, I know how hard it is to see your children hurting, but my experience doesn't come close to that. I'm sorry you have to go through that." In that moment, I felt the power of lamentation and empathy.

I (Josh) remember a brief hallway conversation with one of the coauthors of this book, Charles, just two days after the May 2022 mass shooting in Buffalo, New York, which involved a White teenager shooting and killing ten Black adults who were shopping for groceries at a local store on a Saturday afternoon. As we stopped to talk, Charles expressed the deep pain of the incident and that he was, essentially, at a loss for words. In response to his pain, I offered a hug, knowing I, too, had no words to adequately capture the tremendous hurt caused by this tragic loss of human life. Although very few words were shared between the two of us, I, nevertheless, still imperfectly strived to understand and empathize with his pain, stand with him in condemning the senseless shooting, and acknowledge the sorrow, powerlessness, and exhaustion in learning about yet another violent act that seemed to be motivated by hate and racism and directed toward persons of color.

As you can see, as we actively and intentionally seek to build unity by growing in empathy, stepping into the experience of the other, and working to understand the world from their perspective, we can model God's compassionate pursuit of us (as demonstrated in the grand narrative of Scripture). What is more, throughout Scripture we see that God actively pursues us, even though we may stray. Applied to race relations, as a parallel process, we should continue to patiently pursue loving and compassionate unity with others and relationships characterized by empathy, even when our relationships are fragmented or we feel isolated because of racial differences and possible discord. After all, God continues to display "long-temperedness" toward us, which means we should be patient toward others. With this in mind, we now turn to the following lectio divina exercise, drawing from the parable of the lost sheep and focusing on God's active, loving pursuit of sinners as the heart of the meta-narrative of Scripture.

JOURNALING BREAK: LECTIO DIVINA

In the following lectio divina exercise, we invite you to continue to move from your head to your heart as you seek to deepen your understanding of the meta-narrative of Scripture. Consider Jesus' use of parables to demonstrate God's continual pursuit of you, despite your flaws and imperfections, as you read the parable of the lost sheep.

READ: Read the parable of the lost sheep in Luke 15:1-7. Read slowly and allow yourself to take in the content of the passage, including God's pursuit of sinners.

REFLECT: Take one key verse from this story to ponder and meditate on, such as "Doesn't he . . . go after the lost sheep until he finds it?" (Luke 15:4). As you slowly and gently recite this verse, think deeply about God's use of story to convey his love for, and compassionate pursuit of, you, even though you may frequently wander away. Reflect on God's desire for you to also patiently pursue loving, compassionate relationships, characterized by empathy, with racially different others, despite potential strife or fragmentation in these relationships.

RESPOND: Spend a few minutes praying to God, asking him to fill your inner world with empathy for others as you consider the ways in which you can offer empathy, turning from self to other and from self to God in your relationships with racially different others. In other words, cry out to God, asking for Christlike empathy and compassion to fill your heart, as well as a desire to pursue cross-racial relationships. Pray for God's perfect love to fill the center of your being.

REST: Slowly and gently repeat the word *pursue* or *go after*, reminiscent of Jesus' pursuit of sinners described in Luke's Gospel. Sit in silence with God, resting in his presence as you are filled with God's compassion and love for others from the inside out.

Before you move on to the next section of this chapter, which focuses on a contemporary psychological view of narrative, empathy, and grieving/lamentation, pick up your journal and reflect on the following questions:

1. Briefly reflect on your time of lectio divina and God's pursuit of sinners (yourself and others).

2. Offer a brief prayer of lamentation for the racial division in our world. Begin with a complaint and end with praise.

ATTACHMENT NARRATIVES AND GRIEF/MOURNING:
A PSYCHOLOGICAL PERSPECTIVE

Within the psychology literature, emotionally focused therapy (EFT) uses the term *attachment narrative*[15] to refer to the relationship stories we use to interpret our experiences. These narratives, based on the history of our relationships with parents, loved ones, and romantic partners, are made up of powerful memories, emotions, needs, expectations, and interpretations related to both our positive and negative relational experiences.[16] We all have our own individual attachment narratives. These stories accumulate over time and provide us with a way to view the world and relationships. Unfortunately, when our past experiences in relationships have been negative, our attachment narratives can include a lack of trust and safety with others. This can lead to continued emotional and relational struggles, including difficulties in expressing vulnerable feelings, like fear and sadness, in relationships.[17]

It is possible to heal and change our attachment narratives (or views of relationships), including our emotional injuries and unmet relational needs, through the retelling and renarrating of our stories in the presence of a caring, empathic, emotionally responsive person who is attuned to our emotions and needs. In this kind of relational encounter, the storyteller learns to see themselves and their relationships in a new light. Put more succinctly, *emotionally attuned communication* (communication with empathy) can help to deepen relationships through understanding and responsiveness.[18] In this process, as an individual expresses their past experiences and emotions, intentionally self-reflecting in the presence of a caring listener, a healing process can take place, with one individual at a time.

[15]Makinen and Johnson (2006).
[16]Becker-Weidman et al. (2012); Kobak et al. (2015).
[17]Kobak et al. (2015).
[18]Kobak et al. (2015).

Part of the growth involved in this process occurs when the listener demonstrates empathy toward the pain of others, grieving alongside the hurting party and feeling their pain with them. In fact, when the story-teller can safely express their *primary emotions*, which are the initial, deeper, authentic, more vulnerable feelings (fear, sadness, hurt, or righteous anger), these serve as important signals to help convey *relational needs* and actions.[19] Primary emotions, for example, can convey sadness in response to the loss of a loved one, which might reveal the relational need for comfort; righteous anger in response to a social injustice, which may illuminate the relational need for healthy distance or regained control; and fear in response to a potentially dangerous social encounter, which might illuminate the relational need for safety and protection. On the other hand, *secondary emotions*, which are the self-protective, reactive feelings that function to defend against primary emotions, mask (rather than signal) relational needs and actions.[20] Secondary emotional reactions, often made up of an amalgam of frustration, unrighteous anger, and defensiveness, can quickly cover up the more authentic, initial feeling and undermine the pursuit of an unmet relational need.[21] Therefore, shared grief and lamentation, anchored to the safe expression of the primary emotions that signal relational needs, is an important part of the healing process and building unity in cross-racial relationships.

Grief and mourning. One of the original attachment theorists, John Bowlby, described grief and mourning as a normal and expected reaction to losses experienced in relationships.[22] He proposed that, upon loss (whether through death, some other form of loss, or in relationships), our *attachment behavioral system* is activated and we engage in behaviors to reestablish physical and emotional closeness with the object of our loss. However, when this is not possible, we enter into mourning, going through a series of stages as we respond to the loss of a person with

---

[19]Greenberg and Paivio (2003); Kobak et al. (2015).
[20]Greenberg and Paivio (2003); Kobak et al. (2015).
[21]Brubacher (2018).
[22]Bowlby (1980).

whom we shared an attachment bond. These stages begin with initial shock and numbness, during which time the person experiences the loss as unreal. From that point, shock and numbness transition to a sense of deep yearning and searching for ways to fill the emptiness that the loss has left. At some point, the individual begins to accept and/or understand that the loss truly is real and may enter into a time of despair. The last of these stages involves a time of "recovery" and "reorganization," during which the person begins to move out of despair and feels the ability to move into new experiences and relationships, despite realizing that the loss is permanent. These stages of mourning are adaptive, expected, and reasonable because of the importance of attachment relationships for a felt sense of safety and security in the world. However, at times, people do not complete these stages or tasks of mourning and continually experience difficulties developing safety and security in new relationships.

As applied to race relations, these grief responses are a fitting descriptor of how we may grieve the losses in our lives due to cross-racial division, disunity, and racism. Grief and mourning are normal and adaptive responses to the broken cross-racial relationships of our fallen and divided world and the relational pain and loss associated with racism and racial disunity. In other words, we long for "affectional bonds" throughout the lifespan, including bonds with others who are different from us racially and ethnically. Yet, the pain of racial disunity can leave us stuck in grief and mourning. When we experience the pain of racism and racial division, we may struggle to properly grieve the loss of relationship and move through the four stages in a healthy way. As Bowlby described, people can actually fail to move through the proposed stages, never fully healing or experiencing recovery from loss. However, this grief, as a normal reaction to the losses of relationship, trust, and security that is often felt in cross-racial relationships, reminds us of the need for healing. We believe that part of the healing of racial division and disunity includes recognizing the normality of grief and mourning and jointly transitioning through the stages within healthy attachment relationships. We can rewrite our loss stories together by building emotional bonds as we jointly grieve our losses in safe and secure relationships. We can do this by sharing our stories and responding to each other with empathy and responsiveness in the process.

JOURNALING BREAK: PERSONAL REFLECTION

Before moving on to the next section, briefly reflect on Oscar's story from the beginning of this chapter. Spend a few moments journaling about the feelings you had as you read about Oscar's experience, highlighting your primary and secondary emotions.

1. Reflect on any memories or personal experiences from your own story that were evoked by Oscar's story. In your own memory and/or story, identify the following:

    a. Key characters and the environment, time, and social context of the memory/story.

    b. Your primary emotions connected with the memory/story.

    c. Your relational need that is connected to your emotional experience of this memory/story.

2. What might it be like to share your unique, personal story with a racially different partner who listens with empathy and responds to your primary emotion and need?

EMPATHY, NARRATIVE, AND LAMENTATION: AN INTEGRATED BIBLICAL AND PSYCHOLOGICAL PERSPECTIVE

As you have seen, we believe empathy is a core component of healing in cross-racial relationships, and stories have a powerful impact on the development of empathy. In our daily lives, our own and others' stories help us to make better sense of our relationships. Whether we are growing in Christlikeness through the power of a scriptural story or listening to the stories of our friends, we are deeply impacted by these relational narratives, especially since human beings were created in God's image to be in relationship. The degree to which we can offer empathy in our relationships is also influenced by our own attachment narratives and relationship stories, which are developed through our lived experiences. Unfortunately, within cross-racial relationships, these attachment narratives can sometimes include fear, uncertainty, pain, misinformation, and emotional wounds from previous conflicts, thereby hindering the expression of empathy. Part of building connected cross-racial relationships will include, therefore, working to change these relationship stories. In fact, because we live in a fallen world, the stories that we write can sometimes be filled with so much pain that it is all we can see, and it prevents us from displaying Christlike love and empathy in our relationships with others. Yet, when we weave our stories into the grand narrative of Scripture, we are afforded the opportunity to better understand God's plan for our life, which includes unity with God and others in the midst of brokenness and pain.

Therefore, we believe that growth and healing can occur in cross-racial relationships through the development of empathy as we share and express personal stories, placed against the backdrop of the grand narrative of Scripture, as we walk together toward spiritual formation, sanctification, and Christlikeness. This will include the exploration of stories of race-related experiences, racial injury, and racism, all located within a biblical worldview and with Christlikeness as the central aim. The historian and author Jamar Tisby alludes to this idea in *How to Fight Racism*. He states,

> All racial justice is relational. What sparks the desire for people to see change? How does someone develop a burden to combat racism? Often it comes through relationships with other people who are most adversely impacted by racist ideas and deeds. It is through knowing others that those we previously viewed as "problems" become people. It is by knowing other people, developing friendships and collegiality, that we can form the coalitions necessary to take on a society rife with racial bigotry.[23]

---

[23]Tisby (2021, p. 5).

Delving deeper, we believe that recounting stories of race-related injury, pain in cross-racial relationships, and racism can help repair their effects,[24] with the "counternarrative" to racism, discrimination, and prejudice being the personal story of the individual who has experienced the negative effects of these things. The partial mechanism of action is empathy, which dynamically interacts with the practices of humility, acceptance, and Christlike love.

Although our stories can by clouded by distortions in our thinking due to pain in previous relationships, sharing these stories in the presence of an empathic and responsive listener can begin to heal these previous emotional wounds. Furthermore, just as in the biblical account of King David and Nathan (2 Samuel 12), storytelling can help people become more aware of their own sin, expressed within cross-racial relationships, and lead to repentance and action. This greater self-understanding and self-awareness can further generate empathy for others, helping the listener pivot from self to other, which is something God calls us to do within many biblical stories. Certainly, listening in a caring manner to another person's story brings healing for both the listener and sharer. Racism or race-related injury, whether experienced directly or indirectly, inevitably impacts attachment narratives. Beliefs about racially different others (such as prejudices and stereotypes) and expectations for how people may behave are included in these attachment narratives, increasing insecurities, fears, and mistrust. With this in mind, the retelling of these stories in a safe environment, with both a caring and empathic listener of a different racial/ethnic background and God at the center, can bring healing, especially when primary emotions and relational needs are expressed in an open, direct manner to a trusted, safe person.

More specifically, our narratives that develop over time often include impactful episodes that are consolidated into relational goals, expectations/needs, themes, and interpretations, woven together by powerful emotions.[25] In other words, attachment narratives are commonly used

---

[24]Bell (2003); Sue (2015).
[25]Dallos (2006).

to make sense of "emotionally significant information."[26] In a sense, as we think about racially different others, we may develop a consistent view of certain racial groups that is based on our past experiences, ending up with a coherent *script* for how these racially different people will interact with us and how we will interact with them. At times, these scripts can include inaccuracies, misinterpretations, and powerful negative primary emotions. These scripts will typically include the following:[27]

- A set of main characters, located in a particular environment, time, and social context.

- A stable structure, with particular events, responses, and steps to fix or remedy the events.

- An emotional reaction that conveys the most important meaning(s) behind the events.

- An attempt to integrate the events into a larger life story.

Returning to the story of Oscar from the beginning of the chapter, we might describe Oscar's script in the following way: The main characters in Oscar's script about "White people" include his father and mother, his siblings, himself, and the White man who fired his father and called him a "dirty Mexican." The stable structure that Oscar may have developed about events such as these may include a sense that all interactions with White people will include insults, degradation, and insecurity. Therefore, as Oscar responds to this expected structure of events in future relationships, he may attempt to remedy the fear and sadness (primary emotions) connected with interactions with White people by avoiding others who are White or vowing not to trust White people. As Oscar integrates this story into his day-to-day life, he may continue to interact with White people who enter his congregation in the same manner. As he holds on to this attachment narrative and the script that has been developed, he may not be able to fully trust or interact with White Christians. In essence, this script may continue to play itself out in future relationships,

---

[26]Dallos (2006).
[27]Dallos (2006).

possibly even with people of other races/ethnicities, unless Oscar has opportunities to rewrite this script in secure, trusting relationships with White Christians within the body of Christ.

Unfortunately, as can be seen in Oscar's story, attachment narratives may sometimes get in the way of deepening relationships within the body of Christ, especially if prior experiences of racism and racial injustice have led to the primary emotions of sadness, hurt, and fear, which are sometimes masked by frustration, unrighteous anger, and even rage. Also, when we struggle to locate our personal story within the grand narrative of Scripture, we may have a harder time making sense of the problem of race relations and racism in a fallen, broken world and the solution—the image of Christ on display both internally and externally. For example, because the emotion of anger can sometimes create distance in close relationships, it is frequently a "double-edged sword," helping us when we are in danger or need to stand up to injustice, but hurting us when we are striving for Christlike unity and reconciliation within the body of Christ.

To deepen unity with the body, and move away from disunity, gaining a deeper awareness of our primary emotions is key. It is important that we welcome these emotions as powerful signals that convey vital information about our life stories and relational needs, then describe them in an open, vulnerable manner to both God and our brothers and sisters in Christ.[28] In doing so, we allow others to respond with empathy and we can, in turn, respond with empathy to the stories of others. In the process, we move toward uncovering our deeper hurts and needs and learn to stand together as we fight the injustice of racism, respond to racial injuries, and heal cross-racial relationships as a unified body. When a Christian of one ethnic/racial group stands with a Christian of another ethnic/racial group as they tell their story, placed against the backdrop of the grand narrative of Scripture, the two cultivate a new "overcoming" attachment narrative. With this story of overcoming, they

[28]Greenberg (2006).

strengthen the relationship through enduring the hardship/relational adversity together by displaying the fruit of the Spirit and cultivating safety, trust, and closeness along the way. As Christians, this exemplifies Christ's "ministry of reconciliation" (2 Corinthians 5:18) in that the two grow in unity in Christ, grieving and walking together toward God's restoration of this broken, fragile world.

Lamentation, racism, and race relations. The theme of grief, loss, and lamentation, when understood relationally and against the backdrop of the meta-narrative of the Bible, can help us to make sense of and respond to the relational damage of racism and racial disunity. Reminiscent of Bowlby's conceptualization of the stages of grief/mourning following loss, attachment loss is anchored to the universal, God-given, primary emotion of sadness and is associated with experiences of racism and struggles in cross-racial relationships. Where there is racism or racial disunity with the body of Christ, there is the shock of loss of relational unity, a yearning for restored unity, despair and hopelessness because the loss is perceived to be permanent, and an attempt to recover by moving on in life (but still experiencing the loss/yearning). However, we believe that healing begins by mutually grieving this pain in relationship with a racially different brother or sister in Christ.[29] To be sure, corporate lamentation of racism and racial injustice can be healing in Christian congregations; however, one-on-one lamentation with an empathic partner offers opportunities for deeper relational connection. The two-part process of sharing and listening one-on-one to race-related stories allows for empathic grieving alongside the storyteller against the backdrop of the grand narrative of Scripture, which reminds us that we are created in God's image to be in relationship with him and others but struggle with the reverberations of the fall (disunity, division, loss) to this very day. Responding to the pain experienced in a caring manner while actively

---

[29]Although we recommend that healing conversations on race and joint lamentation occur between racially different partners, we recognize that healing can also occur when this is done with individuals of similar racial/ethnic backgrounds, given the inherent differences in experiences and views. For example, two White partners may choose to read this book together and engage in the recommended pivots, practices, and steps of the healing conversation together.

grieving losses builds emotional connection, especially when we hold the Bible's meta-story in mind. Identifying primary emotions and unmet needs connected to racism, racial injury, or struggles in cross-racial relationships allows for joint grieving and lamenting, as is seen in the Psalms.

Unfortunately, secondary emotions, which are often made up of an amalgam of frustration, unrighteous anger, and defensiveness, can quickly cover up the more authentic primary emotions and undermine the pursuit of emotional connection and unmet relational needs.[30] Therefore, taking time to grieve and lament racism and racial injury, rather than responding to it with unrighteous anger, blaming, or defensiveness, is an important piece in the healing process and the building of racial unity within the body of Christ. Stated differently, instead of struggling in isolation, we are walking with a brother or sister in Christ through the shock, yearning, despair, and recovery that are experienced with racism and racial discord/division, with God at the center. In doing so, we are together working toward sanctification, Christlikeness, and spiritual formation. This process allows for all the participants involved, whether White or a person of color, to express their deeper, primary emotions and opens opportunities for the demonstration of the fruit of the Spirit (love, joy, peace, patience, kindness, goodness, faithfulness, gentleness, and self-control). After all, in our fallen state, there is an inevitable longing to return to restored unity. Yet this longing can only be fully satisfied through our union with Christ (justification). We can, however, begin to display Christlikeness in our relationships with racially different others (sanctification) as we walk together toward true community in heaven (glorification), wherein we will be in perfect relationship with God and others.[31] As God meets believers in this place of lamentation over attachment losses, the fruit of the Spirit serves as the proverbial glue. Joint grief and lamentation, therefore, provides an opportunity for the people involved in a conversation on race to seek God's loving presence and grace, while recognizing the reality of the sin of

---

[30]Brubacher (2018).
[31]Grudem (1994).

racism together. In the process, primary emotions can be accessed and expressed and deeper needs conveyed so Christian brothers and sisters are actively pursuing a "ministry of reconciliation" (2 Corinthians 5:18).

CONCLUSION

Within our model, healing in cross-racial relationships will be influenced by one's ability to demonstrate empathy toward others and successfully pivot from self to other. Empathy, emotional and behavioral responsiveness to the emotions and needs of others, helps us to deepen relational connections. Listening empathically to the stories of others can help begin this process of healing, gradually restoring one relationship at a time and increasing unity within the body of Christ. Whether we draw from the core themes of the grand narrative of Scripture or directly from the biblical accounts of God's people and Jesus' parables, we see the power of God's use of story to display his faithful pursuit of the restoration of his relationship with humanity. As we put on the fruit of the Spirit (Galatians 5:22-23) and are formed into Christ's image, we can pursue Christlikeness while also seeking restoration in our cross-racial relationships. Together, we can lament the racial division in our world and the specific and unique pain experienced by those within the body of Christ. As we enter into the perspectives of others, hearing their stories and their pain, we can jointly grieve and lament this pain together, growing in connectedness and healing emotional wounds. God's story of all stories exemplifies his call to his people to pursue unity and loving relationships with others, just as he has done for us.

As you conclude this chapter, we invite you to consider the ways in which you can empathically respond (E of the HEAL model) to others' race-related stories and how doing so can build relational connections and promote relational healing, especially when we grieve together over the inevitable attachment losses that emanate from the fall. As another key practice for conversations on race, empathy will be crucial for your success as you move toward having an intentional healing conversation (described in chapter six). Combined with the other key practices of the model (humility, acceptance, and love), growing in empathy will move you closer to the goal of unity and healing in cross-racial relationships. To continue to build on this skill, as you conclude this chapter, review your responses to the "Lectio Divina" and "Personal Reflection" prompts and then complete the following activities. Make sure to hold on to your notes from these exercises, as they will provide important reminders of your growth and learning as you continue to move through the key practices and toward healing conversations on race.

PRAYER AND JOURNALING EXERCISES

In the exercises that follow, we will be inviting you to go deeper with Scripture and your relationship with God, while also exploring your own race-related stories as a way to help you to pivot from yourself to others and to God. Engaging in the following exercises will also be a starting point for helping you identify primary emotions and needs within yourself, with the goal of later being able to demonstrate empathy by identifying and responding to the same in others. Keep in mind, you will use your responses to some of these prompts in your upcoming intentional conversation on race.

1. Read Psalm 77:1-15. Pay attention to the themes of loss and sadness, with the psalmist struggling to experience God's presence. In other words, consistent with John Bowlby's stages of grief, see if you can pay particular attention to the shock of the relational rupture, longing to restore the rupture, sadness and despair associated with the realization that the loss may be permanent, and need to move on in life with some sense of restored normalcy.

   As you consider Psalm 77:1-15 in the context of racism, offer (a) a complaint to God, expressing your primary emotions and unmet relational needs in the context of personal or societal experiences of racism; and (b) praise to God, letting him know that you trust him and surrender to his loving care.[32]

2. Briefly write the story of your conversion experience (how you came into a relationship with Christ) or a powerful experience you have had with God. Make sure to include your primary emotions and relational needs, along with the event

---

[32]Brueggemann (1984).

details such as the people involved, location/environment, period of time, preceding event(s), your response/actions after the event, and how the event was integrated into your overall life story.[33]

Be prepared to tell this story, including the primary emotions, prior to your upcoming intentional healing conversation on race with a Christian brother or sister.

3. Reflect on *two* of the following questions of your choice. If possible, as you reflect on your chosen questions, try to access any potential primary emotions, such as sadness, fear, and hurt. As you identify deeper emotional experiences, pay particular attention to the themes of attachment loss, grief, and sadness in the context of race relations, then connect these emotions to key relational needs in your relationship with God and others.

Be prepared to discuss *one* of your responses during an intentional *Healing Conversation on Race.*[34]

- What is your racial/ethnic/cultural background? What messages did you receive growing up about your background? What thoughts and primary emotions are attached to these messages? What unmet relational needs, if any, do you remember having? (Some of the messages may have been obvious, while others may have been more subtle. See if you can identify ways that ideas/emotions about your background were communicated within your family or community.)

- When you were growing up, what were the kinds of conversations that your parents/family members had with you about your racial/ethnic/cultural identity, if any, or about the racial/cultural identities of others? What thoughts and primary emotions are attached to this? What unmet relational needs, if any, do you remember having? (Keep in mind, if your family members did not talk with you about your racial/ethnic/cultural identity or that of others, you can still respond to this question. Reflect on what you did not talk about and your emotions surrounding this.)

---

[33]Dallos (2006).
[34]Questions were adapted from activities in Pope et al. (2011) and Sue (2015).

- What is your earliest race/ethnicity/culture-related memory? What primary emotions, if any, are attached to this memory? What unmet relational needs, if any, do you remember having? (Keep in mind, a race/ethnicity/culture-related memory could include anything related to race/culture, including the recognition that others had different skin tones, that others speak different languages, etc. The memory does not have to include an experience of racism, but it could.)

- What role does your race/ethnicity/cultural identity play in how you see yourself? How often do you think about your race/ethnicity/cultural identity? What thoughts and primary emotions are attached to this? What primary emotions, if any, are attached to your sense of self and experience of race/ethnicity/culture? What unmet relational needs, if any, are attached to your sense of self and experience of race/ethnicity/culture?

- Have you ever experienced or witnessed racism? Describe the experience, along with your thoughts/emotions/actions during the event. What primary emotions, if any, are attached to this experience? What unmet relational needs, if any, are attached to this experience?

- How might you begin to make sense of racism as loss, especially within the context of the grand narrative of Scripture? How might racism as loss help you to better identify the problem of, and solution to, racism from a biblical perspective?

Below, we have provided an example of a journal entry for James, a 35-year-old White man. James grew up in a middle-income suburban area with his father, mother, and sister. He spent most of his life in church being active in all kinds of ministries, as his mother was the church pianist and his father was a church elder. He currently lives with his wife and daughter in an area experiencing urban renewal.

EXCERPT FROM THE JOURNAL OF JAMES: A 35-YEAR-OLD WHITE MALE

I think I'll write about a powerful experience I had with God, instead of my conversion experience. I need to remember to add the emotions, so I think I'll start there. I felt amazed, loved, and accepted, I guess. It was when I was 22 years old. I was in a car accident. My best friend, Mario, was driving, and the music was blasting. We didn't hear the motorcycle next to us. We were having a good time and the guy on the bike flew past us. Mario swerved because it took him by surprise. At just the same time, another car passed us on the other side, so he pulled the wheel hard in the opposite direction. Luckily, the guy on the bike made it by us just in time because our car started spinning. We were out of control! I don't think I've been more scared in my life. I thought we were going to die and experienced real fear. We spun in circles for what seemed like forever until the car came to a stop. By that time, we had both been knocked around a bunch, but we weren't hurt. It was so weird because we ended up in the middle of the road and there wasn't a car in sight. We both looked at each other. It was crazy! We were both fine and the car was fine. It was like nothing happened, so we drove home. Like I said, I was scared, but I also realized that God took care of us that night. I felt really safe and protected. I spent a lot of time on my knees that night thanking him. What a good God!

So, now the questions about race. When I was growing up, my family didn't talk about race a lot, and I guess I felt sort of numb whenever race would come up in conversations. I remember that one time a friend of my dad's came over and it was the first time I ever heard someone talk in another language. The guy got a call and, when he picked up the phone, he started speaking Spanish. I didn't know it was Spanish at the time. I'm pretty embarrassed to say that I thought it was gibberish. I thought he was messing around. I went in the other room and pretended to talk like him to my sister. We both made up silly words. I wish my parents had said something to us about it or helped us to understand that people spoke different languages. I guess that was my "relational need" at the time. I was only seven years old, so I can't ultimately blame myself. But it would have been nice. To this day, at times, I sort of feel guilty that I was so unaware of differences growing up, and I needed my parents to help me to understand the world around me. I guess I'm still kind of embarrassed about this, and I sometimes still feel shame that I was so ignorant. If I'm truly honest, I also feel some shame that I've never had my own positive racial identity. Of course, I wouldn't really want to tell anyone else about these feelings because I don't want them to think I'm some kind of racist. After all, I was just a kid. I didn't know any better. Actually, it makes me kind of mad to think that I can't tell someone. Why can't I? I didn't know any better. People shouldn't judge me for something that happened when I was a kid, and I'm still struggling to make sense of my own identity and how I can be my true self with people who are different from me. I guess my current "relational need" is that someone accepts me for who I am and doesn't judge me for my past.

Help me, God, to continue to figure out how to handle the feelings that came up today. Help me to figure out how to really hear someone else's story and to show Christlikeness when I fear others' reactions to me.

FINAL STEPS

End this chapter's activities with a time of prayer. Briefly thank God for his presence and ask for his continued guidance and grace as you meditate on your reflections throughout the coming days.

4

ACCEPTANCE

EMBRACING EMOTIONS
WITH CHRISTIAN DISCIPLINES

Jesus wept.

JOHN 11:35

DAKOTA, A 27-YEAR-OLD NATIVE AMERICAN WOMAN, *slammed her handbag and a take-out cup of coffee onto her desk, the contents sloshing out of the opening, as she arrived at her banking office. Her officemate, Nina, a 32-year-old Japanese female, jumped with surprise at the noise. "What's going on?" she asked Dakota. Dakota shook her head and didn't look up. After a moment of silence, she lifted her coffee cup and presented it to Nina. Nina read the words scrawled in Sharpie across the cup: Pocahontas. Nina shook her head and eyed Dakota, not knowing what she was getting at. Dakota motioned again to the words on the cup. "Don't you get it?" she said. "The guy at the shop wrote 'Pocahontas' instead of my name. It's a racial slur." Nina, finally understanding, stood and approached Dakota's desk. She took the cup from her and read it again. "Well, that's nothing compared to the stuff I've had to endure," she quipped.*

> *At Nina's comment, Dakota felt her heartbeat quicken and anger*
> *began to boil. How dare Nina minimize her experience! Dakota*
> *wasn't going to take this anymore. First, it was the coffee shop*
> *employee and now her colleague. She opened her mouth to give*
> *Nina a piece of her mind just as their supervisor, Jerome, walked*
> *in. Dakota closed her mouth, but her anger didn't subside. She'd*
> *wait and deal with Nina later, but she wouldn't let this slide. She*
> *was done putting up with repeated slights and never doing*
> *anything about it. She would let her anger remind her of what*
> *needed to be done.*

Racism and race-related topics stir a variety of emotions for all people involved, whether one is a victim of racism or the individual who hears about the experience. However, when emotions become strong (like Dakota's), especially secondary emotions like anger that mask underlying emotions, they can circumvent healthy race-related dialogue and create disunity, rather than unity. On the other hand, more vulnerable primary emotions, such as the sadness, fear, guilt, and shame that underlie secondary emotions like anger, can facilitate deeper and more meaningful conversations when they are verbalized, recognized, heard, accepted, and validated.[1] Therefore, in this chapter, we provide a biblical and psychological perspective on how to accept (A of the HEAL model) and respond to your emotions (first secondary, then primary) when confronted with racism or talking with others about race-related topics. In other words, as Christians, we can learn to accept God's loving presence in the midst of our emotions, especially if we change our perspective on the function of, and God's role in, our emotional world. Certainly, if acceptance simply means to "receive willingly,"[2] and if God is active and present *within* our array of human emotions, we can learn to "receive willingly" the emotional signals that God is offering us on a moment-by-moment basis. To "find God in all things,"

---

[1]Sue (2015).
[2]Merriam-Webster (1995, p. 4).

as the famous Jesuit saying goes, means we can even locate God in our emotional pain. During healing conversations on race, we can recognize that God's providence (his protective care and good governance)[3] extends to the fluctuating daily feelings we experience in this fallen, broken, conflict-ridden world.

In fact, as Christian authors trained in the behavioral sciences, we firmly believe our emotions are God-given signals,[4] which can help us to make sense of our relational experiences and needs, especially in the context of difficult conversations on race. For example, sadness tells us we have lost something vitally important and need to slow down to reflect before taking effective action to replace what we have lost. Fear alerts us to a present-moment danger and the need to attain safety and security. Anxiety helps us to anticipate a perceived future catastrophe, recognize when we are feeling uncertain about what lies around the corner, and problem solve and plan for what's next. Anger helps us to recognize an unmet expectation, unfairness, or injustice so we can create a healthy amount of distance from a person or situation, if needed, and regain a lost sense of control. Moral emotions such as guilt, moreover, can convey powerful interpersonal messages so we can notice when we have wronged another and need to take action to repair a relational rupture.

Rather than futilely attempting to somehow ignore, avoid, wall off, or eradicate our emotions—especially the more painful ones—this chapter will focus on accepting our emotional world. We begin with a review of biblical and psychological perspectives on human emotions, then offer an integrative understanding of Christians' emotional world, doing so with an applied focus on race relations and the sin of racism. In turn, we discuss four Christian mental skills—attention, present focus, awareness, and acceptance—that can be helpful for accepting and managing painful emotions when having healing conversations on race.[5] Ultimately, with each of these skills, we are learning to both notice and accept our emotions as

---

[3]Erickson (2013).
[4]Knabb, Johnson, et al. (2019).
[5]Feldman et al. (2007); Knabb et al. (2021a).

God-given signals and God's presence within them in our efforts to move from disunity to loving unity with God and racially different others.

EMOTIONS: A BIBLICAL PERSPECTIVE

The Bible is rich with the healthy expression of human emotion. Throughout the pages of the Old and New Testaments, indeed, we frequently read about the emotional experiences of biblical figures who generously invite us into their emotional realm to gain insight into the psychology of the human condition. Whether we are combing over the lament psalms that vividly depict experiences of loneliness, fear, sadness, and shame or following along with the Gospel narratives that convey Jesus' sadness and righteous anger and the disciples' uncertainty and anxiety, the timeless stories of the Bible elucidate a rich tapestry of human feeling states, with love at the very center.

Emotions, Christlike unity, and love. For Christians, love is central to what it means to be human and allows us to thrive in our relationships with others.[6] In fact, God created us in his image to love him and others (Matthew 22:36-40), exemplified in the birth, life, death, and resurrection of Jesus Christ, the Son of God. Because of this, as Christ-followers we are called to emulate Jesus in all that we do, with Christian spiritual formation involving growing in Christlikeness so we can love others the way that Jesus loves others and pursue unity the way that Jesus pursues unity.[7] In this process of moving from justification (being righteous before, and reconciled to, God through Jesus Christ), to sanctification (becoming more like Jesus Christ), to glorification (being face-to-face with God in heaven),[8] our emotions play a central role, with love serving as the core emotion in helping us to make sense of our full range of emotional experiences.[9] With love as our foundation, we are able to display compassion for suffering others, reminiscent of Jesus'

---

[6]Chandler (2014).
[7]Chandler (2014).
[8]Grudem (1994).
[9]Chandler (2014).

compassionate response throughout the Gospels.[10] Of course, love is the emotion most fully displayed in Scripture when examining the Bible's grand narrative, which involves God actively and compassionately pursuing wayward humans in order to reconcile us to him. Yet, there are an abundance of other emotions captured in the pages of the Bible, revealing the full spectrum of feelings within the human condition.

A thorough review of Scripture reveals God's role in our emotional lives. To be sure, emotions are God-given in that he created humans in his image as whole beings, with thoughts, feelings, and bodies.[11] When God created humans in Genesis, he declared that we were "very good." This pronouncement involved the whole of our beings, including our emotions. A deeper look at various pillars of the faith throughout Scripture reveals the emotional lives of people like Moses and King David, both of whom are listed in the Hebrews "hall of faith" (Hebrews 12), despite their varied emotional histories. Moses, for example, struggled with anger, which culminated in the murder of an Egyptian, whom Moses witnessed beating a fellow Israelite. David, as another example, spent much time struggling with fear and sadness as he hid from King Saul in the wilderness. More specifically, David cried out to God about his pain, "I am worn out from my groaning. All night long I flood my bed with weeping and drench my couch with tears" (Psalm 6:6).

Jesus, as fully God and fully human, also experienced common human emotions like sadness and anger. For instance, in John's Gospel we read that "Jesus wept" in response to human sin, unbelief, and death.[12] Since Jesus was fully human, he experienced the full gamut of emotions and serves as a model for healthy emotional expression among humans.[13] Certainly love was central to Jesus' life, especially in his compassionate responses to others' pain and suffering; all other emotions, including sadness, grief, and anger, flow from his love for the Father and others.[14]

---

[10]Chandler (2014).
[11]Howard (2018).
[12]Carson (1991).
[13]Chandler (2014).
[14]Chandler (2014).

As Christ-followers, love should be our primary core emotion and the anchor of our emotional life.[15] Ultimately, because God is love, loves us perfectly, and has reconciled us to himself through our union with Christ, we are invited into a loving, personal relationship with him, which means we can more fully and confidently love ourselves and others.[16] Worded another way, vertical God-human love strengthens horizontal God-human-human love,[17] which was on full display in Jesus' prayer for unity in the Gospel of John (John 17:20-23). As we learn to begin and end with love in our relationships with racially different others, we come to more fully understand varying other emotions.

Emotions, sin, and shame. Just like all aspects of the human experience, our God-given emotions have been tinged by sin. We can react in haste to our emotional experiences, at times hurting others or even ourselves with ungodly reactions and behaviors. We can also misread or misunderstand our own and others' emotions. Therefore, some Christians might argue against a focus on feelings. "You can't trust your feelings because the heart is desperately wicked," a Christian might say. Or they might respond with, "We're supposed to take every thought captive." Yet, we believe that learning to identify and accept our emotions, all the while inviting God into the process, is much more helpful than futilely striving to minimize, downplay, ignore, or eliminate our God-given emotions by creating an adversarial relationship with them. In other words, when we do not invite God to be at the center of *all* of our emotional experiences, we may end up sinning in the midst of pain. Conversely, when we surrender our emotional world to God, attempting to "find God in all things," we believe we are much more prepared to have healing conversations on race.

Regrettably, due to our brokenness that came at the fall of humankind, the emotion of shame is often at the core of our human emotional experience. Shame may quite possibly be humans' most dreaded, difficult,

---

[15]Chandler (2014).
[16]Boa (2009).
[17]Boa (2009).

far-reaching emotion that leads to all sorts of psychological suffering.[18] In the Genesis account of the fall, Adam and Eve attempted to be like God, not reliant on him.[19] Once they turned from God, they quickly realized what they had done and hid in their exposed, vulnerable state. This early experience of shame, for humankind, has continued to the present day, with shame being connected with personal struggles with unlovability, worthlessness, defectiveness, incompleteness, power-lessness, and a lack of belonging.[20] Similar to Adam and Eve, we quickly attempt to cover up and hide in our relationship with God and others when we experience shame, which can undermine our ability to commune with God and deepen our intimacy with others. Indeed, there is a recognition that something is deeply wrong with our sense of self in our experience of shame, a "not-quite-right-ness" and "powerless longing" to return to the comfort and security of our dependence on God, reminiscent of the Genesis account of creation.[21]

As a universal human emotion and vital signal, shame as the "master emotion"[22] tells us that we are incomplete, finite, and de-pendent on God for our identity and survival, given we were never designed to be our own God. Shame also reveals our need for inclusion, value, and, ultimately, love.[23] When we struggle with this inevitable human emotion, this "powerless longing" can spur us to invite God into our experience, as the love of Christ is the antidote to our aching, enduring inadequacy and estrangement. Because, as Christians, we can commune with God as a friend based on our union with Christ, we no longer need to turn away and hide. Instead, we can run to God's throne of grace (Hebrews 4:16) and enduring love. We can then extend this love and grace to others as we imperfectly attempt to move from disunion to union.

---

[18]Schoenleber and Berenbaum (2011).
[19]Bonhoeffer (1955).
[20]Arel (2016); Bath (2019); Bonhoeffer (1955); Knabb, Johnson, et al. (2019).
[21]Bonhoeffer (1955).
[22]Scheff (1997).
[23]Knabb (2018).

In the context of race relations and racism, we may end up feeling traces of shame. From a Christian perspective, these experiences of shame are reverberations of the fall of humankind. Instead of identifying and acknowledging shame, however, we may only be aware of anger. In fact, humans often struggle with a recurrent pattern of interconnected emotions, beginning with anger and corresponding themes of blame, unmet expectations, unfairness, and injustice. Anger can be traced back to sadness (and corresponding themes of loss) or fear (and corresponding themes of danger).[24] In turn, sadness and fear can often be traced back to shame and corresponding themes of inadequacy, unlovability, a lack of belonging, and powerlessness.[25] See figure 4.1 as an example of the common interconnection/relationship between these emotional experiences.[26]

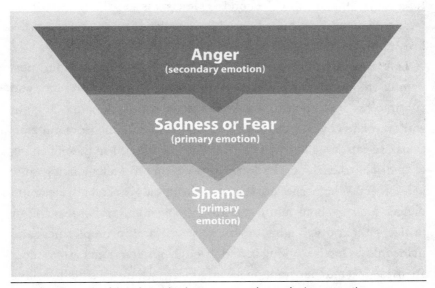

Figure 4.1. Example of the relationship between secondary and primary emotions

Applied to race relations, the fall led to division and disunion in the world, with humans blaming and vilifying one another on a daily basis; still, underneath the anger may be a deeper sadness, which conveys the

---

[24]Teyber (2006).
[25]Teyber (2006).
[26]This figure is adapted from Greenberg and Pascual-Leone (2006) and Teyber (2006).

loss of connection we long for in our relationship with God and others. In other words, we were never designed to be estranged from one another, given our purpose is to be in right relationship—with love as the bonding agent—with God and others. Where there is anger, therefore, there may also be sadness, which can often be traced back to a foundation of shame.

Foundationally, shame, therefore, can be beneath other emotions and originates "from social threats to social bonds, self-esteem and/or social status,"[27] which has parallels with Adam and Eve's shame in Genesis. In the context of healing conversations on race, the Christian experience of shame can help us make sense of the pain of racism because it is a reminder of our estrangement from one another and captures "social threats to social bonds."[28] Racism is so painful because we were created in God's image to be in loving relationship and it severs the love, unity, and belonging we long for.

Emotions: A biblical response. When accepted as signals, our most painful emotions can help us to either consent to God's presence and run into his arms so as to restore lost unity with him (and others) or withdraw and cover up in disunity.[29] Instead of running from our emotions, we can recognize that God is revealing himself in them, helping us to display the fruit of the Spirit as we attempt to walk in loving unity with others. Whether we are struggling with sadness and loss, fear and danger, anxiety about future catastrophe, anger and unfairness and injustice, guilt and wronging others, or shame and incompleteness and inadequacy, God is working in and through our emotional experiences. To invite God into our emotional world means we are, essentially, asking him the following:

- What are you revealing to me in this emotional experience?

- What is this emotion telling me about my relational experiences and needs and others' relational experiences and needs?

---

[27]Johnson and Wakefield (2020).
[28]Johnson and Wakefield (2020).
[29]Pettit (2018).

- How can this emotion help me to better understand the concrete relational steps I need to take, anchored to your love, to restore lost unity with you and others?

In the last chapter, we saw that we can use the lament psalms as a model for joint lamentation over racism and racial injustice. These psalms also provide an example of a biblical response to the full gamut of human emotions. The psalmists frequently verbalized heartfelt emotions, doing so in the context of painfully authentic laments to God. In moving from transparently expressing their emotional pain to God, to making a direct request for God to respond, to committing to trusting in God in the midst of uncertainty, the psalmists appropriately captured a both/and strategy for Christians' emotional life.[30] As an example, the psalmist in Psalm 13 laments,

> How long, LORD? Will you forget me forever?
>> How long will you hide your face from me?
> How long must I wrestle with my thoughts
>> and day after day have sorrow in my heart?
>> How long will my enemy triumph over me?
> Look on me and answer, LORD my God.
>> Give light to my eyes, or I will sleep in death,
> and my enemy will say, "I have overcome him,"
>> and my foes will rejoice when I fall.
> But I trust in your unfailing love;
>> my heart rejoices in your salvation.
> I will sing the LORD's praise,
>> for he has been good to me.

Here the psalmist employs the both/and approach to the emotional pains of life—he expresses his heartfelt pain to God, asking for God's responsiveness along the way, and trusts and praises God, even when an immediate solution is not in sight.[31]

---

[30]Beckett (2016); Brueggemann (1984).
[31]Brueggemann (1984).

In the context of race relations and racism, we can first lament to God (as described in the last chapter), and then use this psalm (and others) as a model for our conversation with a racially different brother or sister in Christ. Certainly, we can connect to our more vulnerable emotions, which may include fear, sadness, righteous anger, or shame, as God-given signals. We can express them to God (then trusted others), ask for God (then trusted others) to respond to us in our pain, and trust that God is (and trusted others are) present to comfort us in the midst of our fallen experience. Below, for example, is a modified lament to God, inspired by Psalm 13:

> How long, LORD, will racism continue to exist in our broken society? How long will you wait to respond to my daily experience of racial division? How long will I have to struggle with the loss of unity and feeling that I don't belong? How long will I have to endure microaggressions, which are weighing me down and chipping away at my soul? Look on me and answer, LORD my God. Help me to find hope in the midst of the racial disunity that surrounds me. But I trust in your unfailing love, believing that you have a plan and your love will heal all racial wounds; my heart rejoices in your salvation, knowing that redemption comes from you. I will sing the LORD's praise, for he has been good to me, even in the midst of the pain of racism.[32]

This lament can effortlessly be extended to healing conversations on race as we learn to recognize God's active, loving presence in our pursuit of racial unity.

First, we can authentically share our emotional pain with racially different others (which, when understood as a signal, elucidates a relational need behind the pain), recognizing that God is present in the midst of the pain. Second, we can ask them to be responsive to our need, with an awareness that being one in Christlike love is our central aim. Finally, we can trust that God will continue to guide the conversation with his perfect love, staying connected to the reality that God's

---

[32]Adapted from the NIV (2011).

redemption will eventually lead to a unified, perfect community of believers as we slowly (and painfully) move from justification, to sanctification, to glorification.

To summarize, in each of these steps, we are learning, from a biblical perspective, how to employ our emotional world to deepen the unity we long for with God and others. Next, before moving on to a psychological view of emotions, take a moment to spend time reflecting on this biblical view of emotions in the following lectio divina exercise.

JOURNALING BREAK: LECTIO DIVINA

As in previous chapters, this lectio divina exercise will help you to move from your head to your heart as you reflect on the salience of emotions in the Christian life. With this particular psalm, David was on the run from Saul, hiding out in Philistia.[33] During this time, David was particularly afraid, leaving Israel because of the danger he was in and struggling with anger because he was apparently being slandered by the Philistines.[34] For this particular exercise, we will be focusing on David's individual lament, crying out to God in fear, anger, and sadness.

READ: Read Psalm 56 in its entirety, slowly allowing yourself to take in the emotions of the passage, including the possible fear of being pursued by others, the anger of being unjustly conspired against, and the sadness of being all alone.

REFLECT: Really ponder the emotional experience of the psalmist and your own experiences of these various emotions, including the anger of being unjustly targeted, fear of being in danger, or sadness of being isolated and alone. What is God revealing to you in the secondary emotion of anger? The primary emotions of fear and sadness? What specifically do you need from God as you experience these emotions? What other relational needs are present? How can love, as your core emotion, help you to better understand your relational needs?

RESPOND: Spend a few minutes praying to God. First, like the psalmist, ask him to be with you as you experience the God-given emotions of fear, anger, and sadness.

---

[33]Wiersbe (2007).
[34]Wiersbe (2007).

Second, ask God to reveal what you need as you experience the emotional pain of Psalm 56, anchored to love as your foundation. Finally, give thanks to God, declaring you will trust in him, regardless of the outcome.

REST: Once you have connected to the emotions of fear, anger, and sadness, and then invited God as *the* source of love into the experience, slowly and gently repeat the word *trust* as you rest in God's active, loving presence. In the midst of the uncertainties of life, God is with you in your emotional pain. Like David in Psalm 56, when the fears and dangers of life seem to overwhelm you, remember to trust in God to deliver you.

Before you move on to the next section of this chapter, pick up your journal and reflect on the following questions:

1. As you engaged in the lectio divina exercise, what did God reveal to you as you reflected on your own secondary and primary emotions?

2. What do you need from God, specifically, as you continue to reflect on these secondary and primary emotions?

3. How can love, as your core emotion, help you as you learn to respond to your race-related emotions?

EMOTIONS: A PSYCHOLOGICAL PERSPECTIVE

The contemporary psychology literature captures the seemingly endless depths of human emotion. Our emotions include physiological components, such as a change in heart rate upon learning of a job loss; cognitive components, such as the thought, *I'm sad because I've just lost a job that was important to me*; and motivational components, such as the thought, *My sadness over my job loss tells me I need to get another job that offers me meaning in life.* Each of these components helps us to make better sense of our immediate environment.[35] Whether psychologists are attempting to understand the normal—from happiness to anger to sadness to fear, for example—or abnormal—from anxiety to depressive disorders,

---

[35]Elliott (2006); Hareli and Hess (2012); Oatley and Johnson-Laird (1996); Roberts (2007).

for example—range of emotions, as humans, we must inevitably come to grips with the reality that our God-given emotions are a core part of who we are and how we function as embodied, finite, and, ultimately, fallen creatures.

Primary and secondary emotions. In addition to considering a biblical view of emotions, a psychological view can help us better understand the salience of primary emotions when having healing, unifying conversations on race, tethered to God's love.

I (Josh) grew up in several different multiracial neighborhoods in Southern California, commonly belonging to friend groups with a wide variety of races/ethnicities. In middle school, however, I was sometimes bullied by a group of peers that were racially different from me. During these experiences, I could only connect to the feeling of anger, with corresponding thoughts that it was unfair that I appeared to be singled out because I looked different. Over time, the anger seemed to only grow, given my expectation that I should be accepted, not judged based on my physical appearance. Yet, in retrospect, anger may have been, at least in part, a secondary emotion, covering up the more vulnerable, primary emotion of shame. During this tumultuous time, my father divorced my mother, leaving my mother, brother, and me so he could start a new, much younger family about an hour's drive away. Because of this, I felt rejected and alone at home, which was exacerbated by the frequent bullying that took place at school. Wherever I seemed to turn in my early adolescence, in fact, I felt unloved and excluded, which revealed my deeper need for belonging, connection, and unity. Although I wasn't able to access the feeling of shame at the time, looking back on these painful years, I can now make sense of the link between my anger (and corresponding theme of unfairness), which was fueled by a deeper sadness (and corresponding theme of the loss of acceptance and approval), which was fueled by a

> *deeper shame (and corresponding theme of unworthiness,*
> *unlovability, exclusion, and powerlessness).*

As revealed in the previous chapter, secondary emotions, such as anger, are reactive feelings that seemingly protect us from more vulnerable, primary emotions, like fear, sadness, or shame.[36] In other words, secondary emotions are "those responses that are secondary to other more primary internal processes and, as such, may be defenses," whereas primary emotions are "a person's most fundamental, direct, and initial reactions to a situation."[37]

As the above example reveals, we may be only aware of secondary emotions, like anger, when experiencing race-related conflict. Worded another way, as a familiar, socially acceptable, go-to secondary emotion, we may be overly relying on anger in our relationships with racially different others. Unfortunately, although anger can certainly be an adaptive emotion when we are dealing with trauma, injustice, or immediate danger and need to quickly create distance or a sense of control, it may sometimes be unhelpful in our attempts to deepen our intimacy with others, especially when attempting to have *healing* conversations on race. However, if we are able to become more aware and accepting of our core, primary emotions, these emotions can help us to identify what we need in our relationships so we can take effective action, offering us the motivation to accomplish our relational goals in life.[38]

Although by no means pleasant, accessing and accepting primary emotions, such as sadness, fear, and shame, helps us to better understand our relationships so we can pursue loving unity with others. However, when we only stay connected to secondary emotions, such as anger, we may have a hard time understanding what, exactly, we need when interacting with others. Anger, in reality, tends to elicit distance, defensiveness, and more anger from the other person. On the other hand, during conversations on race, accepting and understanding our own and others'

---

[36]Greenberg and Paivio (2003); Kobak et al. (2015).
[37]Greenberg and Pascual-Leone (2006, pp. 616, 612).
[38]Greenberg and Pascual-Leone (2006).

primary emotions can bring about healing in relationships. This is espe-cially true because conversations on race and racism can evoke emotions connected with prior race-related emotional wounds.[39]

Racism and primary and secondary emotions. Racism can be a chronic source of emotional pain for many persons of color, given they may encounter it in daily life at a variety of different levels; that is, it may be experienced at the interpersonal or societal levels.[40] Possibly mani-festing as being excluded from, or stigmatized in, relationships,[41] con-versations on racism with racially different others may elicit a range of powerful emotions—both primary and secondary. For example, anger is a common, understandable emotion that may materialize, given the deep injustice of racism. On one hand, anger may be a primary emotion, given the unfairness of racism and unmet expectation that everyone should be treated with dignity and worth, regardless of the color of their skin. On the other hand, anger can sometimes be a secondary emotion when engaging in conversations about racism, given it may mask or cover up the more vulnerable feeling of shame. With shame, there may be a deeper need to be accepted, be valued, and belong.[42] The primary emotions of sadness and fear can also emerge in race-related conversa-tions. They may serve as signals that reveal a sense of loss of connection and value or the danger of being isolated, stigmatized, or harassed be-cause of racism. In these instances, anger may be a reaction to some of the more difficult hurts that emanate from racism. Ultimately, racism can emerge in a variety of different ways, leading to a whole host of primary and secondary feeling states. What follows, then, is a brief review of the diversity literature, focusing on the intersection between racism-related stress/coping and primary and secondary emotions in order to better understand the ways in which racism manifests and is responded to in contemporary society.

---

[39]Malott and Schaefle (2015).
[40]Brondolo et al. (2009).
[41]Brondolo et al. (2009).
[42]Greenberg and Paivio (2003).

Racism-related stress/coping and primary and secondary emotions.
Within the diversity literature, several terms have been used to describe
the emotional response and corresponding reactions people have to
racism. These terms include *race-based stress, racist incident-based stress/
trauma,* and *racial trauma.*[43] Researchers in the diversity field have considered racism to be a *complex stressor* in that the results accumulate
across the different racist events and can combine with the effects of
other stressors and traumas.[44]

Racism, in its various manifestations, can affect all aspects of human
functioning, including thoughts, feelings, and physical experiences.[45] As
a result of racist events and the accumulation of stress from racism,
people have reported depression, anxiety, obsessive-compulsive
symptoms, numbness, grief, and anger, among other types of psychological suffering.[46] Behavioral responses to these emotional experiences
include an increase in smoking and alcohol consumption.[47] Beyond
these responses, racism can also affect spiritual functioning, with some
people questioning their faith as a result.[48] For some, these accumulated
experiences or individual significant racist events can lead to symptoms
that mimic posttraumatic stress disorder (PTSD), with victims experiencing intrusive thoughts, the avoidance of racism-related reminders,
and increased alertness to potential threats.[49] Overall, this body of literature has revealed the psychological and spiritual impact that racism
has on BIPOC.

Because of the emotional pain of racism and the cumulative effects
of years of oppressive experiences, it may be difficult for BIPOC to
openly, honestly, and authentically talk about race with racially different
others. What is more, those who have not directly or personally experienced racism may also experience discomfort, uncertainty, and fear

---

[43]Bryant-Davis (2007); Carter (2007).
[44]Brondolo et al. (2009).
[45]Bryant-Davis (2007); Carter et al. (2017); Paradies et al. (2015).
[46]Carter (2007); Carter et al. (2017).
[47]Carter et al. (2017).
[48]Bryant-Davis (2007).
[49]Bryant-Davis (2007).

(among other emotions) when faced with having a conversation on race. It is not uncommon for people (of all racial and ethnic backgrounds, whether White or BIPOC) to stifle or shut down emotions during race-related conversations. Unfortunately, doing so can decrease learning[50] and undermine the ability to effectively communicate relational needs. Certainly, racism hurts everyone, due to both its individual and its societal consequences. Therefore, people are often afraid of the emotions that are elicited during these conversations, especially when anger is expressed or people feel accused and blamed.[51] People may also fear losing control of emotions during these conversations.[52] What is more, BIPOC individuals may feel obligated to educate others about their experiences, which may feel like an added emotional burden. Overall, reciprocity is especially salient in healing conversations on race, given both parties can find healing by being authentic about their emotional experiences. In other words, we are learning to walk together on the roads of life, at the same pace, rather than one person getting out ahead of the other and feeling pressure to lead the way. Therefore, although the psychology literature clearly demonstrates the emotional impact of racism on BIPOC, all parties involved in a healing conversation on race must become aware of, share, and find ways to cope with, and respond to, their emotional experiences.

In the psychology literature, we find a number of descriptions of how people cope with and respond to racism-related stress and the associated emotions. Common coping strategies, and examples of each, include the following:[53]

- Racially conscious action (educating others about racism)

- Constrained resistance (threatening someone or getting revenge)

- Confrontation (talking to the perpetrator of racism to express feelings)

---

[50]Sue (2015).
[51]Sue (2015).
[52]Sue (2015).
[53]Forsyth and Carter (2014); Kwah (2019); Zapolski et al. (2019).

- Hypervigilance (being more cautious around people in authority)
- Bargaining (looking for an explanation other than racism)
- Anger regulation (fantasizing about getting revenge)
- Empowered action (taking legal action)
- Spiritual coping (reading the Bible)
- Mindfulness and loving-kindness (commonly used meditative techniques that have been recently employed to address discrimination and racism). (In this chapter, we offer Christian meditative and contemplative alternatives to these approaches, which have historically been referred to as spiritual disciplines within the Christian tradition.)

Overall, empowered action is related to better psychological functioning, and spiritual coping is related to greater overall well-being, whereas hypervigilance, bargaining, and constrained resistance are associated with increased psychological distress.[54] From our perspective, being mindful of primary emotions (based on a Christian alternative to mindfulness, which was listed as the final coping strategy above) and accepting them as a valid, signal-providing part of the human experience is especially important when having healing conversations on race.

Ultimately, we concur with the psychologist Derald Sue, who powerfully declared the following on the importance of understanding, acknowledging, and responding to our emotions when it comes to conversations on race:

> As long as emotions are left untouched, unacknowledged, and unexplored, they will serve as emotional roadblocks to successful race talk. Our research suggests that successful race talk must allow for the free expression of nested and impacted feelings, acknowledge their legitimacy and importance in dialogues, and be deconstructed so their meanings are made clear. Rather than seeing emotions as a hindrance and barrier to race talk and rather than shutting them down, allowing

---

[54]Forsyth and Carter (2014).

them to bubble to the surface actually frees the mind and body to achieve understanding and insight.[55]

It is essential to acknowledge our deeper emotions when we are engaged in important conversations on race. If we avoid doing so, we may be unable to achieve the loving unity we are longing for. Therefore, from our perspective, an integrated biblical and psychological perspective can help us to be mindful of our primary emotions, which serve as vital signals that help us to deepen our relationship with God and others as we pursue Christlike unity on this side of heaven. Before moving on to reading further about this integrated perspective, take a moment to spend time in personal reflection.

JOURNALING BREAK: PERSONAL REFLECTION

1. In your journal, spend 10 minutes reflecting on the topic of racism and its impact in society and your life or the lives of people you know. As you do so, reflect on and note the secondary (anger, for example), then primary (sadness, fear, shame, righteous anger), emotions that arise.

2. What secondary and primary emotions were you aware of during your journaling time? What relational needs are present when you experience these emotions? Who has been helpful in meeting these relational needs in the past? In what specific ways have they met your needs?

3. What role does God play in your emotions? What do you need from him as you experience them?

EMOTIONS: AN INTEGRATED BIBLICAL AND PSYCHOLOGICAL PERSPECTIVE

Whether we are discussing emotions from a biblical or secular psychological perspective, we believe they are God-given signals that convey rich meaning and elucidate our deeper relational needs. When having healing conversations on race between racially different Christians, with love at the center, we need to be able to authentically acknowledge them

---

[55]Sue (2015, p. 145).

to God and others, inviting God into the process as the author of love and our proverbial guide. We need to learn to recognize our emotions, lean into them to understand their meaning, discern God's role in them, and employ them to cultivate unity with racially different others. Along the way, we are tethering these steps to love as our core emotion, asking God to display his love in and through our emotional world.

The Bible is filled with example after example of the heartfelt expression of the emotional pains of life. Jesus, as both fully God and fully human, modeled the healthy expression of emotions while living a life fully devoted to his Father. Therefore, we, too, can have confidence that our emotions should be at the center, rather than on the periphery, of healthy human functioning. To identify and integrate our emotions into conversations on race means we are attempting to better understand our own (and racially different others') need for unity and connection as we humbly attempt to display the fruit of the Spirit and allow God to work through us as *the* source of love. We are also moving from secondary to primary emotions, leading to the core emotion of love, wherein God is revealing himself to us from moment to moment.

Christian mental skills as a response to race-related emotions. As described earlier, we may attempt to cope with these painful emotional experiences in a wide variety of ways. We can summarize these various approaches to coping with race-related emotions as either problem-focused or emotion-focused coping. With problem-focused coping, we might strive to take action to change the situation and, thus, reduce or eliminate the emotional pain.[56] Essentially, we are taking steps to eliminate the problem that gives rise to the emotional pain, which may include avoidance of the anticipated problem altogether.[57] Conversely, with emotion-focused coping, we may attempt to focus on managing the emotions themselves through reducing, eliminating, or changing our relationship to them, not prioritizing changing the problem itself or our environment.[58]

---

[56]Lazarus (1999).
[57]Carver (2011).
[58]Carver (2011).

As noted in the previous section, one such emotion-focused coping strategy, mindfulness meditation, may be especially helpful for learning how to relate differently to painful race-related emotions.[59] In essence, mindfulness involves attempting to relate differently to inner experiences through the cultivation of several key mental skills, including attention (concentrating on one task at a time), present focus (focusing on the here-and-now), awareness (recognizing thoughts and feelings with nonjudgment), and acceptance (tolerating unpleasant thoughts and feelings).[60] When engaging in difficult, albeit necessary, conversations on race, we believe this well-defined set of emotion regulation skills (coping skills) is especially important for unity. Within this skill set, indeed, learning how to accept our emotions is key, observing them with compassion, distance, and nonjudgment so we can stay fully engaged in the conversation.

For Christians, these skills are not practiced in isolation; rather, the mental skills of attention, present focus, awareness, and acceptance are cultivated with God, recognizing that he is active and present in each unfolding moment.[61] Certainly, sanctification and becoming more like Christ involve a holistic approach, with spiritual health working hand in hand with emotional health as we invite God to take residence within our inner world.[62] Moreover, given that mindfulness meditation emanates from the Buddhist tradition, we believe turning to the Christian faith for a more relational, biblically anchored approach to the development of these emotion regulation skills is key. In essence, we are better able to manage and accept our emotional pain because God is with us, revealing himself to us in our inner world as we "find God in all things."

We base our approach on the research of two of the current authors (Josh and Veola). The use of Christian mental skills can help you respond to emotions that arise when talking about, and responding to, race-related

---

[59]Analayo (2020).
[60]Feldman et al. (2007).
[61]Knabb, Vazquez, et al. (2019); Knabb et al. (2021a).
[62]Scazzero (2011).

topics. These four Christian mental skills can be used prior to cross-racial conversations and interactions and during these interactions. We believe these skills will be helpful, especially when attempting to cultivate safe, trusting, emotionally attuned conversations through the expression of primary emotions and unmet relational needs. In fact, using these skills can help both the listener and speaker to authentically accept emotions (A = Acceptance, the third practice in the HEAL model) while building racial unity. What's more, these skills can be used as a helpful immediate response to current race-related events and as a means to respond to long-held emotional residue from the accumulation of racially stressful, painful, and/or traumatic events.

In previous research, we have found that these adaptive mental skills can help people shift their focus from being preoccupied with repetitive negative thoughts (rumination, worry) and the feelings connected with them to an awareness of God's active, loving presence.[63] These skills may help Christians to both accept their emotions and God's presence during conversations on race, which can help you to stay more fully engaged as you attempt to display Christlike love. Actively reorienting the focus does not minimize the importance of emotion; rather, it increases awareness and helps the person draw on God's love and strength.

The purpose is to connect with God *while* experiencing difficult race-related emotions, allowing God to enter into the experience and help you respond in a Christlike manner. As you develop and practice each of the following skills, you will learn to accept each difficult emotional reaction because of God's loving presence.[64]

- *Christian attention.* Concentrating on God's promises (a Scripture verse) in the midst of race-related emotions (primary and secondary)

- *Christian present focus.* Focusing on God's active, loving presence in the here-and-now in the midst of race-related emotions (primary and secondary)

---

[63]Knabb, Vazquez, and Pate (2019); Knabb et al. (2021a).
[64]The descriptions of the four Christian mental skills are adapted from Knabb et al. (2020, 2021a) and Feldman et al. (2007).

- *Christian awareness.* Maintaining an awareness of God's active, loving presence in the midst of race-related emotions (primary and secondary)

- *Christian acceptance.* Accepting race-related emotions (primary and secondary) by yielding to God's active, loving presence

To be more concise, combining these four skills into one involves cultivating and maintaining a present-moment loving awareness of God within your inner world, especially with your emotions, which serve as vital signals in your relationship with God and others.[65] Before concluding the chapter, what follows are brief guided directions for formally practicing each of the four Christian mental skills in the context of race-related emotions.

Christian mental skills in practice: Accepting emotions because God is present. Within the "Prayer and Journaling Exercises" section at the end of this chapter, we will ask you to practice the four Christian mental skills. However, we believe that the ongoing practice of these skills will provide a foundation for later use during conversations on race. Below, we offer instructions for each. When you are ready to complete these, for each of the following four exercises,[66] try to find a quiet environment, free from distractions. Sit up straight in a supportive chair, with your eyes closed and hands resting comfortably in your lap. If you are able, allow your palms to face upward and outward as a symbol of your willingness to accept God's active, loving presence in this very moment. With each exercise, we encourage you to spend 10 minutes each time you practice, slowly moving through the steps and extending mercy and grace to yourself should you get distracted. Remember to focus on the role of each Christian mental skill in allowing you to accept your emotions (first secondary, then primary), given God is with you. Although the four exercises have some similarities, each is designed to focus on one mental skill at a time. However, as we have mentioned, working to

---

[65]Knabb and Bates (2020).

[66]These four exercises are adapted from Feldman et al. (2007), Knabb (2021), and Knabb et al. (2021a).

eventually combine these skills during conversations on race will allow you to maintain your focus on God's work within you and in your relationships as you accept your own and others' emotions. We encourage you to regularly return to each of these exercises to continue to build and practice these skills.

If you would like, you can also follow along with an audio track for each of the four exercises, located at ivpress.com/heal-multimedia.

CHRISTIAN ATTENTION: AN EXERCISE[67]

1. Pray to God, asking him to be with you and help you develop a greater attentiveness toward him in the midst of your race-related emotions during the next 10 minutes.

2. Think about a recent race-related conversation you had. (If nothing comes to mind, try to remember a recent race-related event that was in the news.)

3. Notice the secondary emotion that emerges, such as anger, then primary emotion, such as fear, sadness, or shame. Spend a few minutes just noticing these emotions, including where they are located in your body and any other sensations that may emerge. Consider what the meaning of these emotions may be as God-given signals. For example, sadness may reveal an important loss, fear may reveal a present danger, anger may reveal an injustice, and shame may reveal an incompleteness or lack of belonging.

4. Begin to focus on the verse "Do not be afraid, for I am with you" (Isaiah 43:5), inviting God to be with you in your emotions.

5. In your mind, slowly and gently repeat the verse with focused, sustained attention, recognizing that God is with you in this very moment as you experience your emotions.

6. Allow yourself to deeply feel God's presence in the emotions, first secondary, then primary.

---

[67]This exercise is based on Puritan meditation, which comes from the Protestant Christian tradition. For a more thorough review, see Ball (2016), Beeke and Jones (2012), and Watson (2012).

7. Whenever another thought, feeling, or sensation emerges, acknowledge its presence (for example, "I'm worrying"), then gently return to slowly reciting the verse.

8. Over and over again, notice your emotions, invite God into them by slowly and gently reciting the verse, and return to the verse whenever your attention has wandered to something else, extending grace and mercy to yourself in the process.

9. Conclude the exercise by praying to God, asking him to help you keep your attention on this verse throughout the day, especially in the midst of your race-related emotions.

CHRISTIAN PRESENT FOCUS: AN EXERCISE[68]

1. Pray to God, asking him to be with you and help you to develop a greater focus on him in the midst of your race-related emotions during the next 10 minutes.

2. Think about a recent race-related conversation you had. (If nothing comes to mind, try to remember a recent race-related event that was in the news.)

3. Notice the secondary emotion that emerges, such as anger, then primary emotion, such as fear, sadness, or shame. Spend a few minutes just noticing these emotions, including where they are located in your body and any other sensations that may emerge. Consider what the meaning of these emotions may be as God-given signals. For example, sadness may reveal an important loss, fear may reveal a present danger, anger may reveal an injustice, and shame may reveal an incompleteness or lack of belonging.

4. In your mind, begin to slowly and gently recite the Jesus Prayer, "Lord Jesus Christ, Son of God, have mercy on me," inhaling with the first part of the prayer ("Lord Jesus Christ, Son of God"), then exhaling with the second part of the prayer ("have mercy on me").

---

[68]This exercise is based on the Jesus Prayer, which comes from the Orthodox Christian tradition. For a more thorough review, see Talbot (2013). See also Knabb and Vazquez (2018); Vazquez and Jensen (2020).

5. With the first part, you are symbolically inhaling God's active, loving presence as you invite him into your emotions, first secondary, then primary. With the second part of the prayer, you are symbolically letting go of your need to do anything with your emotions, resting in God's presence as he reveals himself to you in this moment in and through them.

6. Whenever another thought, feeling, or sensation emerges, acknowledge its presence (for example, "I'm worrying"), then gently return to slowly reciting the Jesus Prayer.

7. Over and over again, notice your emotions, invite God into them by slowly and gently reciting the Jesus Prayer, and return to the Jesus Prayer whenever your attention has wandered to something else, extending grace and mercy to yourself in the process.

8. Conclude the exercise by praying to God, asking him to help you maintain greater focus on Jesus' presence in each unfolding moment throughout the day by reciting the Jesus Prayer, especially as you notice difficult or negative race-related emotions.

CHRISTIAN AWARENESS: AN EXERCISE[69]

1. Pray to God, asking him to be with you and help you develop a greater awareness of him in the mist of your race-related emotions during the next 10 minutes.

2. Think about a recent race-related conversation you had. (If nothing comes to mind, try to remember a recent race-related event that was in the news.)

3. Notice the secondary emotion that emerges, such as anger, then primary emotion, such as fear, sadness, or shame. Spend a few minutes just noticing these emotions, including where they are located in your body and any other sensations that may emerge. Consider what the meaning of these emotions may be as God-given signals. For example, sadness may reveal an important loss, fear

---

[69]This exercise is based on *The Practice of the Presence of God*, by Brother Lawrence, a seventeenth-century Catholic monk. For a more thorough review, see Lawrence (2015).

may reveal a present danger, anger may reveal an injustice, and shame may reveal an incompleteness or lack of belonging.

4. In your mind, begin to slowly and gently say to yourself, "My God, I am completely yours."

5. Whenever another thought, feeling, or sensation emerges, acknowledge its presence (for example, "I'm worrying"), then gently return to the phrase, "My God, I am completely yours."

6. Over and over again, notice your emotions, first secondary, then primary, invite God into them by slowly and gently reciting the phrase, and return to the phrase whenever your awareness has wandered to something else, extending grace and mercy to yourself in the process.

7. Conclude the exercise by praying to God, asking him to help you maintain an awareness of his presence by reciting the phrase throughout the day, especially in the midst of your race-related emotions.

CHRISTIAN ACCEPTANCE: AN EXERCISE[70]

1. Pray to God, asking him to be with you and help you develop a greater acceptance of him and your race-related emotions during the next 10 minutes.

2. Think about a recent race-related conversation you had. (If nothing comes to mind, try to remember a recent race-related event that was in the news.)

3. Notice the secondary emotion that emerges, such as anger, then primary emotion, such as fear, sadness, or shame. Spend a few minutes just noticing these emotions, including where they are located in your body and any other sensations that may emerge. Consider what the meaning of these emotions may be as God-given signals. For example, sadness may reveal an important loss, fear

---

[70]This exercise is based on *The Cloud of Unknowing*, by an anonymous fourteenth-century English writer, and centering prayer, a contemporary repackaging of the instructions from *The Cloud of Unknowing*. For a more thorough review, see Bangley (2006) and Pennington (1982).

may reveal a present danger, anger may reveal an injustice, and shame may reveal an incompleteness or lack of belonging.

4. In your mind, begin to slowly and gently repeat the word *love*, given "God is love" (see 1 John 4:7-21). This word symbolically captures your willingness to fully consent, yield to, and accept God's active, loving presence in the midst of your emotions, first secondary, then primary.

5. Whenever another thought, feeling, or sensation emerges, acknowledge its presence (for example, "I'm worrying"), then gently return to the word *love*, which symbolizes your willingness to completely and totally surrender your inner world to God.

6. Over and over again, notice your emotions, invite God into them by slowly and gently reciting the word *love*, and return to the word to turn over your inner world to God, moment-by-moment.

7. Conclude the exercise by praying to God, asking him to help you accept his active, loving presence and your race-related emotions by reciting the word throughout the day.

Lectio divina as a response to race-related emotions. In addition to the above Christian practices that can help you to cultivate key Christian mental skills for having healing conversations on race, before concluding this chapter, we want to teach you one final strategy, which we believe can be especially powerful in allowing you to navigate the roads of life with a recognition that you are a dwelling place and conduit for the Holy Spirit. This can be especially important as you attempt to understand and respond to others' psychological pain. To review, lectio divina involves four major steps: reading, meditating, praying, and contemplating. In this final exercise for the chapter, we draw on the first two steps of lectio divina—reading and meditating—and the apostle Paul's fruit of the Spirit passage in Galatians to help you recognize God's Holy Spirit within, especially God's "love, joy, peace, patience, [and] kindness,"[71]

---

[71]Wilhoit and Howard (2012); NASB (2020).

so that you can, with God's help, better accept your own and others' emotional pain.

Interestingly, among this famous list of nine of God's fruit, love and kindness are included as the first and fifth, reminiscent of a historically Buddhist meditative practice with the same name—loving-kindness meditation (LKM)—that has grown in popularity in the psychology literature in the twenty-first century. With LKM, practitioners are instructed to repeat several key phrases (for example, "May I be happy," "May I be at ease," "May I be free from suffering," "May others be happy," "May others be at ease," "May others be free from suffering") so as to cultivate compassion for both the self (including unpleasant thoughts, feelings, sensations, memories, and images) and others.[72] In fact, a recent review of two-dozen LKM studies revealed that the practice can be helpful in increasing a range of positive emotions,[73] with some authors even advocating for its use in better responding to the psychological pain of racial oppression.[74]

As a Christian alternative to Buddhist-derived LKM, we believe Christians can successfully practice the first two steps of lectio divina to cultivate an awareness of God's fruit of the Spirit throughout the day and move toward accepting and relating differently to the overwhelming emotions that may derail healing conversations on race. In support of this notion, in a recent pilot study—conducted by the first two authors, Josh and Veola, of the present book—among Christian trauma survivors that compared lectio divina and LKM for trauma-based negative emotions, preliminary results revealed that the Christians who practiced lectio divina over a two-week period of time reported a greater decrease in trauma symptoms than the Christians who practiced LKM.[75]

Lectio divina in practice: A two-step strategy for cultivating the fruit of the Spirit. In terms of the specific practice steps, which can be practiced both formally (for example, in a quiet environment, free from distractions,

---

[72]Salzberg (1995).
[73]Zeng et al. (2015).
[74]Kwah (2019).
[75]Knabb et al. (2022).

sitting in a supportive chair with your eyes closed and palms resting comfortably in your lap for a 10-minute period of time) and informally (for example, when washing the dishes, driving to work, having healing conversations on race), the directions are as follows:[76]

1. Slowly *read* the first part of Galatians 5:22, "The fruit of the Spirit is love, joy, peace, patience, kindness . . ." allowing the verse to sink into the depths of your being and relating to it as if you are taking a small bite out of food.

2. Gently, unhurriedly, and interiorly *meditate* on the phrase "God, may you fill me with your perfect love, joy, peace, patience, and kindness," allowing God's Holy Spirit to work in and through you and relating to it as if you are slowly chewing a bite of food.

Whenever another thought, feeling, sensation, memory, or image arises in the inner world or distraction emerges in the outer world, accept it, then gently return to the above meditative phrase so that you will be filled with, and functioning as a conduit for, God's "love, joy, peace, patience, [and] kindness." Again, we recommend practicing this two-step meditation, with lectio divina as the delivery method, both formally and informally so that your healing conversations on race are led by the Holy Spirit, who dwells within and works in and through you from moment to moment to pursue and attain racial unity.

CONCLUSION

Throughout this chapter, we have explored both a biblical and secular psychological understanding of emotions, with God's love at the center, viewing them as important signals that reveal our needs in our relationship with God and others. In the context of healing conversations on race, although certainly painful, our emotions can actually help us to deepen the unity we long for. Rather than trying to ignore or wall off our emotions, we can invite them into the conversation with acceptance (A). As we combine

---

[76]Adapted from Guigo II (2012); Knabb et al. (2021b); NASB (2020); Paintner (2011); Wilhoit and Howard (2012).

this with humility (H) and empathy (E), the Christian mental skills practiced in this chapter help us cultivate an awareness of God's active, loving presence in the midst of our most powerful emotions, recognizing that we can walk through, not around, our emotions. In doing so, we are learning to, like the psalmists, *both* cry out to God in pain *and* thank him for being with us. Because God is with us to make sense of and endure our emotions, we can more confidently walk with racially different others toward unity as we move from justification to sanctification to glorification.

PRAYER AND JOURNALING EXERCISES

In the exercises that follow, we will be inviting you to go deeper with Scripture and your relationship with God, recognizing that God's Word can change lives and help us to make sense of the problem of, and solution to, racism and racial disunity.

1. Return to the "Lectio Divina" and "Personal Reflection" exercises from this chapter. Review your responses to the prompts and reflect on the secondary and primary emotions you experienced as you engaged in these exercises. As you again connect with these emotions, return to the instructions for practicing the four Christian mental skills and the fruit of the Spirit lectio divina meditation provided earlier in this chapter. Spend 10 minutes practicing each mental skill and the fruit of the Spirit meditation.

2. Complete a short self-reflection in your journal about your experience with the Christian mental skills.

Below, we have provided an example of a journal entry for Dakota, based on her experience of racism, described earlier.

EXCERPT FROM THE JOURNAL OF DAKOTA:
A 27-YEAR-OLD NATIVE AMERICAN FEMALE

Today, I practiced the four Christian mental skills. I learned a lot in the process. In reflecting on many of my experiences of racism, I have definitely felt anger at the injustice of it all. Yet, I'm not sure I have ever deeply felt the sadness and grief of the devastating impact of the sin of racism on this world. Therefore, I tried to identify the primary emotion I have been feeling all these years, as well as my relational need. Yes, the anger is still there. Who wouldn't feel anger for the way I've been treated? Interestingly, though, I ended up feeling much more sadness, since we live in such a broken world, filled with painful comments that damage relationships. As I allowed myself to simply feel the primary emotion of sadness, I recognized that I needed to be comforted by God, rather than solely dwell on my anger. Boy, is this process hard. I noticed how quickly I wanted to move past sadness and just condemn others for their racist thoughts and actions. So, what can I do so that I can stay connected to all of the feelings I'm having, not just the anger? Practicing Christian awareness was helpful. I was reminded that Jesus is with me, and he experienced the full range of human emotions, including both anger and sadness. I know that God is in control, and he will help me with this in the future, comforting me in my emotions. I don't have to feel my emotions alone. I can continue to grow. God is with me. I need his help!

FINAL STEPS

End this chapter's activities with a time of prayer. Briefly thank God for his presence and ask for his ongoing guidance and grace as you continue to reflect on what you have learned throughout the coming days.

5

LOVE

DEEPENING RELATIONSHIPS THROUGH
CHRISTLIKE COMPASSION

*And let us consider how we may spur one another on
to love and good deeds.*

HEBREWS 10:24

YUL, A 41-YEAR-OLD KOREAN MALE, *found himself
fighting back tears as he sat with his racially mixed Bible study
group. Many of his Asian American friends compared stories of
the fear they regularly experienced of being racially targeted
when in public places. A White member of the group, Noah, also
spoke up, stating, "You should just ignore all that and just go on
with your lives. You're letting it control you. Just let go and let
God." Yul made eye contact with several of his fellow Asian
American Bible study members and caught the hurt and
confusion in their eyes. Then another group member, Daniel, a
Mexican American male, spoke up. "He's right. You're not
trusting God," he said. Yul felt a flood of emotions, including
anger, sadness, and confusion. He felt unheard and*

> *misunderstood. He listened to member after member agree with*
> *these statements, while he and his fellow Asian American group*
> *members sat silently hurting. Yul wished to respond like Christ,*
> *but wasn't certain what that looked like.*

Like Yul, you may have found yourself at a loss for how to respond during race-focused conversations, seeking practical tips for what to say and how to say it, especially when faced with significantly painful topics. In conversations like these, we often face difficulty phrasing our responses in a way that best represents the love of Christ, while also giving voice to our own stories and emotions. What's more, we often struggle with knowing how to actively listen with empathy to the stories of others. Now that you have read several chapters of this book and participated in the prayer and journaling activities, you have gained a deeper understanding of the complex dynamics involved in these conversations. Yet, like Yul you may be asking for guidance and practical steps for demonstrating Christlike love during these dialogues. Certainly, as the theme verse for this chapter commands, Christians are to consider how to encourage each other to grow in love and good works, doing so in the context of our relationships with others, including racially different others (Hebrews 10:24). In fact, the "one another" verses in Scripture, like this one, remind Christians that responding to others with active, loving Christlikeness should always be at the forefront of our minds.

In previous chapters, we offered an integrated biblical and psychological foundation for cultivating Christlikeness during conversations on race through self-reflection (Humility), storytelling and lamentation (Empathy), and the use of Christian mental skills (Acceptance). As we now focus on love (L), we offer what we believe are the practical biblical and psychological principles useful in building cross-racial relational connections that facilitate healing in race-focused conversations. As one of the four pivots of focus within the book, you will be encouraged to shift from judgment of others ("like God") to Christlike love ("dependent on God"). We first separately provide a biblical perspective and psychological perspective on love. For the biblical perspective, we draw from the spiritual formation literature, using Jesus as our model of love. We then turn to the psychology literature, focusing again on attachment theory. Finally, within our integrated perspective on love, we offer practical, proven approaches for demonstrating love during conversations on race. Although we have covered much ground in previous chapters, with love as the final element of the HEAL model, this does not mean that we believe love is last in importance in our model. As you will find in this chapter, the exact opposite is true. Christlike love is the firm foundation on which we built the HEAL model. Indeed, in agreement with the apostle Paul, we believe that love is everything, and we "gain nothing" if we "do not have love" (1 Corinthians 13:1-3).

LOVE: A BIBLICAL PERSPECTIVE

Within the spiritual formation/disciplines literature, *relational formation*, or building loving, emotionally connected relationships within the body of Christ, is considered to be one of the primary ways God works in us as we are formed into the image of Christ.[1] Consistent with this notion, the New Testament theologian M. Robert Mulholland states the following:

> When the New Testament writers speak of "the image of Christ," they mean the fulfillment of the deepest dynamics of our being. We are created to be compassionate persons whose relationships are characterized by love and forgiveness, persons whose lives are a healing, liberating, transforming touch of God's grace upon our world.[2]

God the Father, Son, and Holy Spirit (the Trinity) work as one to transform us and our relationships. Certainly, the Trinity is the purest example of loving relationship and community. Therefore, God's image in us means we were created for loving, relational community, which

---

[1]Chandler (2014).
[2]Mulholland (2016, p. 41).

includes loving community with racially different others. We can experience this loving community to its fullest as we are immersed in God's love (1 John 4:8) and seek to demonstrate his love to others. We believe that harmonious cross-racial relationships are built on powerful healing conversations, during which it is essential that our actions are grounded in biblical love, defined and exemplified through the life and ministry of Jesus.

Defining Christlike love. The New Testament provides us with clear and compelling reasons to live a life characterized by love. In various verses throughout the New Testament, Jesus gave his disciples, and all of us, the definition of love and presented it as a "commandment," rather than a suggestion. In the book of Matthew, Jesus was tested by the religious leaders, who asked, "Teacher, which is the greatest commandment in the Law?" (Matthew 22:36). It is very likely that, even as Christians, we might all have different responses to this question. However, Jesus responded in this way:

> "Love the Lord your God with all your heart and with all your soul and with all your mind." This is the first and greatest commandment. And the second is like it: "Love your neighbor as yourself." All the Law and the Prophets hang on these two commandments. (Matthew 22:37-40)

These verses, often referred to as the "twin commandments," make it clear that love is an imperative for those who claim to be followers of Christ.[3] Because these two verses are so intimately linked, we argue that you cannot truly love God if you do not also love your neighbor, whatever their ethnic or racial background. Toward the end of Jesus' earthly ministry, he further impressed on his disciples the imperative to love. As he spent his last few moments, and the Passover meal, with his disciples, he instructed them, "A new command I give you: Love one another. As I have loved you, so you must love one another. By this everyone will know that you are my disciples, if you love one another" (John 13:34-35).

---

[3]Carlson-Thies (2021); Wright (2017).

Pastor and author William Chang explored John 13 in detail and suggests that, although the concept of loving others was not new to the Jews, the context and self-sacrificing type of love demonstrated by Jesus himself certainly was novel.[4] Jesus presented the love of God and others as the primary way we demonstrate our faith.[5] As Christians, we should be deeply committed to loving one another the way Jesus loved us. Jesus' love was demonstrated through his patience, commitment, care, compassion, grace, forgiveness, and, ultimately, self-sacrificing death on the cross. This self-emptying love should prompt us to ask ourselves, "Do I love others the way Jesus loved me?"

> *"Do I love others the way Jesus loved me?" Michaela pondered this question while she sat on a sand dune overlooking her family's New Mexico ranch. She hadn't heard from her close friend, Marcos, since their argument the week prior. Michaela and Marcos, both second-generation Mexican immigrants, had widely differing views on the building of the border wall between Mexico and the United States. Marcos felt that legal immigration, with "papers," was the only way his fellow Mexicanos should come to the United States. On the other hand, Michaela felt strongly that her people should be allowed to seek refuge and a better life in the United States and they shouldn't be stopped from practicing this God-given right.*
>
> *Michaela felt a deep emotional ache as she thought of the way she had yelled at Marcos and insulted him with a racial slur as he described his views. As she watched the sun set and breathed in the calming scent of the nearby farm animals, she regretted the pain she caused Marcos and her own sinful behavior. If she had shown Christlike love to him, she would have been more patient and kind and her words would have brought her and Marcos closer together, rather than driving*

---

[4]Chang (2014).
[5]Wright (2017).

> *them apart. She knew she needed to repair their relationship*
> *and it would need to start with loving Marcos the way Christ*
> *loved her.*

Demonstrating Christlike love. Christian love has been said to look like the most absurd love of all[6] because of its seemingly paradoxical nature. Christians are commanded to a form of love that is demonstrated by selfless attention to promoting the well-being and flourishing of others.[7] Love is not simply directed toward those we have positive feelings toward; we must also love our enemies (see Matthew 5:44). This suggests that our demonstration of love is not dependent on the characteristics or response of the beloved. Rather, love is offered to all people and at all times, even during painful or emotional conversations on race or with racially different others.

Although love can have emotional, cognitive, and behavioral manifestations, in this section, we will focus on exploring the *behaviors* that demonstrate Christlike love. Spiritual formation is not solely about an inner transformation but also about outward, behavioral manifestations of Christ's love and character.[8] Our examination of the behaviors that demonstrate love comes from a closer look at 1 Corinthians 13:4-7. This is a relatively well-known section of Scripture. You may have even heard it read at a wedding ceremony because it provides a fairly clear picture of how love should be expressed in actionable ways. The Scripture suggests that love is not something we can do solely through emotions, words, or thoughts; it must be demonstrated.

Below are the various behavioral expressions of Christlike love presented in 1 Corinthians, as applied to race relations and conversations on race.[9] We have provided a few personal stories to demonstrate what some of these expressions of love might look like.

---

[6]Davis (2014).
[7]Davis (2014).
[8]Willard (n.d.).
[9]1 Corinthians 13:4-8. Expanded based on Amplified Bible (2015); English Standard Version Bible (2001); New International Version Bible (2011); New King James Version Bible (1982).

- "Love is patient, love is kind." When others have differing views or seek to persuade us to alter our perspectives, we can demonstrate love with a patient attitude. Even when others speak hurtful words, love allows us to remain kind in our responses.

When I (Veola) tried to speak with a friend about the reasons behind celebrating Black History Month, I was met with anger and frustration. "That's stupid," my friend said dismissively. My friend didn't believe that Black History Month should be celebrated if other racial and ethnic groups didn't also have a month of celebration. At first, I was hurt by my friend's lack of understanding of my point of view. I was tempted to respond with hurtful words in return. Yet, after taking a few deep breaths, I responded with kindness and patiently asked my friend to explain their point of view. Although my friend and I didn't come to an agreement on the topic, our friendship was not hurt, but instead grew.

- "It does not envy, it does not boast, it is not proud." Love allows us to hear others' stories without an attitude of envy or jealousy. Love helps us to sit quietly with others, responding to their experiences without needing to highlight our own righteousness or rightness. Love drives us to shift from the judgment of others to dependence on God.

At times, I (Josh) notice that my initial reaction is one of defensiveness when I hear some of the more contemporary language in Western society for capturing and contrasting White and BIPOC race-related experiences, like "White fragility," "White privilege," "whiteness," and so forth. Yet, on further examination, I often find pride simmering beneath the surface, with my personal pride undermining my ability to be a dwelling place for God's love. In turn, the Holy Spirit convicts me, reminding me to humbly strive to understand the meaning and intention behind these terms, the motivation to diagnose the

many race-related problems in the twenty-first century, the need
for BIPOC Christians (and non-Christians) to accurately
communicate and distinguish their experiences in a majority-
White society, and the enduring impact of, and tremendous
suffering caused by, systemic racism.

- "It does not dishonor others, it is not self-seeking, it is not easily angered, it keeps no record of wrongs." Love helps us to respond with graciousness and consideration of others, without insult or accusation. Instead, love places the other and their needs first. Love helps us to remain calm, even during tense conversations on race, and reminds us not to harbor bitterness or resentment toward others, even when they wrong us.

Every year during Black History Month, my family and I
(Krystal) watch a film to remind us of our rich Black heritage.
Whether it's Roots *or some documentary film, we are reminded*
of the long history of racial hatred and oppression faced by Black
Americans. The record in America, and throughout the world, of
evil acts directed toward people like me is indisputable and
makes it very hard not to keep a record of wrongs. I find myself
trying to remember the past so I can praise God for his
faithfulness and protection while not allowing past, and present,
racism to create bitterness and resentment in me.

- "Love does not delight in evil but rejoices with the truth." Love empowers us to hate evil, even when that evil is suffered by those who seem to deserve it because of their own evil actions (including the evil of racism). Love motivates a response of joy when we see the positive result of truth being spoken.
- "It always protects, always trusts, always hopes, always perseveres. Love never fails." Love motivates us to press on, even in the face of our own and others' failures. Love reminds us to see the best in others, even others who appear to have opposing motives and

perspectives. Love provides hope, even during the most difficult conversations on race, and motivates us to remain persistent in our efforts to heal race relations, despite all of the odds.

As a pastor, life can often feel lonely for me (Charles), as very few people want to hang out with their pastor, let alone understand the weight that often plagues pastors and their families. A few years ago, I was elated when I found a group comprised of pastors just like me who were looking for fellowship and companionship. We met every week and discussed our families, our ministries, and our hopes and dreams as pastors. It was an amazing group. The interesting thing about this group was its diversity. It was comprised primarily of African American and White pastors, who, other than being in ministry, probably would never have met or become friends.

But in 2015, as cases arose of unarmed Black men being killed by law enforcement and the forthcoming election year that was riddled with racial overtones, our conversations turned political and divisions quickly surfaced between us. The group that was once a place of refuge and relaxation became for me a battleground in which I felt I was constantly having to defend issues that impacted the Black community. I soon found myself not only uncomfortable attending the group, but angry about how my White brothers and sisters in Christ responded to social and political issues that affected people who looked like me. I eventually left the group, and, over the next few years, I limited my interactions with the White members of the group while maintaining my relationships with all the Black members. I loved these brothers, but our differences were too much for me, and I settled in my mind that this is why Black people and White people don't worship together.

I had become good friends with one of the young White pastors in the group, and I really loved him. I was hurt to lose my friendship with him, but I couldn't stand his political views, nor how his posts on social media often hurt those closest to me. For five years, he and I barely spoke. However, in the process of writing this book, I felt God turning my heart to revisit my friendship with this brother. For a while, I resisted, but the truth is I loved him, and the devil wanted me to focus on the political areas where we differed instead of the numerous areas we had in common. Lately, I've found ways to reconnect via social media with my friend, and I've found peace as he and I are working to reconnect with one another. It's not easy, and we haven't met face-to-face yet to have the courageous conversations necessary to heal our relationship. Still, we are committed to finding a way to come together because our love for each other as brothers is more important than our differences.

This is the power of love. The ability to press past our hurt, our differences, and our challenges, believing that, through Christ, we can love greater and deeper than before.

As you can see, the verses of 1 Corinthians 13 tell us both what *to do* and what *not to do* as we seek to demonstrate the love of Christ in general and our conversations on race in particular. These directives provide a clear image of how a person living in Christlike love should behave in their relationships with others. Although we all are subject to our fallen nature, which often causes us to rebel against these Christlike behaviors, anyone who claims to be committed to living out the command to "love your neighbor" (Matthew 22:39) should also be committed to exemplifying these behaviors in every relationship.

Not only is Christlike love to be demonstrated in micro-level, individual interactions, but we also have a collective responsibility as the body of Christ to demonstrate Christlike love to the world. What makes Christian congregations distinctive from other communities is that membership is voluntary and ties to other social stations should not determine the character or composition of the church. Instead, as a body of believers, the church must, first and foremost, collectively be committed to Christlike love. Beyond the expressions of love depicted in 1 Corinthians, there are a variety of specific, intentional practices for becoming more like Christ and "incarnating the love of Christ" within the body of believers. These *incarnating disciplines*[10] are directed outward to others[11] and include compassion, forgiveness, and justice. As Christians, when we engage in these spiritual disciplines, we not only draw closer to God, but more clearly demonstrate God's love for all people and build up the body. When responding to racially different others in our lives, we can demonstrate these disciplines in the following ways:

- *Compassion.* Although compassion may appear, at first glance, to be a simple feeling, it is, instead, an intentional and purposeful act directed toward another. Compassionate action toward a fellow brother or sister in Christ who is racially or ethnically different involves actively seeking opportunities to provide support and encouragement. For example, when a person of color describes an experience of racism, a compassionate response may include offering words of empathy, support, concern, and love; or, it may even include delving deeper to ask about their emotional and practical needs.

- *Forgiveness.* Forgiveness may be one of the more difficult incarnating spiritual disciplines. Yet, forgiveness may also be one of the most important disciplines to cultivate as you learn to have healing conversations on race. As we have described in earlier chapters, these conversations are rife with emotion and evoke our responses to prior experiences, reminding us of our earlier narratives. Therefore, it is important to actively strive to "incarnate" Christ's love through working toward forgiveness of past and current racially focused injuries.

---

[10]Calhoun (2005).
[11]Foster (2018).

- *Justice.* In the context of incarnating the love of Christ, "justice seeks to help others through correcting and redressing wrongs. It treats others fairly and shows no favoritism."[12] Applied to conversations on race and race relations, incarnating Christ's love in this way may include open discussions about wrongs that have been experienced or witnessed. Love does not mean accepting or ignoring wrongdoing. Instead, love gently and patiently addresses wrongs as a means to seek justice. Simultaneously, love and justice motivate us to forgive wrongdoings, while also addressing these wrongdoings directly. Conversations on race, therefore, may include discussions of previous or current racially focused wrongs.

To summarize, the Bible provides clear commands on how we are meant to treat each other as we seek to create biblical relationships by demonstrating Christlike love. As described in earlier chapters, relationships and relational needs are God-given. Therefore, Christians have an imperative to seek ways to build up each other and spur each other on to love and good works (Hebrews 10:24). As we pivot from a focus on judgment of others to Christlike love, we can build racial unity. What is more, a deep understanding of, and commitment to, Christlike love is a key ingredient to healing race-related disunity that results from racism. In the following section, we will explore the direct connection between Christlike love and racial disunity.

Christlike love, racial disunity, and racism. Considering that we are commanded to demonstrate love to exemplify the nature of Christ, we believe it logically follows that disunity in race relations and the injuries created by racism can be healed as we cultivate this love in our cross-racial relationships. Since Christlike love is incompatible with racial disunity and racism, as we move closer to consistently living a life that demonstrates Christlike love, we should be compelled toward the pursuit of racial unity. In other words, it is impossible to live out Matthew 22:37-40, John 13:34, and 1 Corinthians 13:4-7 and remain in a place of apathy

---

[12]Calhoun (2005, p. 218).

toward, or active participation in disunity between, those who are racially different. Unfortunately, because of our fallen nature, disunity in relationships tends to be our default position in life. However, as we are continually transformed to the image of Christ, and consistently practice the incarnating disciplines, we experience a change in our attitudes, thoughts, and behaviors that moves us toward unity in race relations. As an example, let us return to the story of Michaela and Marcos.

> *As the sun set and Michaela stared out into the darkened sky, she prayed for God's guidance on how to respond to Marcos. She meditated on the words of 1 Corinthians 13 and felt convicted that she had not been patient or kind toward Marcos. Instead, she had been easily angered and spoken words that were rude, hurtful, and racially motivated. As a chill breeze caused her to shiver, she stood and walked back toward her house. As she walked, she dialed Marcos's number on her cell phone, ready to repair the rift and disunity she had created in their relationship.*
>
> *When Marcos answered, his voice sounded cold and distant. Yet, Michaela did not let his apparent anger dissuade her. "Please forgive me. I should not have made those hurtful comments. I would love to better understand your perspective. Can we talk?"*
>
> *Marcos appeared to instantly soften. "Of course, Mickey. You're forgiven. Let's get together tomorrow."*

Michaela and Marco's story illustrates the incompatibility of Christlike love with racial disunity and racist thoughts, words, and actions. As in Michaela's example, it is impossible to be patient, kind, gracious, and considerate, as 1 Corinthians instructs, while also being comfortable with racial epithets and derogatory, racially focused comments. It seems incomprehensible to harbor hateful feelings about someone based on their racial/ethnic background or differing race-based perspectives, while simultaneously loving that person the way that Jesus loved us. As Michaela found, like oil and water, Christlike love and racial disunity cannot mix.

This does not mean that the moment one becomes a follower of Christ they will instantly be free from the struggle to live like Christ in cross-racial relationships. If it is present, we do not instantly become free of racial bias, bigotry, and apathy toward racism or understand how to talk with others about race-related topics. Spiritual formation is a *process* of becoming like Christ. The process requires intentionality and discipline to take steps every day to come closer to reflecting the image of Christ and his love to the world. For this reason, your decision to embark on this journey of having healing conversations on race is worth celebrating. This journey is just one step in your pursuit of demonstrating Christlike love in your relationships with others that will move you closer toward racial unity and further away from apathy and racial disunity.

JOURNALING BREAK: LECTIO DIVINA

Before moving on to the next section, reflect on the biblical perspective on Christlike love and the incarnating disciplines of compassion, forgiveness, and justice.

READ: Read John 15:9, "As the Father has loved me, so have I loved you. Now remain in my love." Read the verse slowly and allow yourself to take in the content of the passage.

REFLECT: Take one portion of this Scripture (a short phrase) to ponder and meditate on, such as "Now remain in my love." As you slowly and gently recite this portion of the verse, think deeply about what it means to remain in God's love as you relate to racially different others and/or have conversations on race.

RESPOND: Spend a few minutes praying to God, asking him to fill your inner world with love as you consider the ways in which you can actively show love to those who are racially/ethnically different from you. Cry out to God, asking for Christlike love to fill your heart so that you are consumed by God's perfect love at the center of your being.

REST: Slowly and gently repeat the word *love*, reminiscent of Christ's interactions with humanity while on earth. Sit in silence with God, resting in his presence as you are filled with God's love from the inside out.

Before you move on to the next section of this chapter, pick up your journal and reflect on the following questions:

1. In what ways have you actively demonstrated Christlike love to those who are racially/ethnically different from you?

2. This week, what is one way you can show compassion to someone who is racially/ethnically different from you? (Return to the discussion of compassion if you are uncertain of what this might look like.)

3. What might it look like to seek justice for those who are racially/ethnically different from you? (Return to the discussion of justice if you are uncertain of how to respond.)

LOVE: A PSYCHOLOGICAL PERSPECTIVE

Although never a replacement for God's Word, psychology has contributed much to our understanding of love in human relationships and some of the building blocks required to effectively engage in loving connection with others. In this section, we will revisit the concept of attachment and demonstrate how our early relational experiences can have a lasting impact on how we engage with others. Our attachment style can certainly play a role in how we experience love and connection and demonstrate love to others, especially in the context of seeking racial unity.

Attachments and attachment injuries. From a psychological perspective, our daily interactions with others are the building blocks of healthy, loving relationships. Returning to attachment theory, we develop our approach to relationships and love through our early experiences. Throughout our development, we build personal attachment narratives, or expectations for what love looks like in relationships and our view of ourselves and others within relationships. As we learn how to relate to others throughout our development, we look for others who can be trusted as a *secure base,* someone that makes us feel confident to explore and experience the world, and *safe haven,* someone we can return to when we are hurt or afraid and need soothing comfort. This "circle of security," visually depicted in figure 5.1, can be helpful in making sense of our love relationships with others.[13]

As we see in figure 5.1, when others provide a loving environment, they can serve as a secure base for us to confidently explore the world and relationships and, when we are feeling uncertain, fearful, or insecure, we can return to these same people as a loving safe haven for soothing comfort. As we return to our most trusted relationships in our time of need, we tend to employ a variety of *attachment behaviors*. These are behaviors we engage in to emotionally reconnect with safe others, such as verbalizing our emotional pain and relational needs or reaching out to a trusted friend. These behaviors are an important part of maintaining and growing in our relationships with others, who optimally function as both a secure base and a safe haven in daily life. When others are regularly loving and responsive to our attachment behaviors, that is, our "circle of security" is in place with close, trusted others, we develop a felt sense of security in our relationships, called secure attachments.

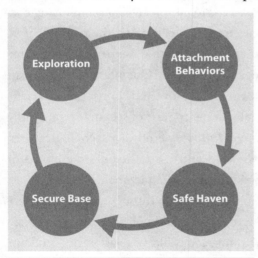

Figure 5.1. Circle of security

When we develop a secure attachment style, we tend to believe that we are worthy of love and others are available and willing to lovingly respond to our needs.[14] With secure attachments, we are less likely to feel anxious about the love of others or avoidant of potentially loving relationships with others.[15] When we are securely attached, healthy

---

[13]In this section, the discussion and figure on the "circle of security" is adapted from Feeney and Collins (2004).

[14]Bartholomew and Horowitz (1991); Fairchild and Finney (2006); Sibley et al. (2011).

[15]Bartholomew and Horowitz (1991); Fairchild and Finney (2006); Sibley et al. (2011).

attachment behaviors are present in both romantic relationships and friendships, drawing us closer to those around us. However, when our relational needs are not met, such as when others do not respond to our attachment behaviors in loving ways, we can develop negative emotional and behavioral patterns in our relationships, often in the form of an insecure attachment style.[16] We may feel unlovable or fear others will not offer love to us. These same patterns can present themselves in our relationships with racially different others, causing us to be anxious in these relationships or to avoid relationships with people who are racially different altogether. What is more, when we have traumatic experiences, such as the ongoing negative effects of racism or racial injury, we may end up struggling to feel safe, loved, and supported in cross-racial relationships.

In emotionally focused couples therapy (EFT), the ARE acronym (accessibility, responsiveness, engagement) is used to describe some of the key building blocks of securely attached relationships. In other words, to build secure/safe relationships, the individuals involved must demonstrate accessibility, responsiveness, and engagement toward each other.[17] With accessibility, the key question is, "Can I reach you?" and involves being open, available, attentive, and emotionally vulnerable with one another, especially when conversations escalate with emotional pain.[18] For responsiveness, the pressing question is, "Can I rely on you to respond to me emotionally?" and consists of being attuned, responsive, supportive, and reassuring toward the other person's emotional experiences (fear, sadness, shame) and needs (comfort, closeness, connection, etc.).[19] Finally, with engagement, the most salient question is, "Do I know you will value me and stay close?" and is made up of being caring toward, as well as connected with, the other person, especially when they need a safe, supportive response.[20] Overall, the ARE acronym can be condensed to two powerful, succinct questions, which capture

---

[16]Bartholomew and Horowitz (1991); Fairchild and Finney (2006); Sibley et al. (2011).
[17]Johnson (2008).
[18]Johnson (2008, pp. 49-50).
[19]Johnson (2008, pp. 49-50).
[20]Johnson (2008, pp. 49-50).

secure attachments during crucial moments in life: "Are you there, are you with me?"[21]

Our behaviors within our current relationships will regularly be influenced by our attachment style and our view of love that grows out of our experiences with others, whether we are securely attached and exhibit some, most, or all of the key ingredients of the ARE acronym or insecurely attached and these ingredients are missing. If we encounter others who inadvertently reinforce negative relational beliefs about our own unlovability or the lack of trustworthiness of others' love, we can become more and more entrenched in unhealthy styles of relating. On the other hand, if others regularly reinforce positive relational expectations of love and connection or disprove our negative expectations, we can become more and more entrenched in healthy styles of relating. Unfortunately, when we expect to receive love and support, but instead experience pain and rejection, we will often experience what has been called an *attachment injury*.[22] Attachment injuries occur when someone "violates the expectation that the other will offer comfort and caring in times of danger or distress."[23] More specifically, over time, race-related traumas and conflict may lead to Christians carrying hurt based on the expectation that racially different others will not be available to understand and respond to them during salient moments of sadness, fear, and/or shame. Although one racially different Christian may not have been the one to directly cause the original race-related attachment injury, they can serve an important role in facilitating racial healing for the other. Healing within cross-racial relationships can be facilitated by engaging in behaviors that increase a sense in others that we can be both a secure base and safe haven for them. These behaviors include demonstrating empathy, warmth, and responsiveness toward the needs of others. The practical steps of our HEAL model, which we will describe below and in the next chapter, are founded on the idea that you can serve as a healing

---

[21]Johnson (2008, pp. 49-50).
[22]Johnson et al. (2001).
[23]Johnson et al. (2001).

figure in the life of another person by offering this empathy, warmth, responsiveness, and Christlike love during interactions and conversations on race.

JOURNALING BREAK: PERSONAL REFLECTION

Before moving on to the next section, take a few moments to reflect in your journal on the idea of serving as a loving secure base (someone that makes others feel confident to explore and experience the world) and safe haven (someone others can return to when they are hurt or afraid and need soothing comfort) for racially different others.

1. What might it be like to serve as a secure base in the life of someone who is racially/ethnically different from you? Reflect on and note any secondary (anger, for example), then primary (sadness, fear, shame, righteous anger), emotions that arise.

2. What might it be like to serve as a safe haven in the life of someone who is racially/ethnically different from you? Reflect on and note any secondary (anger, for example), then primary (sadness, fear, shame, righteous anger), emotions that arise.

3. What do you currently need to do/change to prepare yourself to serve as both a secure base and safe haven for individuals who are racially/ethnically different from you?

LOVE: AN INTEGRATED BIBLICAL AND PSYCHOLOGICAL PERSPECTIVE

Both Scripture and attachment theory support the importance of taking active steps to cultivate loving relational connections in cross-racial relationships. For Christians, with our firm foundation in Scripture, God must be at the center of these relationships. As we seek to glorify God, grow to be more like him, and display Christlike love in our cross-racial relationships, we will also grow closer to racially different others. Attachment theory, when housed within a biblical worldview, helps us make sense of the processes involved in this, depicted in the figure below.

Thus, returning to EFT's ARE acronym, we believe that accessibility, responsiveness, and engagement are key in our relationships with God and others, especially as we partake in healing conversations on race.[24]

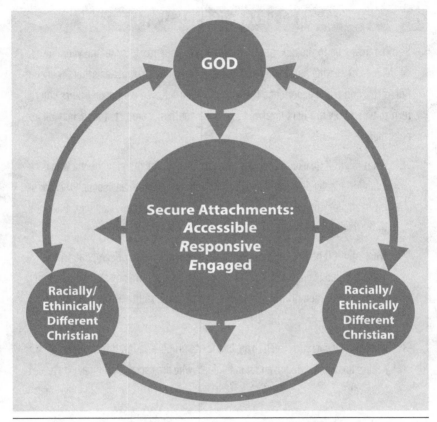

Figure 5.2. The reciprocal and bidirectional nature of ARE in relationships

In figure 5.2, notice that each Christian should strive for a secure attachment with God, wherein accessibility, responsiveness, and engagement are on full display in a reciprocal, bidirectional manner. Indeed, when we are suffering and in pain, we can turn to God as a refuge, knowing that he is available, will lovingly respond and comfort us in our time of need (Psalm 46:1), and values us and prioritizes and

---

[24]Adapted from Johnson (2008).

cherishes our relationship with him. We also need to be accessible, responsive, and engaged with God, given communion with God involves a back-and-forth friendship.[25] In return, we are open, attentive, and available to God, responsive to God's guidance and will for our life, and deeply engaged with God, prioritizing our relationship with him in each unfolding moment of the day. (Of course, our display of ARE toward God looks much different than his display of ARE toward us, given God is self-sufficient, unchangeable, transcendent, etc.) Moreover, in our effort to build secure attachments with racially/ethnically different others, God is at the center, forever remaining accessible, responsive, and engaged in our human-human exchanges. Finally, because God is in the middle of these ongoing interpersonal efforts to build and maintain loving racial unity, we, in turn, can give and receive ARE in our relationships with racially different others in a reciprocal, Christlike manner.

As the figure depicts, this dynamic, bidirectional process builds secure attachments in all directions, with God always directing the process by modeling his perfect ARE. To be certain, because God is omnipresent, he is always available to guide our relationships toward unity, with love as *the* guiding fruit of the Spirit. In other words, God unwaveringly answers yes and yes to the concise ARE questions of "Are you there, are you with me?"[26] Because God has already answered yes to these two ARE questions, we can have the confidence to answer yes to these questions with racially different others.

Ultimately, from our perspective, this process is the foundation for growth in cross-racial relationships and the healing of race-related injuries. When inevitably seeking answers to the above two ARE questions, God's definite, invariable yes with us should lead to our own yes response to racially different others, an outside-in to inside-out process as we move from justification (being right with, and reconciled to, God because of Jesus Christ) to sanctification (becoming more like Jesus

---

[25]Knabb and Wang (2021).
[26]Adapted from Johnson (2008, pp. 49-50).

Christ) to glorification (being face-to-face with God).[27] To summarize, figure 5.2 serves as a formidable reminder that the God of love is always accessible, responsive, and engaged in our relationships and, thus, we are always involved in God-human-human relational exchanges, not left alone to make sense of our human-human interactions outside of his love. As mentioned previously, we believe that this growth and healing best takes place during face-to-face, individual conversations on race, with God at the center.

Adapted attachment injury model. With Christlikeness and Christlike love as the foundation, we have adapted the attachment injury model of EFT[28] to provide practical steps to guide you toward holding these healing conversations. To succinctly describe these steps, two people engage in a purposeful conversation on race, with the goal of increasing emotional connection and resolving relational injuries by using specific skills that are consistent with the behavioral manifestations of Christlike love. Although we will cover the basic ideas, structure, and skills needed for the conversation here, we offer a step-by-step guide for you to use during an intentional, preplanned conversation in the next chapter.

Within our conversation model, the two people involved typically come from different racial/ethnic backgrounds. However, even two people from the same racial/ethnic background (even two people of European descent or White racial identity) can hold this kind of conversation, given the inherent differences in experiences and perspectives (reminiscent of the story of Michaela and Marcos from earlier in this chapter). During the conversation, one individual at a time describes a previous experience related to race and expresses their pain and/or primary emotions and relational needs. As the speaker and listener seek to be emotionally responsive to each other (demonstrating humility, empathy, acceptance, and love) and engage in the specific steps of the attachment injury model, the dynamic and reciprocal process of healing,

---

[27]Grudem (1994).
[28]Makinen and Johnson (2006).

with God at the center, can begin. In turn, the individuals involved in these healing conversations strive to grow in their ability to serve as a secure base and safe haven for each other, displaying accessibility, responsiveness, and engagement along the way,[29] with the possibility of exploring future cross-racial relationships because of this newly developed bond.

As described in previous chapters, storytelling/narrative is an important tool in building relational understanding and will be a primary tool in building connectedness and repairing cross-racial attachment injuries. Your own experiences related to race make up your story. Although telling your own story about how race or race relations have affected your life is a vulnerable step that takes courage, it will strengthen the relational bond between you and the people listening to your story. In other words, by expressing primary emotions (sadness, fear, hurt, shame, righteous anger), the storyteller can authentically connect to their emotional experience, which will reveal a God-given relational need. In turn, within the adapted attachment injury model, the listener is encouraged to reflect or paraphrase what has been said (an empathic response, described in the next section), including both the content of the experience (what was said/what happened) and the primary emotions that have been described. The listener also seeks to know more, asking open-ended questions to better understand the storyteller's experience. Drawing out the deeper emotions of the experience (the primary emotions of hurt, sadness, fear, and shame) is key to understanding the experience. Secondary emotions, like anger, often cover up primary emotions.[30] If anger is expressed, the listener must remember to ask what might lie beneath those experiences. For example, one might ask, "What other feelings did you have when that happened? What were you afraid of? In what way were you hurt?" All

---

[29]Johnson (2008, pp. 49-50).

[30]Anger can be both a primary and a secondary emotion. In Christianity, righteous anger can help us to stand up to injustice and create a safe distance when we are in danger. However, anger may sometimes be less useful when attempting to develop trusting, intimate relationships within the body of Christ, given it is commonly a reaction to a more vulnerable, difficult feeling (fear, sadness, hurt) and may create unneeded distance or unintentionally push other people away when comfort and responsiveness are what's needed.

these questions require a foundational understanding of, and commitment to, demonstrating Christlike love.

Both the storyteller and listener play an important role in the attachment injury model. No matter the racial background of the first speaker (White or BIPOC), it is important to note that the listener will experience their own emotions while listening. This may take the form of anger, uncertainty, fear, sadness, rejection, powerlessness, shame, and so on. You may recall from the previous chapters that intense emotions can be evoked by conversations on race. There is a risk that the listener will shut down or withdraw and have difficulty listening, especially when they feel as though they are being criticized or blamed. This may come across as indifference and a lack of care to the speaker. In this case, the listener is encouraged to maintain a posture of acceptance (A of the HEAL model), recognizing their own feelings while also continuing to hear/listen to those of the other. Acceptance starts with the use of the Christian mental skills described in the last chapter, but also includes continued self-awareness and awareness of the other person's experiences, founded on a commitment to Christlike love (patience, kindness, forgiveness, etc.). The speaker is encouraged not to see apparent withdrawal as a sign of lack of care or racism. Instead, this can be reframed as an emotional reaction to the content of the conversation, which may cause deeper relational fears (primary emotions).

Remember, according to EFT theory, when discussing painful experiences in relationship with another, relationship-focused fears and needs are activated. For example, discussions about race and/or racism can lead to fears of rejection, loneliness, and shame, activating deep hurts that are already present. The listener is encouraged to stay accessible, responsive, and engaged,[31] to not withdraw, and to express their own deeper, more vulnerable feelings. The listener is also encouraged to show Christlike love, remembering that the purpose of listening is to be a vehicle through which Christlikeness can be on display and Christlike unity can grow.

---

[31]Johnson (2008, pp. 49-50).

Finally, the listener is encouraged to reflect on their experiences related to race and racism. This part of the conversation should include an expression of vulnerability and confession of any feelings of uncertainty, inadequacy, powerlessness, and numbness. This may also include repentance for any unrecognized biases or indifference/apathy that have impacted their attitudes and behaviors or overt racism they may have exhibited. In doing so, the listener will also be taking a step toward greater vulnerability, making the exchange reciprocal. The other person, in turn, can validate the listener's willingness to be vulnerable. The goal is for the interaction to be a reciprocal, mutual conversation, not a monologue, so the parties can grow together toward Christlike love and the image of Christ.

In displaying Christlike love and using specific skills focused on healing attachment injuries (described below), both participants will be contributing to having a more vulnerable conversation, which can strengthen the relationship and lead to further unity. After all, hearing another's pain allows the listener and speaker to lament together, grieve together, and learn to walk together in this imperfect world, with God leading the way. Recognizing and experiencing pain together means, as Christians, we can stand with each other as we cry out to God, deepening the love within the body of Christ in this fallen, broken world as we patiently wait for Jesus' return to restore all things and be with him, face-to-face, in heaven. Next, we turn to the basic communication skills that are necessary to facilitate this process.

Basic communications skills. Within an attachment framework, demonstrating empathy and understanding of others' emotions facilitates relational connection and healing.[32] The way we communicate with others should also reflect the behavioral manifestations of Christlike love described earlier in this chapter. Below we provide practical guidance and exercises to help you build communication skills that will facilitate your healing conversation on race. We also provide guidance on how to use each practice individually and combine them naturally in your

---

[32]Johnson (2019a, 2019b).

conversations and as you relate to others. Empathic responsiveness is at the heart of these combined practices.

Empathic responsiveness. To demonstrate empathic responsiveness[33] during conversations on race, you are encouraged to maintain an attitude of acceptance toward the other. Empathic warmth and reflective listening communicate to the person that they have intrinsic value. Although there are several ways to demonstrate empathy toward others during conversations on race, and some people might find it easier to demonstrate empathy than others, we recommend the basic, proven formula below to demonstrate either basic or advanced empathy:[34]

- Basic empathy: Respond to the basic content and feeling provided in a statement by the speaker. ("You feel _____ because of _____.")

- Advanced empathy: Respond to the basic content and deeper emotion (primary emotion), even if it was not stated and was only implied. ("You feel _____ because of _____ and it sounds like you might have been feeling _____. Am I right?")

Paraphrasing. To paraphrase the statements of others during conversations, briefly reproduce, in your own words, the gist of what the other person has said. Paraphrased statements could sound like, "So far, you've mentioned to me that it's really hurtful for you to hear people talk about building a border wall. You also said that one of the reasons this is so hurtful is because you would not be living in the United States if there had been a wall. Is that right?"

If you are not certain how best to paraphrase what the speaker has said, you can ask the person to repeat themselves. According to the EFT approach, slowing down the conversation for the sake of understanding can facilitate emotional connection.[35] Also, repeating what has been said, doing so slowly, softly, and simply,[36] can help the other person stay engaged and connected with their emotional experiences.

---

[33]Kuntze et al. (2009).
[34]Ivey et al. (2009).
[35]Johnson (2019a, 2019b).
[36]Denton et al. (2009).

Open-ended questions. To facilitate further conversation and deeper understanding, ask questions in a way that invites the person to provide an elaborate response. These types of questions cannot be answered with a simple yes or no answer. A closed-ended question could be, "Did you have a good day today?" whereas an open-ended question would be, "What was the highlight of your day today?" In terms of an emotionally focused, race-based conversation, an open-ended question might be, "What was it like to hear others say they wished your people would go back to where they came from?"

Combining these communication skills to create an empathically responsive dialogue takes practice. Listen in as John, a 35-year-old Black man, practices combining these skills to talk about colorblindness with his brother.

> *John: What do you think about colorblindness; you know, when people act like they don't see color?*
>
> *Ben: I don't believe it.*
>
> *John: Can you tell me more about what you mean by that? (Open-ended question)*
>
> *Ben: Just because they say they don't see color, it doesn't mean it's true.*
>
> *John: So, it sounds like you think people are being dishonest when they say that. (Paraphrase)*
>
> *Ben: I don't think they know they're being dishonest. I don't know. Maybe they're just deceiving themselves.*
>
> *John: What do you mean? (A brief open-ended question)*
>
> *Ben: So, maybe they don't want to feel like color makes a difference. Or, maybe they think that seeing color makes them a racist or something. I don't know.*
>
> *John: You think maybe people worry about being seen as a racist if they say they see color. (Paraphrase)*

Ben: Right. You know, they're worried about how they'll look if they acknowledge skin color. But people aren't blind. We all can see that we look different. And what's wrong with that? I mean, if you can't see that I'm a Black man, there's something wrong.

John: So, you're saying that you don't see anything wrong with acknowledging skin color differences. (Paraphrase)

Ben: Of course not. You're Black, I'm Black. You're a little darker than I am. So what? Did saying that out loud make me a racist?

John: How do you feel about all of this? Like, if you had to put an emotion on it. (Open-ended question)

Ben: Now, you're going to make me talk about feelings?

John: (laughs)

Ben: I guess I think the whole thing is ridiculous. I don't know. It makes me mad.

John: So, you feel mad because of this idea that people think there's something wrong with recognizing skin color. (Empathic response, including a reflection of feelings and content)

Ben: Yeah. I get really frustrated when thinking about it.

John: It must be hurtful to think that some people won't acknowledge a piece of who you are. What do you need? (Empathic response, including a reflection of primary emotion and open-ended question about the need)

Ben: Yeah, I guess it kind of hurts. I really just need to be understood, accepted, and valued for who I am, which includes my race. Being Black is a part of my identity, a part of my experience. I need people to see that, not ignore it or dismiss it.

Using these basic communication skills and developing caring empathic responsiveness toward racially different others prepares you for healing conversations on race. As we have described, these skills also create a conversational environment in which attachment injuries can be healed. Next, we provide the specific steps of the HEAL conversation model, which is developed based on an adapted EFT model.

Major steps of the adapted attachment injury model. In our adaptation of the attachment injury model,[37] we provide practical steps to use during a healing conversation on race. By following the steps of the adapted model, you can begin to pursue the healing of cross-racial relational wounds and increase your sense of security and safety within cross-racial relationships. In the following chapter (chap. 6), we will provide a step-by-step guide for using these steps during an intentional conversation on race. In chapter seven, we will provide guidance on using the key practices in an abbreviated model when on the go or when unexpected conversations on race arise. As you read through the steps, keep in mind that we assume that the people involved in the conversation will come from different racial/ethnic backgrounds. However, this does not have to be the case. In fact, two people from the same racial/ethnic background may choose to engage in this process and even read this book together. This includes two people of European descent (two White people). Given that even two people with the same racial/ethnic background will have differing experiences and views surrounding racial issues, we believe that healing conversations on race can benefit cross-racial relations even if they begin with conversations between people of the same racial/ethnic group. Despite this, we recommend that if you begin by having conversations with people of your same racial/ethnic group you work toward having these conversations cross-racially. Also, we do not have an assumption of who will speak first during the conversation. Instead, the individuals involved in the conversation can choose who will speak first and who will listen first. The goal is that the conversation is a reciprocal exchange, with neither person dominating the

---

[37]Adapted from Johnson (2008) and Makinen and Johnson (2006).

conversation and each person committed to humility, empathy, acceptance, and love.

Step 1. Christian brothers/sisters pray together, humbly reflecting (H) and asking God to help each person be accessible, responsive, and engaged and display Christlikeness and the fruit of the Spirit in their healing relationship.

Step 2. One Christian expresses the emotional pain, impact, and significance of a race-related issue or racism in a vulnerable manner.

Step 3. The brother/sister Christian is accessible and expresses empathy (E), attempting to hear, understand, and be moved by the emotional pain, impact, and significance of the race-related issue or racism in the life of the speaker, while also maintaining a posture of acceptance (A).

Step 4. The original speaker expresses their relational/emotional need, which may have been previously unmet.

Step 5. The brother/sister Christian responds to the emotional need in an engaged, caring manner, demonstrating Christlike love (L), the fruit of the Spirit, and the incarnating disciplines.

Step 6. Both Christians pray together, asking God to continue to help each person be accessible, responsive, and engaged and display Christlike love and the fruit of the Spirit in their healing relationship.

These steps should be repeated, allowing each Christian brother/sister to express their own experiences with race while the other listens empathically and responds to an expressed need. Throughout the process, each Christian should be working toward the display of Christlike love and the fruit of the Spirit, recognizing that Christlike unity is the central aim.

Returning to our discussion of attachment, the steps above allow Christians of different racial backgrounds to engage in an emotionally responsive dialogue about race-related issues, facilitating healthy, secure attachments in a dynamic and interactional manner by displaying accessibility, responsiveness, and engagement.[38] As their relationship with

---

[38]Johnson (2008).

God is strengthened through this purposeful attempt at a Christlike interaction, the relationship between the two Christians is also strengthened. At the same time, as the two Christians purposefully and intentionally seek to build racial unity, they each individually strengthen their relationship with God and with each other, displaying ARE along the way. In turn, a new relational experience, with new expectations for interactions with racially different others and a new attachment narrative for cross-racial relationships, is created.

CONCLUSION

In this chapter, we have focused on the L of the HEAL model and suggested that Christlike love is essential for moving toward racial unity. We have defined and exemplified love from a biblical perspective and made the case that Christians should feel compelled to live a life that demonstrates Christlike love as we are continually transformed into the image of Christ. Certainly, Christlike love is incompatible with racial disunity and racism, and Christ desires to see unity among those who are culturally and ethnically different. The parable of the good Samaritan (Luke 10:25-37) provides an excellent example to follow. Jesus placed high value on the command to "love your neighbor" and defined "neighbor" broadly, including those who are racially/ ethnically different from us.

Also in this chapter, we have described different types of attachments and the role that attachment styles play in our current relationships, including cross-racial relationships. Our adapted attachment injury model provides a guide for Christians to begin to pursue racial healing by using psychological principles and basic skills to help you demonstrate Christlike love in conversations about race.

This chapter provides the final key practice of the HEAL model. Now that you have completed this chapter, our prayer is that you have obtained the foundational knowledge to work toward building the skills necessary to engage in a real conversation with a racially different brother/sister in Christ. Although building and using these skills may take time and much practice, we are confident that working toward this important step will move you as an individual, and the church as whole, closer to racial unity, which is consistent with Christlikeness. Through this process, Christians stand to be a shining example of the transformational power of Christ by demonstrating a solution to the racial disunity and racism that plagues our society.

PRAYER AND JOURNALING ACTIVITIES

In the exercises that follow, we invite you to go deeper with Scripture and your relationship with God, reflecting on the content of the chapter. Engage in the following activities, then grab your journal and reflect on your experience.

1. Read John 17:20-25, focusing on the theme of unity. Engage in lectio divina by reading, responding, reflecting, and resting. Then, write in your journal as you reflect on your interaction with this passage in Scripture.

2. Engage in a 15-minute conversation with a friend or family member about a recent problem they experienced. Practice the following empathic responsiveness skills:

   a. Paraphrase what has been said: "You said _____."

   b. Make an empathic statement: "You feel _____ because _____."

   c. Ask if there is more they want to share. Use open-ended questions to better understand the experience (questions that start with "When," "What," "How," and "Where?")

   d. Use paraphrasing and empathic statements again. End with the recognition and validation of the person's deeper emotional experience of the problem (primary emotion): "It must be painful/lonely/scary to have experienced _____."

3. Engage in a second 15-minute conversation with the same friend or family member about their thoughts/feelings about one of the ways racism can manifest, as described in chapter two (for example, microaggressions, colorblindness, systemic racism).

a. Use the same skills you practiced in the first conversation.

b. While paraphrasing and using empathic statements, practice using the Christian mental skills described in chapter four.

c. Practice awareness of your own primary emotions (sadness, fear, hurt, shame) and thoughts during this conversation.

4. Complete a short self-reflection in your journal about your experience with empathic responsiveness during these conversations.

Below, we have provided an example of a journal entry for John as he reflects on the conversations he had with his brother, demonstrated earlier in this chapter, as a part of this week's prayer and journaling activities.

EXCERPT FROM THE JOURNAL OF JOHN: A 35-YEAR-OLD BLACK MALE

Today, I had the two conversations with my brother. He told me about a problem he had at work. His boss was giving him a hard time for needing to take time off for his daughter's school activities. First, it was for back-to-school night. Then, it was for a choir thing. So, here's how it went. After listening to him, I tried the paraphrasing thing. I said, "You said that you're getting pretty mad at your boss for giving you such a hard time." He seemed to track with that, so I guess I did a good job with the paraphrase. Then, I tried the empathy thing. I said, "You're feeling frustrated because he's not being very accommodating." That also worked pretty well. I felt like I was getting the hang of things. I asked a few open-ended questions, like, "When did this start to be a problem?" and "What's it like for you at work having to deal with this?" The last thing I did was try to figure out the deeper emotion. I said, "It must leave you feeling scared about your job because I know you want to take care of your family financially, but you also want to be there for your daughter." I nailed it with that one!

FINAL STEPS

End this chapter's activities with a time of prayer. Briefly thank God for his presence and ask for his ongoing guidance and grace as you continue to reflect on what you have learned throughout the coming days.

6

HOLDING A HEALING CONVERSATION ON RACE

DEMONSTRATING CHRISTLIKE HUMILITY, EMPATHY, ACCEPTANCE, AND LOVE

And we all, who with unveiled faces contemplate the Lord's glory, are being transformed into his image with ever-increasing glory, which comes from the Lord, who is the Spirit.

2 Corinthians 3:18

ALBERTO (A CUBAN MALE) AND SIMON (A WHITE MALE) *sat in a local coffee shop after a morning jog together. Both men finally had a weekend free after spending the last several Saturdays and Sundays completing inventory at the warehouse where they worked. Alberto complained to Simon about their boss, who had promised the additional work would be completed quickly. Both men commiserated about the need for their boss to be more upfront about his expectations. They laughed together over minor mistakes each had made as they grew more tired with the work. Alberto picked up a newspaper and scanned the local stories. One headline stood out, "Local*

Illegal Immigrants Face Deportation." Alberto, an immigrant himself, was sickened by the idea of people he knew and loved possibly being returned to their countries of origin against their will.

"Did you see this?" Alberto pointed to the story and gave the newspaper to Simon.

Simon took a moment to read the headline and shrugged. "Yeah. I'm actually relieved. I'm tired of worrying about whether an illegal is going to end up with my job."

Alberto drew in a deep breath before he responded to Simon. He knew he had to say something, but wanted to make sure that the conversation didn't end up in an argument. He and Simon were friends, after all. But he felt hurt by Simon's comment. Instead of jumping to say the first thing that came to his mind, Alberto invited Simon to learn more about the HEAL model and asked if they could talk more about their experiences with the issue in a few weeks. Simon agreed.

As you have read through the previous chapters, your investment in learning and participating in the activities has helped prepare you for a conversation like the one that Alberto and Simon plan to share. You have learned how to demonstrate Christlikeness by practicing humility when addressing race relations and racism, grown in empathy, learned to be more accepting of your own and others' emotions, and developed important skills for demonstrating Christlike love when talking with others about race and racism. In each of the steps in your preparation process, you have grown and integrated new ways of building relational connections and responding to racial tensions and racial injuries. As you have done so, we have encouraged you to make the following important pivots:

- from a human-centered to a God-centered understanding of race relations and racism

- from a focus on self to Other (God) and others

- from disunity to unity

- from judgment of others ("like God") to Christlike love ("dependent on God")

We have also encouraged you to increase your overall biblical and cultural humility by engaging in continual learning and self-exploration. You have reviewed biblical and psychological concepts related to race and developed greater self-awareness and an awareness of the impact of race-related issues on others, including the ways in which race relations and racism may be related to deep and painful primary emotions. You have also developed Christian mental skills, empathic responsiveness, and listening skills to respond to your own and others' emotions during a conversation on race. Put succinctly, you have been involved in a process of spiritual formation, allowing Christ to transform you from the inside out into his image as the theme verse for this chapter describes. Your time and intentional, vulnerable efforts have prepared you for the next steps in this journey. In this chapter, we provide a practical step-by-step guide to be used during an intentional conversation on race with a Christian of a different racial background. Before we provide you with these practical steps, we offer several additional areas to reflect on as you prepare for the healing conversation.

PREPARATION FOR HEALING CONVERSATIONS

As an important relational activity, intentional and healing conversations on race naturally involve preparation. As you have dynamically cultivated humility, empathy, acceptance, and Christlike love, together these characteristics and behaviors have provided the soil for the growth of unity and healing of cross-racial relationships. Certainly, the reading and activities you have completed from the previous chapters provide the needed foundation for your preparation. However, included below are additional areas to consider as you determine your readiness for holding an intentional conversation on race.

Roles and relationships. The beauty of the HEAL model is that you can display the basic ingredients of the model in all relationships. There is no limit to how you can demonstrate humility, empathy, acceptance, and Christlike love to racially different people in your life (or to racially similar people, for that matter). However, as you consider having a formal healing conversation with the steps outlined in this chapter, it will be important to consider your current relationship with your chosen partner for the conversation. You do not need to know this person well. However, you will want to consider the various roles this person may play in your life. For example, does this person supervise your work? Are they in a position of authority in your life (for example, your pastor)? What is their gender, and what form of relationship do you have (friend, romantic partner)? The steps of the formal healing conversation include a need to be vulnerable. You will be talking about your race-related experiences, emotions, and needs, as well as seeking to empathize with the deep emotions and needs of the other person. We invite you to reflect on your relationship with your chosen partner and the level of vulnerability you will demonstrate if you were to engage in an intentional conversation on race with this person. Although Christlike relationships are the goal with all people in our lives, we may be limited in our ability or desire to be vulnerable and open in certain relationships (for example, you are married and want to have cross-gender conversations, but also want to limit your emotional vulnerability with someone who is not your spouse). Not all relationships need to include deep vulnerability, but we can still engage in the key practices of the HEAL model in all relationships. In fact, most of our day-to-day interactions will involve practical interactions, like paying for groceries or talking to the mechanic about an auto repair, and may not include deeper conversations on race. Therefore, we encourage you to consider your choice of a partner for the intentional conversation on race. As we have mentioned previously, the racial composition of the conversation does not matter. To make the most of the healing conversation, we recommend that the two people involved be of different racial/ethnic backgrounds, but this is not required. Instead, it is important to consider that you will grow in connectedness with this person and learn more about their experiences, and your conversation with this person will be the beginning of your journey to grow in racial unity. Even if you find that you choose to limit the extent of your vulnerability in your conversations with certain people, or you choose to have a healing conversation with a person of a similar racial/ethnic background, we believe that small steps in using the HEAL model, like demonstrating humility and love, can promote connectedness and healing.

Your partner's preparation. For intentional healing conversations, the assumption is that both members of the conversation are Christians and they are each committed to demonstrating Christlikeness and the fruit of the Spirit during the conversation. In other words, both Christians must be willing to enter the conversation with an understanding that yielding to God's will is prioritized above all else, exemplified in the life of Jesus Christ. Also, both members must be willing to embrace a biblical worldview, rather than a secular theory, as the starting and ending point for the conversation, with the grand narrative of Scripture serving as the proverbial bridge to having a healing conversation. Conversely, if a secular theory or worldview is employed as the primary lens through which race relations and racism are viewed, the parties involved may not be able to begin the conversation with the unity in Christ that is crucially needed. Therefore, as you consider who your partner will be for your intentional healing conversation, consider the following: Has your partner also engaged in activities to prepare for a healing conversation on race? Are they aware that you have been doing your own work to prepare? Although you and your partner will certainly start the conversation at different points in your own development and life story, assuring a similar starting point of a biblical worldview and commitment to Christlikeness can help assure success and growth as you engage in the healing conversation. The ultimate goal would be that both parties read through this book and participate in all of the exercises and activities. However, if one of the participants in the conversation has not read the book or engaged in the exercises, this should not put a stop to a conversation. Instead, the individual who has invested more time in preparation can lead the way in modeling the different practices and steps of the HEAL model. Success in efforts such as these "is not the product of human cleverness or carefully conceived strategies and tactics—it is first and foremost the fruit of God experienced in the lives of all those who cling to Christ."[1]

Location and timing. As designed, the healing conversation is meant to be a vulnerable experience. You will need privacy and sufficient time to engage in this conversation. Remember, you will be purposefully engaging in the sharing of your emotional experiences and asking your partner to do the same. Plan at least an hour or two for the conversation.

Use of your journal. During your time reading through this book, you have been invited to spend time journaling. Your journal is a key tool to be used during your healing conversation. Your notes and responses to chapter questions will be used during your conversation. You will need to have your journal on hand and be prepared to share your experiences, primary emotions, and relational needs. Once again, if your partner has not gone through these preparatory steps, you can still participate in the conversation by actively demonstrating humility, empathy, acceptance, and love in the manner described in the steps below (also see section in chap. 7 titled "Responding to Challenges When Using HEAL").

Prayer, prayer, and more prayer. Throughout the preparation for the healing conversation, you have been engaged in a variety of exercises that were intended to deepen your relationship with God. Along the way, our hope is that you have been working on surrendering to God's will and allowing the Holy Spirit to display the fruit of the Spirit in your life. As you get ready for the healing conversation, we encourage you to continue this work in the here-and-now, praying in real time that God would help you to live out Christlikeness with love, peace, patience, kindness, goodness, gentleness, and so forth. Remember, when entering into the healing conversation, God is at the center; therefore, try to maintain an awareness of God's presence by conversing with him in the present moment.

---

[1]Romero (2020, p. 140)

Overall, imagine that you are beginning a hike with a fellow brother or sister in Christ as your traveling companion, with Jesus Christ as your tour guide. Indeed, Jesus is with you, but he is a half-step ahead in order to safely guide the way. Therefore, on this important trek, you are dually turning to your fellow traveler and looking ahead to Jesus to ensure you are following his directions to safely arrive at your destination. Prayer along the journey is necessary to ensure you are effectively communicating with Jesus as your tour guide.

Finally, as you consider the work you have completed thus far in reading through this book, if you do not feel prepared to have a healing conversation on race, feel free to pause and return to the activities and readings from previous chapters. Prayerfully consider the areas where you feel stuck or need additional time in prayer and contemplation. As a means to consider your current readiness, take a moment to engage in the following journaling and self-reflection activities.

JOURNALING BREAK: PERSONAL REFLECTION

To determine your readiness for an intentional healing conversation on race using the HEAL model, grab your journal and take some time to reflect on the following:

1. Have you been able to identify primary emotions connected to your various race-related experiences, including prior conversations, experiences with racism, messages you received about race while growing up, etc.? What additional past experiences do you need to explore? What additional primary emotions do you need to identify?

2. How comfortable do you feel using basic empathic responsiveness skills (basic and advanced empathy, paraphrasing, open-ended questions)? Which skills do you struggle with the most? What can you do to strengthen your ability to use these skills?

3. Have you had sufficient practice using the Christian mental skills for responding to your difficult/negative emotional experiences? What skills do you feel you need to practice? What can you do to strengthen your ability to use these skills?

If you continue to struggle with any of these areas, we recommend returning to their respective chapters and engaging in further practice of the various skills. Regular and repeated practice will increase your comfort with the skills and lead to a greater likelihood of a positive experience during a conversation on race. Returning to these ideas and skills with the ultimate goal of developing Christlikeness and deepening relationships with God and others will serve to help you gently and slowly move through this process of growth.

ENGAGING IN THE HEALING CONVERSATION ON RACE

Now that you have reviewed the foundational elements of the HEAL model and considered your preparedness, you are ready to begin to use the model and engage in an intentional healing conversation. Remember, the HEAL model is ultimately about demonstrating Christlikeness; in the following steps, though, we will provide you with practical guidance on what this should look like to activate the power behind the model. You will be expressing vulnerable emotions and needs to a trusted brother or sister in Christ, lamenting together over the sin of racism, practicing the use of Christian mental skills, and using key methods and phrases for facilitating communication with your brothers and sisters in Christ, with Christ at the center and Christlike unity as the aim.

To make the healing conversation on race easier for you, we have provided guidance in easy-to-follow steps below. These steps are an expanded version of the adapted attachment injury model described in the last chapter.[2] Once you join with your partner for the conversation, the two of you should follow each step as written. We have also provided several videos of the HEAL model in action, recorded by us as we were having our own healing conversations on race. To watch the videos, which include the six major steps, please visit ivpress.com/heal-multimedia.

Step 1: Christian brothers/sisters pray together, humbly reflecting (H) and asking God to help each person be accessible, responsive, and engaged and display Christlikeness and the fruit of the Spirit in their

---

[2]Adapted from Johnson (2008) and Makinen and Johnson (2006).

healing relationship. To begin your conversation, you will start with a time of prayer and lamentation. Together, offer a complaint to God[3] (as described in chap. 3) about the pain related to past and present-day race relations and racism. In this complaint, recognize that God is present to hear the heartfelt pain connected with the long-reaching effects of racism on all people and the brokenness it has caused in our world and relationships for BIPOC and White people alike. Cry out to God by expressing your primary emotions (sadness, fear, shame, righteous anger) and emotional needs (comfort, encouragement, closeness, connection, etc.). Seek God's guidance and presence during the conversation. In this time of prayer, each person should humbly reflect with an attitude of Christlike self-emptying and openly acknowledge the sadness and loss associated with racism and the common humanity and sinfulness of all. Ask God to cultivate a secure, safe, trusting, and healing relationship during this conversation, displaying accessibility, responsiveness, and engagement, with Christlikeness and Christlike unity as the central aim. Pray that God would display the fruit of the Spirit in each of you as you move through the HEAL steps. Although an oral prayer offered by both can serve as a means of initial unity, certainly the prayer can be by just one member. The time of prayer is meant to be a mutual/shared experience, without an emphasis on either participant. Both participants should feel free to offer a lament and prayer.

The following is an example of what this prayer might look like:

> *God, thank you for allowing us to join together to talk about race and racism. Together, we recognize the pain that racism has caused and continues to cause. We don't understand exactly why there is so much conflict between the races, but we need your presence right now as we talk about it. We are saddened by racial disunity, apathy, and racism, and we need your comfort and encouragement as we consider the pain in our society and personal lives. Help us to connect with each other right now, and*

---

[3]Brueggemann (1984).

be present with us during this conversation. Help each of us to humbly respond to each other in a Christlike manner, and draw us together in unity. Help us to display the fruit of the Spirit as we walk through the steps of the HEAL model and share our personal experiences and stories. Amen.

After the prayer, the conversation should begin. However, we believe that the conversation should be started gently, with an initial activity to build connection and unity. Each person should begin the conversation by telling their conversion story or a powerful experience they had with God (taken from the journaling activity in chap. 2). As mentioned, telling these stories will accomplish two goals. First, listening to the story of another person's experiences with God creates a common ground of unity between believers. Second, listening to another's story allows the listener to practice the basic empathic responsiveness skills needed to begin to build emotional connection and understanding (pivoting from self to other/Other with empathy). Therefore, each person should take 5 to 10 minutes to describe their experience, sharing primary emotions in the process. While doing so, the listener should use empathic responses ("You felt _____ because of _____"), paraphrases, and open-ended questions to facilitate communication. Either the BIPOC participant or the White participant can share their story first. Neither participant should feel pressure to be the person who leads the conversation. Rather, the people involved benefit most when there is mutual/equal participation, given that the goal is for each person to have the opportunity to actively demonstrate Christlikeness and engage in the HEAL steps. After each participant has recounted their experience, you can move on to step two.

Step 2: One Christian expresses the emotional pain, impact, and significance of a race-related issue or racism in a vulnerable manner. Moving into the next step of the HEAL model, the individual who would like to speak first tells of their own experience with a chosen race-related topic, retaining awareness of their own feelings and sharing them in the process. As the speaker, you should honestly express your primary emotions (sadness, fear, shame, righteous anger) and the impact and significance of the race-related experience in a vulnerable manner. We recommend using one of your responses from the journaling activities in chapter two to provide the content for this part of the conversation. In doing so, you will be describing an experience that you have already explored during your personal time of preparation and for which you have already considered your primary emotions. Remember, both BIPOC individuals and all others have race- and ethnicity-related experiences. You may not have experienced racism personally, but you may have had a number of salient experiences related to race, ethnicity, or culture (reminiscent of James's story in chap. 3).

While the speaker is describing their experience during this step, the listener's job is active, not passive. Without inserting their own ideas or perspectives, the listener attempts to hear and understand the speaker at a deeper level. This process is the content of step 3.

Step 3: The listener is accessible and expresses empathy (E), attempting to hear, understand, and be moved by the emotional pain, impact, and significance of the race-related issue or racism in the life of the speaker, while also maintaining a posture of acceptance (A). The role of the listener is to attempt to display Christlikeness and the fruit of the Spirit (love, joy, peace, patience, kindness, goodness, faithfulness, gentleness, and self-control), while also empathically responding to the speaker. As the listener, you will use paraphrasing, advanced empathy, and open-ended questions to demonstrate empathic responsiveness. This will include validation of the speaker's primary emotions, including grief and sorrow, as expressed. Examples of validating and empathic responses include the following:

- "That sounds like it was so hard for you."
- "That must have been painful."
- "What a hard experience."
- "I'm here for you."

- "I hear you."

- "I can understand why you feel that way."

- "I understand you better now."

- "I didn't understand the depth of the problem."

- "I didn't know about these things."

- "Thank you for sharing that with me."

- "I'm sorry that happened to you."

- "I've minimized these things, and this minimization has hurt you."

- "I'm sorry that I have done things like that or that I've seen things like that and not said anything."

When conveying empathy as the listener, remember to identify and repeat the speaker's key words and phrases (paraphrasing) that capture their salient primary emotions, doing so slowly, softly, and simply,[4] with the fruit of the Spirit on display in the process. Additional examples include the following:

- "You felt so sad when you were excluded from the group."

- "It was heartbreaking to be treated that way."

- "You were devastated when they said that to you."

- "Yes. An earth-shattering experience."

- "You felt totally alone in that moment."

By slowly, softly, and simply repeating the speaker's key words, you will be helping them to stay connected to the deeper sadness and loss often associated with race-related issues and racism, demonstrating that you are standing with them and attempting to understand their struggles in a fallen, broken world. What is more, slowing down the conversation allows you the opportunity to practice the Christian mental skills of attention, present focus, awareness, and acceptance.[5] Whether you take on

---

[4]Denton et al. (2009).
[5]Feldman et al. (2007).

the role of the listener or speaker, you will certainly experience a number of emotions. It will be important during all steps of the conversation to maintain awareness of your own emotional experiences, recognizing that they are signals that you can respond to using these skills while inviting God into the experience. As you do so, you will be able to stay emotionally engaged in the conversation and respond with Christlike love to the emotional experiences of the other.

Step 4: The original speaker expresses their relational/emotional need, which may have been previously unmet. As the speaker, identity the relational/emotional need that is connected with the experience you have described. For example, "As I discuss this issue . . ."

- "I need to know that you won't make fun of me."
- "I need you to show that you hear me."
- "I need to know that you believe me."
- "I need you to understand that my experience is different from yours."
- "I need you to listen without judging me."
- "I need to know that you're on my side."
- "I need you to validate my experience."
- "I need you just to listen."
- "I need to know that we are united."
- "I need to know that I'm not alone."
- "I need to know that I'm an important part of this community."

The most important part of conveying a need is that it is concrete enough for the listener to actually attempt to meet the need in the here-and-now. In other words, what can the listener say or do, specifically and concretely, to respond in the present moment? Also, the need should be connected to the primary emotion, since the listener is being asked to respond to the primary emotion connected with the race-related experience (such as the pain of racism) while displaying Christlikeness.

Ultimately, the listener's goal is to display the fruit of the Spirit as they respond to the primary emotions connected with the race-related experience and any pain and disunity caused by racism in order to begin to create unity and a restored connection.

Step 5: *The listener responds to the emotional need in an engaged, caring manner, demonstrating Christlike love (L), the fruit of the Spirit, and the incarnating disciplines.* The listener should respond directly to the emotional need stated by the other with love, patience, kindness, and so on. For example:

- If the speaker says, "I need you to show that you hear me," the listener can respond with, "I hear you. That must have been . . ." (completing the thought with the primary emotion connected with the speaker's experience).

- If the speaker says, "I need to know that you believe me," the listener can respond with, "I believe you."

At times, the speaker may state the emotional need prior to arriving at step four. Therefore, the listener should actively listen for the expressed need throughout the speaker's story. At times, the need may not be expressed as directly as we have stated. Instead, it might sound something like this:

- "When that happened, all I wanted was for someone to believe me." (The implied expressed need is to be believed.)

- "I wish they had just said they were sorry for all that had happened to me." (The implied expressed need is for others to express sorrow in response to their pain.)

- "It would have been so much better if I'd had a few friends at the time." (The implied expressed need is for relational connection.)

Whether the need is expressed directly or indirectly, it is the listener's duty to respond directly, verbalizing and attempting to meet the need in that moment. Again, what can the listener say or do, specifically and concretely, to respond to an attainable need in the present?

Before moving to step six, the participants in the conversation switch roles. The new speaker should share their own experiences with a race-related issue or racism (step 2), while both the listener and speaker follow the remaining steps of the model (steps 3–6). In reversing roles and repeating this process, both parties are working toward balance and reciprocity in the relationship, rather than one person taking all of the risks. This role reversal allows for interdependence on the path toward relational unity and Christlikeness, wherein both Christians have the opportunity to display Christlike responsiveness to the needs of another.

Step 6: Both Christians pray together, asking God to continue to help each person be accessible, responsive, and engaged and display Christlike love and the fruit of the Spirit in their healing relationship. By the time you arrive at step six, both people involved in the conversation have prayed together, had the opportunity to share their conversion story or a powerful experience with God, and shared primary emotions and a relational need based on prior experiences with a race-related topic or racism. If one of these steps has been missed for either person, return to that step and continue from that point forward. Once completed, pray together again. This time, grieve once more over losses created by racism, while also looking toward the future and healing. In other words, praise God[6] for his presence, as well as his perfect plan of restored unity, revealed in the grand narrative of Scripture. Thank God for offering Jesus Christ to redeem a broken, fallen world. Express hope that God will restore all things as you move from justification to sanctification to glorification, with perfect unity as the end goal. Again, ask God to continue to help each of you be accessible, responsive, and engaged in your relationship. As you pray, actively recognize God's sovereignty in race relations and meditate on the following verses:

> I remember my affliction and my wandering,
>> the bitterness and the gall.

---

[6]Brueggemann (1984).

I well remember them,
 and my soul is downcast within me.
Yet this I call to mind
 and therefore I have hope:
Because of the LORD's great love we are not consumed,
 for his compassions never fail.
They are new every morning;
 great is your faithfulness. (Lamentations 3:19-23)

The following is an example of what your prayer might look like:

> *God, we are again sorrowful over the current and past pain in race relations and racism. However, we also look toward the future and have hope for healing. We know you have a perfect plan for restored unity, and we are thankful for Jesus' redemption of this broken, fallen world. We know that you will someday restore all things and we will be glorified with you one day in heaven. Please continue to help us each be accessible, responsive, and engaged in our healing relationship. We recognize your sovereignty in race relations as we consider your words in Scripture: "I remember my affliction and my wandering, the bitterness and the gall! I well remember them, and my soul is downcast within me. Yet this I call to mind and therefore I have hope: Because of the LORD's great love we are not consumed, for his compassions never fail. They are new every morning; great is your faithfulness." Amen.*

AFTER THE HEALING CONVERSATION ON RACE: A BIBLICAL AND PSYCHOLOGICAL PERSPECTIVE

Once you and your partner have completed the conversation, take time to evaluate the conversation itself. Spend time sharing with each other about your reactions to the content and process of the conversation, with the goal of continuing to demonstrate the fruit of the Spirit and build relational unity. Talking about your conversation (evaluating how things went) may be a new experience for you. Typically, after a race-related conversation, each person individually thinks about the experience, considering their own and the other person's reaction, wondering about the other person's thoughts, and sometimes wishing they said something differently. We suggest that talking about the conversation itself, both the content of the conversation and the process of the conversation, presents another opportunity for growth and healing. In psychology, this process has been referred to as meta-communication, immediacy, or having a focus on the process of the conversation.[7] Focusing on the process and content of the healing conversation can help you see how others perceive your communications. It also allows for the possibility of a new relational experience with a racially different person, allowing for the healing of your attachment narrative and giving you the chance to become aware of and reveal concerns, primary emotions, and needs that came up during the conversation itself. Continuing the conversation in this way allows for further opportunities to demonstrate humility, empathy, acceptance, and Christlike love.

As you evaluate your conversation with your partner, you will likely want to consider a number of questions, such as the following:

- "How do I feel the conversation went?"

- "What aspects of the conversation were the most difficult for me?"

- "What aspects of the conversation were the easiest for me?"

- "Were there any parts of the conversation that did not go well and why?"

- "How has God been active and present in this conversation?"

- "What has God revealed to me in this conversation?"

We have adapted the relational dialogue task[8] model from the EFT literature to provide you with a structure for your time of evaluation. This model was originally developed to help therapists and clients

---

[7] Elliott and Macdonald (2021).
[8] Elliott and Macdonald (2021).

evaluate and address difficulties in their relationship. The model, as we have adapted it, provides guidance for the examination of your use of the HEAL model, while also helping you to consider the ways you were able to make the following movements throughout your conversation:

- from a human-centered to God-centered understanding

- from self to Other/other

- from human disunity to unity

- from human judgment ("like God") to Christlike love ("dependent on God")

ADAPTED RELATIONAL DIALOGUE TASK MODEL

The adapted relational dialogue task model includes six tasks to complete after your conversation. As you evaluate your conversation with your partner, gently and carefully engage in each task, practicing Christlike humility in the process. Keep in mind, as tasks, the activities below are typically completed simultaneously. Therefore, as you mutually evaluate your healing conversation, you will each simultaneously attempt to accomplish each task.

Task 1. Demonstrate self-awareness. First, take a moment to notice your own emotional reaction to the conversation, employing the four Christian mental skills in response to your primary emotions. During this postconversation time, you have the opportunity to continue to grow in Christlike relationality and acceptance of God-given emotions and seek to build unity through honest emotional connection. Ultimately, for Christ-followers, love should be at the center of our emotional world,[9] given God commands us to love him and others (Matthew 22:36-40). Therefore, loving, honest self-reflection and awareness of your emotional response to the conversation is important. As you work to gain awareness of your emotional responses, invite God to be with you and help you to better understand your emotional reactions. As you become aware of

---

[9]Chandler (2014).

your emotional response to the conversation, lovingly, openly, and honestly share this with your partner.

Task 2. Demonstrate empathy. As your partner shares their response to the conversation, actively use empathic responsiveness skills to connect with their primary emotions. Use basic and advanced empathy statements, paraphrasing, and open-ended questions, striving to demonstrate Christlike love in the process. Remember, as you use these skills, you may be providing a new relational experience for the other person, serving as both a secure base and safe haven. God is at the center of this interaction as you remain emotionally accessible, responsive, and engaged[10] and display the fruit of the Spirit.

Task 3. Openly discuss difficulties. Honestly communicate struggles faced during the process of the conversation, including your emotions, any internal thoughts that impacted you during the conversation, and how you responded to your partner's actions/words. Also include what it was like to share your story. Seek to share your own needs and primary emotions and understand your partner's needs and primary emotions as they relate to the process and content of the conversation itself. As you discuss the difficulties that emerged, this is an opportunity to further strengthen relational unity, rather than dwell on perceived mistakes. In other words, use this opportunity to further display the fruit of the Spirit as you work together to address some of the perceived mistakes so you can apply what you have learned to subsequent conversations. Along the way, try to display patience (the New Testament concept of long-temperedness) for one another, just as God has demonstrated his patience for you.

Task 4. Demonstrate Christlike humility. Although it can be difficult to evaluate yourself and possible struggles during the conversation, with Christlike humility, you can observe your own and others' faults with patience, love, and acceptance. Therefore, this task requires that you seek to respond with humility, rather than defensiveness, as you listen to your

---

[10]Johnson (2008).

partner describe their experience of the conversation. Remember, a humble response places the needs of the other above your own. As you humbly listen to the needs of your partner, you can demonstrate a recognition that there is always more to learn.

Task 5. Seek unity. As you work together to discuss and understand the process of the conversation (both the positive aspects and unhelpful aspects), openly recognize that it is difficult (and not typical) to engage in meta-communication about a conversation on race. This meta-communication may cause an increase in negative race-related emotions. Therefore, keep your ultimate goal of unity in mind during the evaluation process.

Task 6. Plan for future conversations. Together, address specific ways you can each grow so that you can have future conversations with each other and other partners. This should not be your last and only intentional healing conversation. Ongoing conversations will be important for growing in relational connection. As part of the process of spiritual formation (being conformed to the image of Christ), we must continue to seek out opportunities for growth. Future conversations will help you to solidify skills and build new and healthy attachment narratives focused on unity with racially different others.

PRAYER AND JOURNALING ACTIVITIES

End this chapter's activities with prayer. Briefly ask for God's guidance and grace as you prayerfully consider the prompts below and respond in a journal entry.

Reflect on your conversation. What went well? What do you wish you'd done differently? What was your overall emotional response to the conversation?

1. What will you do differently in future cross-racial relationships based on this conversation and your evaluation time?

2. How can you improve in your ability to recognize God's active, loving presence in the midst of your attempts to have healing conversations on race? Moving forward, how can you improve in your ability to be a conduit for the fruit of the Spirit in your efforts to build racial unity?

FINAL STEPS

End today's activities with a time of prayer. Briefly thank God for his presence and ask for his continued guidance and grace as you meditate on your reflections throughout the coming days.

7

CONTINUING THE JOURNEY

YOUR STORY AND THE GRAND NARRATIVE OF SCRIPTURE

*Then I saw "a new heaven and a new earth," for the first heaven
and the first earth had passed away, and there was no longer any sea.
I saw the Holy City, the new Jerusalem, coming down out of heaven
from God, prepared as a bride beautifully dressed for her husband.
And I heard a loud voice from the throne saying,
"Look! God's dwelling place is now among the people,
and he will dwell with them.
They will be his people, and God himself will be with them
and be their God. 'He will wipe every tear from their eyes.
There will be no more death' or mourning or crying or pain,
for the old order of things has passed away." He who was seated
on the throne said, "I am making everything new!"*

REVELATION 21:1-5

*FOLLOWING THE MURDER OF GEORGE FLOYD, I
(Charles) was facilitating a Bible study with my predominately
Black congregants. I could see the pain, frustration, and anger on*

the faces of everyone in attendance, so I folded my preplanned notes for the study, looked into everyone's faces, and said, "They lynched him." Tears began streaming down faces, as hard-working mothers, grandmothers, fathers, grandfathers, brothers, and sisters felt affirmed, comforted, relieved, and supported that their pastor spoke aloud what they had been feeling inside all day.

That night, I listened as nearly every person in attendance shared their hurt, not only over another unarmed Black man being killed, but that the White folks they interacted with throughout the day, or viewed on Facebook, many of whom professed to be Christians, appeared to be completely unaffected by it all. They shared how they listened to remarks throughout the day from their White supervisors and/or colleagues, who said, "He must've done something wrong," "He shouldn't have been resisting arrest," "Police officers have a tough job," and "I'm sure there's a lot that the camera didn't catch that led to him being killed." As they shared the hurtful reflections of their White peers, they also shared how they had to fight within themselves to not respond or share their feelings, as in their words, "I knew they would never get it, and trying to talk to them would just upset me more." One young person in full anger said, "This is why I don't talk to White people. I know they can never understand my struggle, and they probably don't care anyway." I looked around as people of all ages nodded and groaned in agreement. It was silent for a moment, then an elderly gentleman, who had lived through the civil rights movement, shared, "This is why we have to have a [Black] church, because we need a safe space where we can be real, where we don't have to hide how we feel, and where we can feel supported as we try to grapple with the craziness of this world." I asked everyone, "Don't you think White Christians are hurting just like we are over this murder?" And at that moment, *one of the young ladies in the group said, "Listen to the posts of my White friends who are Christian. Listen to what they have posted on their social media platforms." She read post after post in response to the killing stating things like "Blue Lives Matter," "Support the Cops," and "God is on the side of our officers." Afterward, she said, "I'm going to delete all of them. They will no longer be my friends."*

As we neared the time for our session to conclude, God moved me to share with everyone that we have the right to feel everything that had been expressed that night, even the extreme feelings of not wanting to speak to our White brothers and sisters. But how would Christ be glorified if this became our stance? I challenged everyone not to run from conversation, but rather to seek to engage in conversation with their White colleagues and to have that conversation in a way in which Christ would be lifted up. One of the leading maternal figures in our church responded by saying, "Pastor, what you are asking us to do is going to be real hard," to which everyone laughed in agreement, and I smiled and said, "Following Jesus has never been easy."

As you have likely experienced as you have read through this book and participated in a *healing conversation on race*, the process of learning to have these conversations is not easy work, but it is necessary work in our collective journey to be Christlike. In fact, Jesus' ministry, as it is recorded in the biblical record, is a string of healing conversations that he initiated with politicians, commoners, religious rulers, tax collectors, blind men, the demon-possessed, the infirmed, the outcasts, the rich, and the poor. It appears that Christlikeness cannot be separated from healing conversations. Now that you have had the opportunity to engage in your own intentional healing conversation with a racially and/or ethnically different partner, you have experienced firsthand the challenges of doing so. You have walked through this emotionally vulnerable task and sought to demonstrate Christlike humility, empathy, acceptance, and love in the process. As the initial story in this chapter exemplifies, initiating these conversations takes courage. At times, they may even feel impossible to begin or sustain. However, despite the effort and sacrifice involved, with Christ as your model of self-emptying love, we pray that you have persevered in this journey.

As we come to the final chapter of this book, we encourage you to remember where this journey began. We first started by situating these healing conversations within the grand narrative of Scripture. With the themes of creation, fall, redemption, and restored unity, our goal has been to help you locate yourself and your relationships with racially different others within this grand story. As you move from justification to sanctification to one day being glorified with Christ in heaven, we pray that growth in Christlikeness in your cross-racial relationships has become a part of your story. Figure 7.1 illustrates the initial model that we provided.

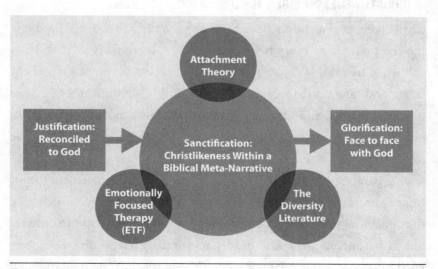

Figure 7.1. Foundations of the HEAL model

As we have walked with you along this journey, we have attempted to prioritize a biblical worldview and then draw from different areas of the professional literature to help you grow in your ability to have healing conversations. Within this final chapter, we will conclude with a biblical encouragement to press on in your journey, despite difficulties and struggles that may arise. We will also provide you with practical guidance on how to respond to these struggles, as well as how to prepare for and hold unexpected and unplanned conversations. Finally, we will also offer a simplified version of the HEAL model to use when on the go, given the majority of our healing conversations in daily life will require spontaneity. Just as Jesus engaged with people as he traveled the countryside of Israel, always prepared to demonstrate his love, our prayer for you is that you will be equipped and ready to demonstrate the HEAL model in all of your relationships. As you seek to see the *imago Dei* (image of God) in all people and demonstrate Christlikeness in all relationships, we seek to remind you to commit to humility, empathy, acceptance, and love.

AN ENCOURAGEMENT TO CONTINUE GROWING IN CHRISTLIKENESS: A BIBLICAL PERSPECTIVE

Christlikeness can simply be defined as becoming like Christ, and it is the chief pursuit of every believer, of every race, to daily yield to Jesus' call when he said, "Whoever wants to be my disciple must deny themselves and take up their cross and follow me" (Matthew 16:24). As we described earlier, and throughout this book, this is not an easy task. In fact, the first two criteria that Jesus gave in this verse for being Christlike imply suffering ("deny themselves" and "take up their cross"). In the following paragraphs, we strive to provide you with encouragement to continue to grow in Christlikeness in your cross-racial relationships, despite the difficulties you may encounter along the way. As you strive to be more like Christ and use the HEAL model in your daily relationships, you may encounter others who are opposed to this approach. You might find that your efforts are not rewarded, or you might even find yourself reverting to old ways of responding during conversations on race. Our encouragement to you is to continue to find ways to follow Christ's example by denying yourself, taking up your cross, and following him, despite difficulties and challenges. Remember, as you are formed into his image, the Holy Spirit both guides you and strengthens you in the process.

Christlikeness: Self-denial and burden bearing. As we initially described humility in chapter two and throughout the book, we have regularly returned to the idea of *self-emptying* or self-denial based on the description of Christ in Philippians 2. We have regularly used the fruit of the Spirit (love, joy, peace, patience, kindness, goodness, faithfulness, gentleness, and self-control) as our foundational and practical means of demonstrating self-denial in daily life. As we look deeply at the fruit of the Spirit, we see that to deny oneself suggests turning from one's own feelings and desires and rejecting what we *could* do for what God says we *should* do. Paul, in his first letter to the church at Corinth, exemplified this idea in his guidance to the readers on how to handle their freedom in Christ. He said, "'Everything is permissible for me,' but not everything is beneficial. 'Everything is permissible,' but I will not be mastered by anything" (1 Corinthians 6:12 CSB). While Paul was addressing food and sexual immorality in this text, he was also sharing a larger concept with the early church about the call to deny oneself. Paul challenged them to carefully consider how to handle their freedoms (the *could* versus *should*). Returning to the story from the beginning of this chapter as an example, a believer *could* choose to avoid conversations with others about racism or race-related injury or they *could* turn their eyes from the hurts of others around them. However, in each of these instances, *should* these be the correct responses? As primary and secondary emotions develop, we may be tempted to engage in all that we *could* do, rather than turning to self-denial or self-emptying. Denying oneself involves continual self-reflection (on both primary and secondary emotions) and acceptance (A) of God's enduring presence and help in the process of healing conversations. Within the HEAL model, we recognize that secondary emotions may drive us to avoid conversations altogether or to use words and actions that may offend, harm, negate, or invalidate the experiences or perspectives of another. Rather than responding to these secondary emotions, we must seek to identify the primary emotion and connected need. This process is one of active self-emptying and humility (H) and, ultimately, is part of the sanctification process wherein we become more and more like Christ. It can be helpful to remind ourselves that, even in this, we can look to the grand narrative of Scripture. This is part of the journey from justification to sanctification to glorification as you actively seek to demonstrate Christlikeness in challenging situations where self-denial is difficult.

Beyond denying oneself, Jesus also told his followers that they are to "take up their cross" (Matthew 16:24). We must understand that the cross, which often adorns necklaces and church edifices today, was not a celebrated symbol when Jesus spoke these words in the first century. In fact, the cross was a sign of death, guilt, shame, torture, and scorn. When Jesus told followers to take up their cross, he called those who truly desired to follow him to completely surrender to carrying (bearing the burden of) the sin and brokenness of this world, even to the point of death. In our view, this high calling includes finding ways to bear the weight of such things as our country's history of slavery and segregation, as well as the current pain of instances of police brutality, systemic racism, discrimination, and oppression. Although these experiences are painful burdens to bear, within the grand narrative of Scripture, bearing the weight of these burdens is a part of the call to live like Christ by sharing in his sufferings (see Philippians 3:8-11).[1] To take up the cross, therefore, suggests bearing burdens, as Jesus did, that are not our own and/or that we did not create. Yet, we shoulder the weight of these burdens (the pain, injustice, uncertainty, and brokenness) because God is glorified in the process. As we intentionally choose to have healing conversations on race, we actively decide to bear the burden of healing racial injuries, breaking down walls of disunity and serving as a model of Christ's love to those who are different from us. As we do so, we are denying ourselves and taking up our cross.

Despite the call to self-denial and burden bearing, in healing conversations on race, the question may arise for both parties, "Why am I being

---

[1] Erickson (1998).

forced to carry this weight by having these conversations?" For those of marginalized groups, they may ask, "Why is the burden on me to initiate healing conversations with others who don't understand me, have hurt me, and appear to not even care about me?" And those of other racial groups may ask, "Why must I carry the burden of racism, historical atrocities, and current events that I didn't create, I don't participate in, and I'm not a part of?" Again, the answer is found in our desire to be Christlike. All humans, whether they willfully choose to or not, carry the burdens of this world in one way or another. Our distinctiveness as Christians is rooted in how we carry the crosses of this world through evidencing the fruit of the Spirit.

Christlikeness: Following him. When Jesus said, "Follow me," we are challenged to carefully consider and measure, in every conversation, interaction, opportunity, and disappointment, our responses against all of what we have come to know about the person and character of Jesus. Paul, in his encouragement to the early church at Ephesus, captured these words about what it means to follow Christ: "Follow God's example, therefore, as dearly loved children and walk in the way of love, just as Christ loved us and gave himself up for us as a fragrant offering and sacrifice to God" (Ephesians 5:1-2). Within the themes of the grand narrative of Scripture, beginning with God's story in creation, to humanity's fall into sin and futile attempts to meet God's standards by obeying laws, all the way through the redemption of humanity through the death and resurrection of Jesus, the universal underlying theme is love. God's love, demonstrated through Jesus, is our model to follow and share with the world. A favorite hymn of the church says,

> I was sinking deep in sin,
> far from the peaceful shore,
> very deeply stained within,
> sinking to rise no more;
> but the Master of the sea
> heard my despairing cry,
> from the waters lifted me—

now safe am I.
Love lifted me,
love lifted me,
when nothing else could help love lifted me.[2]

As we seek to heal racial injury and pain, and as you persevere through difficulties during conversations on race, the solution is not found in emerging theories, media soundbites, political rhetoric, or even religious jargon. As we discussed in chapter one, the solution to the racial issues of our time culminates in love. When "nothing else can help," following Christ in love is the solution. Love is so transformational and all-encompassing that when John sought to describe God, he penned the words, "God is love" (1 John 4:16). John went further to say, "Whoever claims to love God yet hates a brother or sister is a liar. For whoever does not love their brother and sister, whom they have seen, cannot love God, whom they have not seen" (1 John 4:20). Healing conversations require us to love our brothers and sisters of all backgrounds, even when it is challenging. As is true of all siblings, there will be disagreements, disappointments, fallouts, and contentions. However, if the love of Christ resides within each person, the commitment to love can overcome anything that seeks to separate.

Justification, sanctification, and following Christ. Thankfully, the difficult work of healing conversations does not begin with our effort. Our sanctification process was initiated by Jesus' work on the cross, whereby Jesus justified all who believe in him, changing our status before him from a state of sin to a state of righteousness, despite having been dead in sin and separated from God.[3] God loved us so much that he sent his only Son so that we might be reconciled to him (John 3:16). In healing conversations, we can never forget that we are all sinners, saved by God's amazing grace. In fact, God's grace in his act of justification should motivate us to reconcile with one another and to seek out healing in

---

[2]Rowe (1912).
[3]Erickson (1998).

relationships. Those who desire to engage in healing conversations must be committed to remembering what has been done for us through the work of Jesus Christ. If our desire is to be like Christ, therefore, we must proactively seek opportunities to have healing and reconciling conversations, even when they present a challenge.

Furthermore, in this voluntary journey of sanctification, we must submit to no longer living for ourselves, but rather to following God's will. Sanctification is the pursuit of holiness and the active work of being transformed into his image as we daily surrender our thoughts, ways, and plans to God. Our surrender to the work of God within, or this spiritual formation, is a lifelong commitment to submit to God. In Paul's instructions to the early church at Philippi, he told them,

> Therefore, my dear friends, as you have always obeyed—not only in my presence, but now much more in my absence—continue to work out your salvation with fear and trembling, for it is God who works in you to will and to act in order to fulfill his good purpose. (Philippians 2:12-13)

Although the work of salvation (justification, sanctification, and glorification) is completed by Jesus Christ, the process of sanctification itself requires the cooperation of the believer "to work out [our] salvation." Healing conversations, as a tool you can use as you grow in Christlikeness, require continuous yielding to the Holy Spirit, persistent meditation on the Word of God, and an ongoing commitment to "work out" your salvation. In areas where we struggle with this, we will find we have more difficulties in these conversations. Although we may never feel fully prepared for healing conversations, the more we submit to the work of the Holy Spirit in us, the more prepared we will be to engage in conversations on race that can bring healing.

> *I (Charles) once had an encounter with another of the authors of this book, Veola. We were sitting with some friends in a local Panera Bread having lunch. During the discussion, one of our colleagues brought up law enforcement and without thinking twice, I blurted out, "I'm tired of all these White cops shooting*

young Black men. I don't trust any of them." I felt strongly about my response, but I noticed the faces of everyone at the table drop. One of our colleagues lifted her head and said, "Charles, I'm not sure if you know this, but the colleague you are sitting next to, her husband is White, he's a cop, they have Black children, and he's a really great guy that cares about the community."

Immediately, I knew I had been careless, reckless, and ignorant in my response. Instead of that colleague blowing up at me, she looked at me and said, "I can understand why you feel that way, and I'm sorry for the experiences that have led you to that conclusion." She then said, "I would love for you to meet my family and to talk more with you so that God can help us all to understand each other more."

I'm a pretty big guy, but I felt like a 3-year-old at that table, whose feet couldn't reach the ground. How could she respond to me with such patience, gentleness, kindness, and self-control? In our conversations following that day, I came to understand the deepness of her walk with God, the regularity of her study of God's Word, and the seriousness of her personal commitment to the work of the Holy Spirit within her. She was able to "handle" me because she was in the hands of the Holy Spirit. That's sanctification. She was not there to "set me straight," "tell me off," or "cancel" me. Instead, her pursuit of holiness set her apart for ministry, to reach even those who are offensive.

I could pick any of the nine fruit of the Spirit from Galatians 5 to describe my colleague's response to me that day. Without having to break open a Bible, throw holy water on me, or find some holy oil to anoint me, God's Spirit within her convicted me, brought me into a place where I sought her forgiveness and to understand more about her family, and led us into a stronger relationship. Only those that stay before the Lord can anticipate such amazing results.

Undoubtedly, in healing conversations, there will be comments, ideas, and perspectives that will be expressed that are offensive and hurtful. Even Christians with the best intentions can make overgeneralized statements that are divisive and destructive. If we have not spent time before the Lord, being transformed by his Word and committing to the fruit of the Spirit, we are very likely to respond in ways that do not honor God and bring greater division and damage to relationships. Once again, recall Paul's writings to the people of Galatia, where he described the fruit of the Spirit (the product of God's transforming work from the inside out) as "love, joy, peace, forbearance, kindness, goodness, faithfulness, gentleness, and self-control" (Galatians 5:22-23). The sanctifying work of the Holy Spirit and your choice to follow after Christ is evidenced by conversations that can be described in this way.

Glorification and following Christ. The final act of salvation is often described as *glorification.* In the redemptive work of Jesus Christ, glorification looks to the day in which the believer will be unified with Christ in heaven, forever.[4] It is the ultimate prize that all believers seek, to be in God's presence for eternity, praising and worshiping his name. In Revelation 7:9, the writer in his vision of the day of glorification said, "After this I looked, and there before me was a great multitude that no one could count, from every nation, tribe, people and language, standing before the throne and before the Lamb." When we arrive in "glory," there will be great diversity before the throne of God. If this is God's will once we get to heaven, we can imagine that God is glorified on earth when we stand in unity and diversity.

Therefore, in healing conversations, each participant should engage with one goal in mind, that God may be glorified as they build stronger cross-racial relationships and heal racial injuries. When all parties seek this ultimate goal, words are more carefully chosen, attitudes are more likely to be tempered, and each person's commitment to Christlikeness is evidenced. Dissension, division, and destruction are often the products

---

[4]Erickson (1998).

of communication when those involved are looking to glorify the self. Conversely, when we enter into conversations with the desire that God be glorified, looking to the ultimate vision of yearning to one day stand in unity with God, we engage in conversations that bring healing, understanding, and transformation.

So, how do you continue along this journey of sanctification as you respond to the difficulties that may arise during your conversations on race? How do you actively demonstrate self-emptying and the fruit of the Spirit as you work to take up your cross and follow him when it is hard or confusing or when the strategies we have provided become challenging? Next, we will provide you with a guide based on the principle of Christlikeness integrated with practical tools drawn from attachment theory and the EFT literature to help you along your continued journey.

RESPONDING TO CHALLENGES WHEN USING HEAL:
BIBLICAL AND PSYCHOLOGICAL PERSPECTIVES

As we have stated, with the deep emotions connected to racism and cross-racial relationships, it is inevitable that you might encounter challenges in demonstrating Christlikeness when attempting to have conversations on race. In each cross-racial relationship, the goal is the development of stronger relational connections as you are conformed into the image of Christ. Therefore, no matter what barrier is encountered, the primary objective will be to maintain the focus on this goal. When having intentional conversations on race, we predict that the best outcomes will develop when both partners use the tenets of HEAL. However, you may find yourself in a conversation with a partner who chooses not to use the HEAL model or struggles with portions of it. Although you might return to the model, reminding yourself of the steps, you may not know how to respond when your partner falters. It's possible to respond with Christlikeness during these situations, offering empathy and seeking to understand the other's needs.

Returning to attachment theory, recall that when having conversations on race, old attachment narratives may be activated. Anxious attachment styles (negative view of self; positive view of others) and avoidant attachment styles (positive view of self; negative view of others) may present themselves in your own and others' behaviors or words.[5] For example, this may take the form of argumentativeness, with the secondary emotion of anger at the core, or giving up on the conversation and withdrawing, with the primary emotion of shame as the impetus. Others may react by *intellectualizing* (providing facts and statistics about the topic), while steering away from the primary emotion of sadness. In EFT, these common negative relational styles limit emotional connection.

The founder of an EFT approach to couples therapy, Sue Johnson, describes problematic patterns and negative relational styles that couples commonly engage in when involved in conflict.[6] These patterns undermine relationships and create disconnection. We believe these common relational patterns can also arise during conversations on race, highlighting our continual struggle with sin, shame, and pride that draw us away from God and away from unity with others. These common patterns include the tendency for mutual attack, demand/withdraw, and tension/avoidance.[7] Oftentimes, rather than drawing closer to others and growing deeper in our understanding of others' experiences, emotions, and needs, we may undermine Christlike unity by engaging in these patterns and unhelpful cycles. Below, we will describe these possible scenarios and provide examples of how a Christian using the HEAL model can respond.

Mutual attack cycle. The mutual attack cycle occurs when the members involved in the conversation on race are drawn away from the HEAL approach and, instead, focus on attacking each other. These attacks often take the form of mutual criticism. During conversations on race, people may attack each other's point of view, experiences, or way of describing their experiences or even make direct attacks on the other's

---

[5]Bartholomew and Horowitz (1991); Fairchild and Finney (2006); Sibley et al. (2011).
[6]Johnson (2008).
[7]Johnson (2008).

character. Unfortunately, it is easy to become entrenched in this cycle of mutual blame (blame/blame)[8] and attack during conversations on race. It is not uncommon for blame to be invoked for current or past racial injuries, and the two parties may attempt to make their points by using criticism and argument to persuade the other to see their side. Whatever the focus of the blame or attack, the conversation can devolve into an argument about who is right and who is wrong, rather than working toward Christlike unity.

If what begins as a healing conversation becomes a time of mutual attack, it is clear that the conversation has gone off track. At the same time, it is important to recognize that the intense emotional content of these conversations can easily drive these conversations in this direction. Ultimately, beneath the blame/blame cycle may be mutual hurt, with both parties needing the other person to understand their pain. Unfortunately, the surface-level strategy used—futilely attempting to convince the other person they are wrong—rarely, if ever, works, given the other person often ends up taking a defensive posture.

To avoid the blame/blame cycle or to recover from it, the goal is to find ways to return to the HEAL model, acknowledging the primary emotions and relational needs that are residing beneath the surface. In the case of the blame/blame cycle, humility (H) and empathy (E) may be the most helpful tools at your disposal. We recognize that, when being attacked, these two skills can be very difficult to conjure. However, Christlike humility places the needs of others before our own and empathy helps us to hear and to see the other's perspective. Although it may feel impossible to demonstrate these behaviors in some conversations, do not lose hope. We believe that, with a commitment to Christlikeness and the use of humility and empathy, you can move past what seems like an insurmountable obstacle. We provide the following as an example of how a humble and empathic response might help to move the conversation in the direction of healing:

---

[8]Johnson (2008).

Dominique, a Syrian-American woman, speaks with Jay, a Black man, about an incident of racism she experienced.

Dominique: You think you are the only people who experience racism. I had someone call me a terrorist the other day.

Jay: Well, you don't know what it's like. You really don't have anything that compares with what I've been through.

Dominique: How dare you say that. So, you're saying that my experience doesn't mean anything?

Jay: Well, you said it.

Dominque: You're such a jerk. You don't know what you're talking about. What about 9/11? What about everything I go through when I get on an airplane?

Jay: Why are all Middle Eastern people so sensitive about 9/11? That's so irritating.

At this point, Dominique is aware that she and Jay are diving into a mutual attack cycle that may be hard to recover from. She takes a moment and prays a brief prayer, accepting God's active presence in the conversation and in her emotional experience. Then, she seeks to work toward healing by using humility and empathy.

Dominique: I guess I don't completely understand how you see it. It sounds like it's hard for you to hear people who aren't Black describe their experiences of racism as if they are the same as your experiences. I wonder what you need from me right now.

Jay: Of course, it's hard. My people have been through a lot. I just need you to understand that before you start in about your experiences.

Dominique: I get it. Your people have been through a lot. I probably don't really even understand it all. But I want to

> *understand more. I hope you know that I hear how hurtful it*
> *can be if I just gloss over it.*

In this example, Dominique has attempted to find her way back to the HEAL model by using empathy and paraphrasing in her response, which included identifying Jay's primary emotion and asking about his need. Although not all conversations may get back on track as easily as is seen in this example, you can regularly return to humility and empathy if you see the mutual attack cycle begin. You will have to remain committed to using these skills, repeatedly returning to primary emotions and needs with humility until the conversation returns to a healing path.

Demand/withdraw cycle. As we described in chapter four, when talking about race with a racially different partner, the content of the conversation may stir a variety of emotions, which may include fear of what might happen during the conversation, anger about prior events, or insecurity about how one might be perceived. Many of the emotions that are elicited may be linked to prior relational experiences (attachment narratives). Unfortunately, these intense emotions, when not recognized and responded to with intentionality, can lead to problematic patterns in the conversation. The demand/withdraw pattern is commonly experienced when emotions become intense and partners in the conversation struggle with responding with empathy and acceptance of their own and the other's emotional experience. The demand/withdraw cycle is identified by the different responses of the people involved in the conversation. As one member pushes, criticizes, and complains, the other person shuts down and withdraws.[9] The more the withdrawing person shuts down, the more the demanding person pushes for additional interaction through the use of negative tactics. Eventually, the withdrawing individual feels disconnected and defensive, while the demanding party feels rejected.

The demand/withdraw pattern is not uncommon during conversations on race. Within the HEAL model, talking about primary emotions

---

[9]Johnson (2008).

and relational needs may spur this pattern because it's a new experience for many people. Some people may resist this deep emotional process, especially when the emotions involved are intense. In fact, these emotions may drive people to want to give up on the conversation or even the relationship (withdrawal) or to demand more intense and longer interaction. However, instead of giving up the conversation or using negative tactics to draw others into relationship, a healing approach includes acceptance (A) of your own and others' emotions, while staying engaged in the conversation. Furthermore, empathy allows for greater understanding of the other's experience and fosters the deeper connection that is truly desired by both parties. Indeed, beneath the surface, the pursuer may be feeling fear, sadness, or loneliness and need closeness and connection, whereas the withdrawer may be feeling overwhelmed or ashamed and need acceptance and approval.

We provide an example of the demand/withdraw cycle below, including the use of both empathy and acceptance as tools used to heal this pattern.

> *Hana, a Japanese American Christian, speaks with her husband, Shane, a White man, about the anti-Asian discrimination she experienced during the Covid-19 pandemic. Hana is hurt by her husband's insistence on ignoring the problem.*
>
> *Hana: You keep telling me to just ignore it. But I can't stop worrying because it's still happening.*
>
> *Shane: You'll make yourself sick if you keep worrying so much. Let's not talk about it anymore.*
>
> *Hana: You always do this. You never listen to me.*
>
> *Shane: Why are you saying that? Forget it. I'm going to bed.*
>
> *Hana: You always leave when we're having a hard conversation. You just don't care.*
>
> *Shane: Goodnight, Hana. (turns to leave)*

Hana: What kind of husband are you? Do you even love me?

Shane: (says nothing, walks into the bedroom, and closes the door)

Once in his bedroom, Shane leans against the bedroom door and hears Hana crying. He recalls the HEAL model and the importance of inviting God into the conversation with his wife and asking God to help him recognize and respond to his own emotions, as well as Hana's. He takes a moment to practice Christian attention by focusing on God's promise to be with him and Christian present focus by becoming aware of God's presence with him in his current emotions. He takes a breath and opens the door to find Hana, eyes wet with tears.

Shane: I'm sorry. I feel scared when we talk about these things. I don't know how to help you. But I hear that you're worried and scared, too. What do you need from me?

If one partner is able to return to the HEAL model in the middle of the demand/withdraw pattern, the cycle can be broken. Both empathy and acceptance are key tools in this process. As one or both partners identifies the primary emotions present and openly recognizes them, both members have the opportunity to practice Christian attention, awareness, acceptance, and present focus as they respond to their own emotional experience. In the process, they can more easily hear and respond to the emotions of the other.

Tension/avoidance cycle. The cycle of tension and avoidance is often the culmination of ongoing hurtful interactions.[10] When people regularly engage in mutual attacks and/or the demand/withdraw pattern, they eventually come to a point of feeling emotionally unsafe in their interactions. The unfortunate response to this felt sense of insecurity in the relationship is avoidance of the other and a growing tension between the people involved. Within this pattern, one or both members often refuse

---

[10]Johnson (2008).

to speak to each other, and emotional distance grows. In cross-racial relationships, some may consider this to be a helpful way to avoid conflict. However, it is an unhelpful solution to racial tensions. Avoidance increases tension and disunity. The underlying primary emotions typically experienced when avoidance and tension arise include hurt, sadness, fear, shame, exhaustion, and a sense of hopelessness. When these emotions become the hallmark of cross-racial relationships, it can be very difficult to find healing. However, those who are committed to Christlike action, despite the challenge of a pattern that has culminated in tension and avoidance, can use the HEAL model to disrupt this pattern and build unity. The final and pivotal tenet of the HEAL model, Christlike love, is crucial for breaking this cycle. As described in chapter five, Christlike love "always perseveres" (1 Corinthians 13:7). This means that Christlike love drives us to overcome adversity, including the silence, tension, and pain that can arise in cross-racial relationships. When you encounter this barrier in your conversations or when you are unable to start a conversation with your racially different brother or sister in Christ, start with active demonstrations of love. Compassion, forgiveness, and seeking of justice can serve as a practical means to break down tensions (see chap. 5).[11]

Whether you are faced with mutual attacks, a demand/withdraw pattern, or tension and avoidance in your cross-racial relationships, the tenets of the HEAL model can be applied to help increase unity in each of these situations. Overall, with the goal of unity, increased relational connections, and glorifying God, your work to overcome these negative patterns will continue to spur your growth toward Christlikeness.

USING HEAL WHEN ON THE GO

Up to this point, we have provided guidance mostly on how to engage in intentional conversations on race. However, it is likely that you will have unexpected opportunities for a healing conversation. Given that most of our day-to-day interactions are spontaneous, these opportunities can

---

[11]Calhoun (2005).

arise at any time. Although these unexpected and unplanned conversations offer additional challenges, we believe that a commitment to the individual practices of the HEAL model will provide you with the tools needed for all conversations. In fact, as a model based on internal transformation and formation into the image of Christ, you will be able to draw on your transformed inner world and the strength of the Holy Spirit for all unplanned conversations. Despite this, we realize that it is important to have practical tools to return to in difficult situations. Therefore, below, we offer a refined, short-hand model using the HEAL mnemonic. If you are presented with an unexpected conversation on race, we encourage you to bring to mind each of the letters of the HEAL model and to engage in the activity in parentheses below. To help you to further express each practice of the model, ask yourself the questions that follow and prayerfully reflect on your words, actions, and attitudes during the conversation.

Humility (Prayerfully Reflect)

- Am I willing to place the needs of others ahead of my own?
- Am I willing to acknowledge that I can learn something from the other person?
- Is there anything keeping me from demonstrating humility in this conversation?
- How can I display Christlike humility in this situation in its simplest form?

Empathy (Identify Emotion and Need)

- Have I accurately understood the person's primary emotions?
- Have I actively responded to the person's primary emotions?
- Have I sought to understand and actively respond to the person's unmet need?
- Have I displayed the fruit of the Spirit, including love, peace, patience, kindness, goodness, and gentleness, as I sought to understand this person's emotions and need?

Acceptance (Consent to God's Loving Presence)

- Am I actively working to accept my own and others' emotions?
- Am I actively accepting God's presence in the midst of my emotional experience?
- Am I using Christian mental skills to respond to my own emotions?
- Is there anything keeping me from staying emotionally connected?

Love (Respond with Christlikeness)

- Am I willing to accept the other person as they are, without judgment?
- Am I able to see the other person as a fellow sojourner?
- Is there anything keeping me from demonstrating love in this conversation?
- Ultimately, am I serving as a vehicle through which Christlikeness and the fruit of the Spirit can be on full display in this conversation?

If you are confronted with an opportunity to have a conversation on race in an unexpected time or with an expected person, your goal will be to focus on the individual pieces of the model, seeking ways to implement each as the opportunity arises. These conversations will likely not follow the model in the order we have provided for the intentional conversation. Therefore, you will have the opportunity to find the best time to offer empathy, demonstrate humility, show acceptance, and show Christlike love. For each of these areas of the HEAL model, we have provided practical examples in this and previous chapters. If you are unsure what these look like, return to those examples. It may help to role play an unexpected conversation with a partner to help you prepare. Whatever the case, if you actively seek to ask yourself the questions above in the midst of the conversation, you will be on your way to having a healing conversation, even if it is unexpected.

CONCLUSION

As you have come to see, the process of learning to have healing conversations on race is a journey. Along this journey, you are, step by step, being formed into the image of Christ. As you grow and hold these healing conversations, the relational rewards are great. However, to enjoy the fruit of these labors, one must be committed to travel through tense moments, bruised feelings, anger, confusion, frustration, disappointment, disagreement, guilt, shame, resentment, and fear, attempting to explore your own and others' deeper emotions and needs in the process.

Therefore, as you continue walking along the path of growth in your cross-racial relationships, we encourage you to not give up. Recognize that growing in Christlikeness is not only hard work but also continuous work that demands commitment. Remember, you are being *formed* and *transformed*, which is not a destination we reach while residing on earth, but rather a heavenly destination we look forward to. As the theme verse for this chapter reminds us, God is in the process of "making everything new!" (Revelation 21:5). In healing conversations, the goal is not to change how people think or feel, but, rather, to love your brother and sister as God loves them with humility, empathy, and acceptance, thereby growing more into who God created you to be. Having a "healing conversation" does not guarantee any particular outcome. However, with a goal of increased emotional connection and building relational bonds, you may emerge different from when you started. As you commit to engage with others, despite disagreements, differences, or pain, you will be depositing seeds in one another that will sprout in the right season. In other words, healing conversations are about committing to Christlike love in our interactions. Humility, empathy, and acceptance will be your tools. We conclude with one final story of our own experience in writing this book:

> *In the writing of this book, there were many conversations in which we hurt one another, disappointed one another, offended one another, and certainly disagreed with one another. Without the love of Christ within, this book would never have been*

completed. However, it was our commitment to Christ and to demonstrating the fruit of the Spirit that allowed us to not only complete this book, but build relational bonds, heal old injuries, and emerge as true friends. Collectively, when you sum up our life experiences, we are not a likely group that would be friends. Just as you will experience as you grow in your use of the HEAL model with Christlike love at the center, we are drawn to one another and have discovered more of who Jesus is because of our interactions. Yet, we also know that we are not done growing and learning how to have healing conversations. But we are committed to allowing Christ to continue to form us into his image, day by day, year by year, until we see him face-to-face in heaven. We pray the same for you.

If you would like, you can also watch a video of the authors discussing the process of writing the book at ivpress.com/heal-multimedia.

REFERENCES

Allport, G. W. (1979). *The nature of prejudice*. Addison-Wesley.

American Psychological Association. (2019). *Publication manual of the American Psychological Association* (7th ed.). Author.

American Psychological Association. (2020). *Stress in America*. www.apa.org/news/press/releases/stress/2020/report-october.

American Psychological Association. (2021). *APA resolution on harnessing psychology to combat racism: Adopting a uniform definition and understanding*. Author.

Amplified Bible. (2015). *Bible gateway*. www.biblegateway.com/versions/Amplified-Bible-AMP/.

Analayo, B. (2020). Confronting racism with mindfulness. *Mindfulness, 11*, 2283-2297. https://doi.org/10.1007/s12671-020-01432-4.

Anderson, T., Clark, W., & Naugle, D. (2017). *An introduction to Christian worldview: Pursuing God's perspective in a pluralistic world*. InterVarsity Press.

Arel, S. (2016). *Affect theory, shame, and Christian formation*. Palgrave Macmillan.

Ball, J. (2016). *A treatise of divine meditation*. Puritan Publications.

Bangley, B. (Ed.). (2006). *The cloud of unknowing: Contemporary English edition*. Paraclete Press.

Bartholomew, K., & Horowitz, L. M. (1991). Attachment styles among young adults: A test of a four-category model. *Journal of Personality and Social Psychology, 61*(2), 226-244. https://doi.org/10.1037/0022-3514.61.2.226.

Bath, H. (2019). Pain and the unspoken emotion: Shame. *International Journal of Child, Youth and Family Studies, 10*, 126-141. https://doi.org/10.18357/ijcyfs102-3201918856.

Beasley-Topliffe, K. (2003). *The upper room dictionary of Christian spiritual formation*. Upper Room Books.

Becker-Weidman, A., Ehrmann, L., & LeBow, D. (2012). *The attachment therapy companion: Key practice for treating children & families*. W. W. Norton & Company.

Beckett, J. (2016). Lament in three movements: The implications of Psalm 13 for justice and reconciliation. *Journal of Spiritual Formation & Soul Care, 9*, 207-218. https://doi.org/10.1177/193979091600900206.

Beeke, J., & Jones, M. (2012). *A Puritan theology: Doctrine for life.* Reformation Heritage Books.

Bell, L. A. (2003). Telling tales: What stories can teach us about racism. *Race Ethnicity and Education, 6*(1), 3-28. https://doi.org/10.1080/1361332032000044567.

Benner, D. (2010). *Opening to God: Lectio divina and life as prayer.* InterVarsity Press.

Boa, K. (2009). *Conformed to his image: Biblical and practical approaches to spiritual formation.* Zondervan.

Bonhoeffer, D. (1955). *Ethics.* Touchstone.

Bowlby, J. (1980*). Attachment and loss: Loss, sadness and depression* (Vol. 3). Basic Books.

Bowlby, J. (1982). *Attachment and loss* (2nd ed.). Basic Books.

Brondolo, E., Brady Ver Halen, N., Pencille, M., Beatty, D., & Contrada, R. J. (2009). Coping with racism: A selective review of the literature and a theoretical and methodological critique. *Journal of Behavioral Medicine, 32*(1), 64-88. https://doi .org/10.1007/s10865-008-9193-0.

Brubacher, L. (2018). *Stepping into emotionally focused couple therapy: Key ingredients of change.* Routledge.

Brueggemann, W. (1984). *The message of the Psalms: A theological commentary.* Fortress Press.

Bryant-Davis, T. (2007). Healing requires recognition: The case for race-based traumatic stress. *The Counseling Psychologist, 35*(1), 135-143. https://doi.org/10 .1177/0011000006295152.

Bryant-Davis, T., & Ocampo, C. (2005). Racist incident-based trauma. *The Counseling Psychologist, 33*(4), 479-500. https://doi.org/10.1177%2F0011000005276465.

Calhoun, A. (2005). *Spiritual disciplines handbook: Practices that transform us.* InterVarsity Press.

Carlson-Thies, S. (2021). Love God totally, and your neighbor as yourself: How religious freedom enables us to obey both great commandments in our time. *Social Work and Christianity, 48*(2), 200-216. https://doi.org/10.34043/swc.v48i2.228.

Carson, D. (1991). *The gospel according to John.* Eerdmans.

Carter, R. T. (2007). Racism and psychological and emotional injury: Recognizing and assessing race-based traumatic stress. *The Counseling Psychologist, 35*(1), 13-105. https:// doi.org/10.1177/0011000006292033.

Carter, R. T., Lau, M. Y., Johnson, V., & Kirkinis, K. (2017). Racial discrimination and health outcomes among racial/ethnic minorities: A meta-analytic review. *Journal of Multicultural Counseling and Development, 45*(4), 232-259. https://doi.org/10.1002 /jmcd.12076.

Carver, C. (2011). Coping. In R. Contrada & A. Baum (Eds.), *The handbook of stress science: Biology, psychology, and health* (pp. 221-230). Springer.

Chandler, D. (2014). *Christian spiritual formation: An integrated approach to personal and relational wholeness.* IVP Academic.

Chang, W. (2014). The love commandment (John 13:34-35). *Asia Journal of Theology, 28*(2).

Crowell, J. A., Treboux, D., & Waters, E. (2002). Stability of attachment representations: The transition to marriage. *Developmental Psychology, 38,* 467-479.

Dallos, R. (2006). *Attachment narrative therapy: Integrating systemic, narrative and attachment approaches.* Open University Press.

Davis, A. (2014). *An infinite journey: Growth toward Christlikeness.* Ambassador International.

Davis, E., Moriarty, G., & Mauch, J. (2013). God images and God concepts: Definitions, development, and dynamics. *Psychology of Religion and Spirituality, 5,* 51-60. https://doi.org/10.1037/a0029289.

Day-Vines, N. L., Cluxton-Keller, F., Agorsor, C., Gubara, S., & Otabil, N. A. A. (2020). The multidimensional model of broaching behavior. *Journal of Counseling & Development, 98*(1), 107-118. https://doi.org/10.1002/jcad.12304.

Day-Vines, N. L., Wood, S. M., Grothaus, T., Craigen, L., Holman, A., Dotson-Blake, K., & Douglass, M. J. (2007). Broaching the subjects of race, ethnicity, and culture during the counseling process. *Journal of Counseling & Development, 85*(4), 401-409. https://doi.org/10.1002/j.1556-6678.2007.tb00608.x.

Denton, W., Johnson, S., & Burleson, B. (2009). Emotion-Focused Therapy-Therapist Fidelity Scale: Conceptual development and content validity. *Journal of Couple & Relationship Therapy, 8,* 226-246. https://doi.org/10.1080/15332690903048820.

Dougherty, K. D., & Emerson, M. O. (2018). The changing complexion of American congregations. *Journal for the Scientific Study of Religion, 57*(1), 24-38. https://doi.org/10.1111/jssr.12495.

Dwiwardani, C., Hill, P. C., Bollinger, R. A., Marks, L. E., Steele, J. R., Doolin, H. N., Wood, S. L., Hook, J. N., & Davis, D. E. (2014). Virtues develop from a secure base: Attachment and resilience as predictors of humility, gratitude, and forgiveness. *Journal of Psychology and Theology, 42*(1), 83-90. https://doi.org/10.1177/009164711404200109.

Elliott, M. (2006). *Faithful feelings: Rethinking emotion in the New Testament.* Kregel.

Elliott, R., & Macdonald, J. (2021). Relational dialogue in emotion-focused therapy. *Journal of Clinical Psychology, 77*(2), 414-428. https://doi.org/10.1002/jclp.23069.

Ellison, C. G., DeAngelis, R. T., & Güven, M. (2017). Does religious involvement mitigate the effects of major discrimination on the mental health of African Americans? Findings from the Nashville Stress and Health Study. *Religions, 8,* 195-220. https://doi:10.3390/rel8090195.

Emerson, M. O., & Smith, C. (2000). *Divided by faith: Evangelical religion and the problem of race in America.* Oxford University Press.

English Standard Version Bible. (2001). *Bible gateway.* www.biblegateway.com/versions/English-Standard-Version-ESV-Bible/.

Erickson, M. (1998). *Christian theology* (2nd ed.). Baker Academic.

Erickson, M. (2013). *Christian theology* (3rd ed.). Baker Academic.

Fairchild, A., & Finney, S. (2006). Investigating validity evidence for the Experiences in Close Relationships-Revised Questionnaire. *Educational and Psychological Measurement, 66,* 116-135. https://doi.org/10.1177%2F0013164405278564.

Feeney, B., & Collins, N. (2004). Interpersonal safe haven and secure base caregiving processes in adulthood. In W. Rholes & J. Simpson (Eds.), *Adult attachment: Theory, research, and clinical applications* (pp. 300-338). Guilford Press.

Feldman, G., Hayes, A., Kumar, S., Greeson, J., & Laurenceau, J. (2007). Mindfulness and emotion regulation: The development and initial validation of the Cognitive and Affective Mindfulness Scale-Revised (CAMS-R). *Journal of Psychopathology and Behavioral Assessment, 29,* 177-190. https://doi.org/10.1007/s10862-006-9035-8.

Forsyth, J. M., & Carter, R. T. (2014). Development and preliminary validation of the Racism-Related Coping Scale. *Psychological Trauma: Theory, Research, Practice, and Policy, 6*(6), 632-643. https://doi.org/10.1037/a0036702.

Foster, R. (2018). *Celebration of discipline: The path to spiritual growth.* HarperOne.

Goodwin, T. (2015). *The vanity of thoughts.* Chapel Library.

Granqvist, P. (1998). Religiousness and perceived childhood attachment: On the question of compensation or correspondence. *Journal for the Scientific Study of Religion, 37*(2), 350-367. https://doi.org/10.2307/1387533.

Granqvist, P., Mikulincer, M., & Shaver, P. R. (2010). Religion as attachment: Normative processes and individual differences. *Personality and Social Psychology Review, 14*(1), 49-59. https://doi.org/10.1177/1088868309348618.

Graybeal, L., & Roller, J. (2007). *Prayer and worship: A spiritual formation guide.* Renovare.

Greenberg, L. (2006). Emotion-focused therapy: A synopsis. *Journal of Contemporary Psychotherapy, 36,* 87-93. https://doi.org/10.1007/s10879-006-9011-3.

Greenberg, L., & Paivio, S. (2003). *Working with emotions in psychotherapy.* Guilford Press.

Greenberg, L., & Pascual-Leone, A. (2006). Emotion in psychotherapy: A practice-friendly research review. *Journal of Clinical Psychology, 62,* 611-630. https://doi.org/10.1002/jclp.20252.

Grudem, W. (1994). *Systematic theology: An introduction to biblical doctrine.* Zondervan.

Guigo II. (2012). *The ladder of monks* (P. Nau, Trans.) [Kindle version]. Amazon.com.

Hareli, S., & Hess, U. (2012). The social signal value of emotions. *Cognition and Emotion, 26,* 385-389. https://doi.org/10.1080/02699931.2012.665029.

Hays, P. A. (2016). *Addressing cultural complexities in practice: Assessment, diagnosis, and therapy* (3rd ed.). American Psychological Association.

Hazan, C., & Shaver, P. (1987). Romantic love conceptualized as an attachment process. *Journal of Personality and Social Psychology, 52*(3), 511-524. https://doi.org/10.1037/0022-3514.52.3.511.

Hazan, C., & Zeifman, D. (1999). Pair bonds as attachments. In J. Cassidy & P. R. Shaver (Eds.), *Handbook of attachment: Theory, research, and clinical applications* (pp. 336-377). Guilford Press.

Hook, J., Davis, D., Owen, J., & DeBlaere, C. (2017). *Cultural humility: Diverse identities in therapy.* American Psychological Association.

Howard, E. (2018). *A guide to Christian spiritual formation: How Scripture, spirit, community, and mission shape our souls.* Baker Academic.

Ivey, A. E., Ivey, M. B., & Zalaquett, C. (2009). *Intentional interviewing and counseling: Facilitating client development in a multicultural society.* Brooks/Cole.

Johnson, A., & Wakefield, J. (2020). Examining associations between racism, internalized shame, and self-esteem among African Americans. *Cogent Psychology, 7*(1). https://doi.org/10.1080/23311908.2020.1757857.

Johnson, E. (Ed.). (2010). *Christianity and psychology: Five views* (2nd ed.). InterVarsity Press.

Johnson, S. (2008). *Hold me tight: Seven conversations for a lifetime of love.* Little, Brown and Company.

Johnson, S. (2019a). *Attachment theory in practice: Emotionally focused therapy (EFT) with individuals, couples, and families.* Guilford Press.

Johnson, S. (2019b). *The practice of emotionally focused couple therapy: Creating connection* (3rd ed.). Routledge.

Johnson, S., Makinen, J., & Millikin, J. (2001). Attachment injuries in couple relationships: A new perspective on impasses in couples therapy. *Journal of Marital and Family Therapy, 27,* 145-155. https://doi.org/10.1111/j.1752-0606.2001.tb01152.x.

Keller, T. (2010a). *Generous justice: How God's grace makes us just.* Dutton.

Keller, T. (2010b). *Gospel in life: Grace changes everything.* Zondervan.

King, M. L. (1963). *Strength of Love.* Harper & Row.

King, M. L. (1963, April 16). "Letter from Birmingham jail." https://kinginstitute.stanford.edu/sites/mlk/files/letterfrombirmingham_wwcw_0.pdf.

Knabb, J. (2018). *The compassion-based workbook for Christian clients: Finding freedom from shame and negative self-judgments.* Routledge.

Knabb, J. (2021). *Christian meditation in clinical practice: A four-step model and workbook for therapists and clients.* IVP Academic.

Knabb, J., & Bates, M. (2020). "Holy desire" within the "Cloud of Unknowing": The psychological contributions of medieval apophatic contemplation to Christian mental health in the 21st century. *Journal of Psychology and Christianity, 39,* 24-39.

Knabb, J., & Emerson, M. (2013). "I will be your God and you will be my people": Attachment theory and the grand narrative of Scripture. *Pastoral Psychology, 62,* 827-841. https://doi.org/10.1007/s11089-012-0500-x.

Knabb, J., Johnson, E., Bates, T., & Sisemore, T. (2019). *Christian psychotherapy in context: Theoretical and empirical explorations in faith-based mental health.* Routledge.

Knabb, J. J., & Vazquez, V. E. (2018). A randomized controlled trial of a 2-week internet-based contemplative prayer program for Christians with daily stress. *Spirituality in Clinical Practice, 5*(1), 37-53. https://doi.org./10.1037/scp0000154.

Knabb, J., Vazquez, V., & Pate, R. (2019). "Set your minds on things above": Shifting from trauma-based ruminations to ruminating on God. *Mental Health, Religion & Culture, 22*, 384-399. https://doi.org/10.1080/13674676.2019.1612336.

Knabb, J., Vazquez, V., Garzon, F., Ford, K., Wang, K., Conner, K., Warren, S., & Weston, D. (2020). Christian meditation for repetitive negative thinking: A multi-site randomized trial examining the effects of a four-week preventative program. *Spirituality in Clinical Practice, 7*, 34-50. https://doi.org/10.1037/scp0000206.

Knabb, J. J., Vazquez, V. E., Pate, R. A., Garzon, F. L., Wang, K. T., Edison-Riley, D., Slick, A. R., Smith, R. R., & Weber, S. E. (2021a). Christian meditation for trauma-based rumination: A two-part study examining the effects of an internet-based 4-week program. *Spirituality in Clinical Practice.* Advance online publication. http://dx.doi .org/10.1037/scp0000255.

Knabb, J., & Wang, K. (2021). The Communion with God Scale: Shifting from an *etic* to *emic* perspective to assess fellowshipping with the triune God. *Psychology of Religion and Spirituality, 13*, 67-80. https://doi.org/10.1037/rel0000272.

Knabb, J., Vazquez, V., Pate, R., Lowell, J., & Wang, K. (2021b). *Lectio divina for trauma-related emotions: A two-week program.* Unpublished manual.

Knabb, J., Vazquez, V., Pate, R., Wang, K., Lowell, J., De Leeuw, T., Dominguez, A., Duvall, K., Esperante, J., Gonzalez, Y., Nagel, G., Novasel, C., Pelaez, A., & Strickland, S. (2022, March). *Lectio divina for trauma-related negative emotions: A two-part study* [Conference presentation]. Christian Association for Psychological Studies (CAPS) Annual Conference (Virtual).

Kobak, R., Zajac, K., Herres, J., & Krauthamer Ewing, E. (2015). Attachment based treatments for adolescents: The secure cycle as a framework for assessment, treatment and evaluation. *Attachment & Human Development, 17*, 220-239. https://doi.org/10.1080 /14616734.2015.1006388.

Kuntze, J., Molen, H. T. van der, & Born, M. P. (2009). Increase in counselling communication skills after basic and advanced microskills training. *British Journal of Educational Psychology, 79*(1), 175-188. https://doi.org/10.1348/000709908X313758.

Kuyper, A. (2015). *Common grace: God's gifts for a fallen world.* Lexham Press.

Kwah, H. (2019). Buddhist and arts-based practices for addressing racial oppression: Building upon Cleveland and Tobin's mindfulness in education. *Cultural Studies of Science Education, 14*, 1123-1131. https://doi.org/10.1007/s11422-018-9898-5.

Larsen, T. (2007). Defining and locating evangelicalism. In T. Larsen & D. Treier (Eds.), *The Cambridge companion to evangelical theology* (pp. 1-14). Cambridge University Press.

Lawrence, B. (2015). *The practice of the presence of God* (S. Sciurba, Trans.). ICS Publications.

Lazarus, R. (1999). *Stress and emotion: A new synthesis.* Springer Publishing Company.

Makinen, J. A., & Johnson, S. M. (2006). Resolving attachment injuries in couples using emotionally focused therapy: Steps toward forgiveness and reconciliation. *Journal of Consulting and Clinical Psychology, 74*(6), 1055-1064. https://doi.org/10.1037/0022-006X.74.6.1055.

Malott, K. M., & Schaefle, S. (2015). Addressing clients' experiences of racism: A model for clinical practice. *Journal of Counseling & Development, 93*(3), 361-369. https://doi.org/10.1002/jcad.12034.

Marrero-Quevedo, R. J., Blanco-Hernández, P. J., & Hernández-Cabrera, J. A. (2019). Adult attachment and psychological well-being: The mediating role of personality. *Journal of Adult Development, 26*(1), 41-56. https://doi.org/10.1007/s10804-018-9297-x

Mason, E. (2018). *Woke church: An urgent call for Christians in America to confront racism and injustice.* Moody Publishers.

Mayer, F. (2014). *Narrative politics: Stories and collective action.* Oxford University Press.

McCaulley, E. (2020). *Reading while Black: African American biblical interpretation as an exercise in hope.* InterVarsity Press.

McMinn, M. (2008). *Sin and grace in Christian counseling: An integrative paradigm.* InterVarsity Press.

McSloy, S. (1996). Because the Bible tells me so: Manifest destiny and American Indians. *St. Thomas Law Review, 9*(1), 37-48.

Merriam-Webster. (1995). *Merriam-Webster's desk dictionary.* Merriam-Webster, Incorporated.

Merton, T. (1958). *Thoughts in solitude.* Farrar, Straus & Giroux.

Merton, T. (1961). *New seeds of contemplation.* Abbey of Gethsemani.

Mikulincer, M., & Shaver, P. R. (2005). Attachment security, compassion, and altruism. *Current Directions in Psychological Science, 14*(1), 34-38. https://doi.org/10.1037/0022-3514.89.5.817.

Mikulincer, M., & Shaver, P. (2017). *Attachment in adulthood: Structure, dynamics, and change* (2nd ed.). Guilford Press.

Mohamed, B. (2021, February 16). *10 new findings about faith among Black Americans.* Pew Research Center. www.pewresearch.org/fact-tank/2021/02/16/10-new-findings-about-faith-among-black-americans/.

Mouw, R. (2002). *He shines in all that's fair: Culture and common grace.* Eerdmans.

Mulholland, M. (2016). *Invitation to a journey: A road map for spiritual formation.* InterVarsity Press.

New American Standard Bible. (2020). *Bible gateway.* www.biblegateway.com/versions/New-American-Standard-Bible-NASB/.

New International Version Bible. (2011). *Bible gateway.* www.biblegateway.com/versions /New-International-Version-NIV-Bible/.

New King James Version Bible. (1982). *Bible gateway.* www.biblegateway.com/versions /New-King-James-Version-NKJV-Bible/.

Oatley, K., & Johnson-Laird, P. (1996). The communicative theory of emotions: Empirical tests, mental models, and implications for social interaction. In L. Martin & A. Tesser (Eds.), *Striving and feeling: Interactions among goals, affect, and self-regulation* (pp. 363-393). Lawrence Erlbaum Associates.

Paintner, C. (2011). *Lectio divina—the sacred art: Transforming words and images into heart-centered prayer.* SkyLight Paths Publishing.

Paradies, Y., Ben, J., Denson, N., Elias, A., Priest, N., Pieterse, A., Gupta, A., Kelaher, M., & Gee, G. (2015). Racism as a determinant of health: A systematic review and meta-analysis. *PLoS ONE, 10*(9), 1-48. https://doi.org/10.1371/journal.pone.0138511.

Pennington, B. (1982). *Centering prayer: Renewing an ancient Christian prayer form.* Doubleday.

Pettigrew, T. F., & Tropp, L. R. (2006). A meta-analytic test of intergroup contact theory. *Journal of Personality and Social Psychology, 90*(5), 751-783. https://doi.org/10 .1037/0022-3514.90.5.751.

Pettigrew, T. F., & Tropp, L. R. (2008). How does intergroup contact reduce prejudice? Meta-analytic tests of three mediators. *European Journal of Social Psychology, 38*(6), 922-934. https://doi.org/10.1002/ejsp.504.

Pettit, P. (Ed.). (2018). *Foundations of spiritual formation: A community approach to becoming like Christ.* Kregel.

Pew Research Center. (2015, May 12). *America's changing religious landscape.* The Pew Research Center, Religion & Public Life. www.pewforum.org/2015/05/12/americas -changing-religious-landscape/.

Plantinga, A. (2000). *Warranted Christian belief.* Oxford University Press.

Pope, M., Pangelinan, J. S., & Coker, A. D. (2011). *Experiential activities for teaching multicultural competence in counseling.* American Counseling Association.

Priest, R. J., & Nieves, A. L. (2006). *This side of heaven: Race, ethnicity, and Christian faith.* Oxford University Press.

Roberts, R. (2007). *Spiritual emotions: A psychology of Christian virtues.* Eerdmans.

Roberts, S. O., & Rizzo, M. T. (2021). The psychology of American racism. *American Psychologist, 76*(3), 475-487. http://dx.doi.org/10.1037/amp0000642.

Rodenborg, N. A., & Boisen, L. A. (2013). Aversive racism and intergroup contact theories: Cultural competence in a segregated world. *Journal of Social Work Education, 49*(4), 564-579. https://doi.org/10.1037/0022-3514.90.5.751.

Romero, R. C. (2020). *Brown church: Five centuries of Latina/o social justice, theology, and identity.* InterVarsity Press.

Rowe, J. (1912). *Love lifted me.* Public Domain.

Salzberg, S. (1995). *Lovingkindness: The revolutionary art of happiness*. Shambhala.

Scazzero, P. (2011). *Emotionally healthy spirituality: Unleash the power of authentic life in Christ*. Thomas Nelson.

Scazzero, P. (2014). *Emotionally healthy spirituality*. Zondervan.

Scheff, T. (1997). *Emotions, the social bond, and human reality: Part/whole analysis*. Cambridge University Press.

Schoenleber, M., & Berenbaum, H. (2011). Shame regulation in personality pathology. *Journal of Abnormal Psychology, 121*, 433-446. https://doi.org/10.1037/a0025281.

Scorgie, G. (Ed.). (2011). Tears. In *Dictionary of Christian spirituality*. Zondervan.

Sibley, C., Fischer, R., & Liu, J. (2011). Reliability and validity of the Revised Experiences in Close Relationships (ECR-R) self-report measure of adult romantic attachment. *Personality and Social Psychology Bulletin, 31*, 1524-1536. https://doi.org/10.1177%2F0146167205276865.

Smietana, B. (2015, January 15). *Sunday morning in America still segregated—and that's ok with worshipers*. Lifeway Research. https://lifewayresearch.com/2015/01/15/sunday-morning-in-america-still-segregated-and-thats-ok-with-worshipers/.

Sue, D. W. (2015). *Race talk and the conspiracy of silence: Understanding and facilitating difficult dialogues on race*. John Wiley & Sons.

Sue, D. W., Capodilupo, C. M., Torino, G. C., Bucceri, J. M., Holder, A. B., Nadal, K. L., & Esquilin, M. (2007). Racial microaggressions in everyday life: Implications for clinical practice. *American Psychologist, 62*(4), 271-286. https://doi.org/10.1037/0003-066x.62.4.271.

Talbot, J. (2013). *The Jesus prayer: A cry for mercy, a path of renewal*. InterVarsity Press.

Tatum, B. (1992). Talking about race, learning about racism: The application of racial identity development theory in the classroom. *Harvard Educational Review, 62*(1), 124. https://doi.org/10.17763/haer.62.1.146k5v980r703023.

Teyber, E. (2006). *Interpersonal process in therapy: An integrative model*. Brooks/Cole.

Tisby, J. (2021). *How to fight racism: Courageous Christianity and the journey toward racial justice*. Zondervan.

Trimble, J., & Bhadra, M. (2013). In K. D. Keith (Ed.), *The encyclopedia of cross-cultural psychology* (pp. 500-504). Wiley Blackwell.

Vazquez, V., & Jensen, G. (2020). Practicing the Jesus Prayer: Implications for psychological and spiritual well-being. *Journal of Psychology and Christianity, 39*(1), 65-74.

Vazquez, V., Otero, I., & Goodlow, J. (2019). Relationship stigma and Black-White interracial marital satisfaction: The mediating role of religious/spiritual well-being. *Mental Health, Religion & Culture, 22*(3), 305-318. https://doi.org/10.1080/13674676.2019.1620189.

Vazquez, V. E., Stutz-Johnson, J., & Sorbel, R. (2021). Black-White biracial Christians, discrimination, and mental health: A moderated mediation model of church support and religious coping. *Psychology of Religion and Spirituality*. Advance online publication. https://doi.org/10.1037/rel0000415.

Watson, T. (2012). *A treatise concerning meditation*. Waxkeep Publishing.

Wiersbe, W. (2007). *The Wiersbe Bible commentary: Old Testament*. David C. Cook.

Wilhoit, J., & Howard, E. (2012). *Discovering lectio divina: Bringing Scripture into ordinary life*. IVP Books.

Willard, D. (2002). *Renovation of the heart: Putting on the character of Christ*. NavPress.

Willard, D. (n.d.). *Spiritual formation: What it is, and how it is done*. https://dwillard.org/articles/spiritual-formation-what-it-is-and-how-it-is-done.

Witherington, B. (2012). *A shared Christian life*. Abingdon Press.

Wolters, A. (2005). *Creation regained: Biblical basics for a reformational worldview*. Eerdmans.

Wright, C. (2017). *Cultivating the fruit of the Spirit: Growing in Christlikeness*. InterVarsity Press.

Zapolski, T. C. B., Faidley, M. T., & Beutlich, M. R. (2019). The experience of racism on behavioral health outcomes: The moderating impact of mindfulness. *Mindfulness, 10*(1), 168-178. https://doi.org/10.1007/s12671-018-0963-7.

Zeng, X., Chiu, C., Wang, R., Oei, T., & Leung, F. (2015). The effect of loving-kindness meditation on positive emotions: A meta-analytic review. *Frontiers in Psychology, 6*, 1-14. https://doi.org/10.3389/fpsyg.2015.01693.

Zou, L. X., & Dickter, C. L. (2013). Perceptions of racial confrontation: The role of color blindness and comment ambiguity. *Cultural Diversity and Ethnic Minority Psychology, 19*(1), 92-96. https://doi.org/10.1037/a0031115.

GENERAL INDEX

SCRIPTURE INDEX